Armenia and Europe

Armenia and Europe

Foreign Aid and Environmental Politics
in the Post-Soviet Caucasus

Pål Wilter Skedsmo

I.B. TAURIS
LONDON • NEW YORK • OXFORD • NEW DELHI • SYDNEY

I.B. TAURIS
Bloomsbury Publishing Plc
50 Bedford Square, London, WC1B 3DP, UK
1385 Broadway, New York, NY 10018, USA
29 Earlsfort Terrace, Dublin 2, Ireland

BLOOMSBURY, I.B. TAURIS and the Diana logo are trademarks of
Bloomsbury Publishing Plc

First published in Great Britain 2019
This paperback edition published in 2021

Copyright © Pål Wilter Skedsmo, 2019

Pål Wilter Skedsmo has asserted his right under the Copyright, Designs
and Patents Act, 1988, to be identified as Author of this work.

Cover design by Adriana Brioso

All rights reserved. No part of this publication may be reproduced or
transmitted in any form or by any means, electronic or mechanical, including
photocopying, recording, or any information storage or retrieval system,
without prior permission in writing from the publishers.

Bloomsbury Publishing Plc does not have any control over, or responsibility
for, any third-party websites referred to or in this book. All internet addresses
given in this book were correct at the time of going to press. The author and
publisher regret any inconvenience caused if addresses have changed or
sites have ceased to exist, but can accept no responsibility for any such changes.

A catalogue record for this book is available from the British Library.

A catalog record for this book is available from the Library of Congress.

ISBN: HB: 978-1-7883-1174-8
PB: 978-0-7556-3652-5
ePDF: 978-1-7883-1540-1
eBook: 978-1-7883-1539-5

Series: International Library of Twentieth Century History

Typeset by Newgen KnowledgeWorks Pvt. Ltd., Chennai, India

To find out more about our authors and books visit www.bloomsbury.com
and sign up for our newsletters.

Contents

List of Figures	vi
Preface	vii
List of Abbreviations	ix
Introduction	1
1 Development and 'transition' in Armenia: Contexts and concepts	21
Part 1 Environmental rights and politics in the post-Soviet Caucasus	47
2 Transparent environment: 'Helping' countries into a 'pan-European' legal space	49
3 Save Teghut!	81
Part 2 Foreign aid in the post-Soviet Caucasus	117
4 LOG framing: Donor legitimation and unattainable project goals	119
5 'Never mind, it's not a good idea'	151
Conclusion	183
Appendix 1: Excerpt from the Aarhus Convention text	201
Appendix 2: Statement from Teghut Conference	203
Notes	205
Bibliography	243
Index	259

Figures

0.1	'Beating the vulnerability problem'	5
1.1	Map of Armenia	23
2.1	Hrazdan, Kotayk province	75
3.1	Overview of communication ACCC/C/2009/43 Armenia	95
3.2	Overview of communication ACCC/C/2011/62 Armenia	99
4.1	LOG frame, the Armenia project 2009	128
5.1	Picture taken from the closed gate of the grounds of the Miami Hotel, partly submerged in 2010	156
5.2	Invitation to seminar participants, 2006	157
5.3	Facsimile of the letter sent to FNI by the Armenian Ministry of Nature Protection stating the ministry's continued support for the project	169
5.4	OSCE press release	174

Preface

The primary focus of this book is environmentalism and foreign aid in Armenia, areas in which Armenia's obligations under multilateral environmental conventions, its soviet heritage and status as a foreign aid recipient play important roles. The book is a revised and abridged version of my PhD thesis in social anthropology at the University of Oslo.[1]

The people I encountered and befriended in Armenia became a big part of my life after setting foot in *Hayastan* – the land of Hayk – for the first time in 2006. I would like to extend my warmest appreciation to the Jenderedjian family who gave me a home from home every time I was in Yerevan. Special thanks for the way you welcomed my family when they joined me on fieldwork in Yerevan. I also want to express my gratitude to other friends, project partners and informants in Armenia for their hospitality, generosity and patience.

In a way, this book is as much about Norway as it is about Armenia, and there are many people I would like to thank here as well. I am especially indebted to and extremely grateful for the support and advice of my supervisor Knut Gunnar Nustad. Your keen eye for the finest details as well as your ability to convey different ways of framing the material have been a great inspiration and help. Many thanks!

Some of my present and prior colleagues at the Fridtjof Nansen Institute deserve special mention: Steinar Andresen, Jørgen Holten Jørgensen and Peter Johan Schei for our memorable first excursions to Armenia; Director Geir Hønneland for his encouragement and trust; Lars Rowe for reading and commenting on the entire manuscript; and finally Ida Folkestad Soltvedt for superb technical help in formatting the manuscript for publication.

Many thanks to my editor Tomasz Hoskins at I.B. Tauris for encouraging the publication of this book and for his professional support. I have been very fortunate in being able to rely on the professional and also creative language assistance provided by Chris Saunders.

Tove and Einar (who joined me on fieldwork in Armenia) and Anna (we'll go to Armenia together one day!): thanks for all your support, care and for keeping me grounded. My gratitude for the trust, love and patience of these three people I hold dearest in the world can never be adequately expressed.

While there are many who have earned my gratitude, only one person is to blame for any flaws and mistakes: they, of course, are my responsibility alone.

Polhøgda, February 2018

Abbreviations

Aarhus Convention	UNECE Convention on Access to Information, Public Participation in Decision-Making and Access to Justice in Environmental Matters
ACP	Armenia Copper Programme
ASSR	Armenian Socialist Soviet Republic
AUA	American University of Armenia
EaP	Eastern Partnership
EIA	Environmental impact assessment
ELRC	Environmental Law Resource Centre
ENVSEC	Environment and Security Initiative
FNI	Fridtjof Nansen Institute
IDPs	Internally displaced persons
IMF	International Monetary Fund
MEA	Multilateral environmental agreement
MFA	Ministry of Foreign Affairs
MNP	Ministry of Nature Protection of the Republic of Armenia
MoP	Meeting of Parties (to the Aarhus Convention)
NGO	Non-governmental organization
NORAD	Norwegian Agency for Development Cooperation
ODA	Official development assistance
OSCE	Organization for Security and Co-operation in Europe
PEIC	Public Environmental Information Centre
RA	Republic of Armenia
RAMSAR	Ramsar Convention on Wetlands
SAP	Structural adjustment programmes
STCI	Save Teghut Civic Initiative
UNDP	United Nations Development Programme
UNEP	United Nations Environment Programme
UNCCD	United Nations Convention to Combat Desertification
UNECE	United Nations Economic Commission for Europe
USSR	United Socialist Soviet Republics
YSU	Yerevan State University

Abbreviations

Aarhus Convention	UNECE Convention on Access to Information, Public Participation in Decision-Making and Access to Justice in Environmental Matters
ACP	Armenia Copper Programme
ASSR	Armenian Socialist Soviet Republic
AUA	American University of Armenia
EaP	Eastern Partnership
EIA	Environmental impact assessment
ELRC	Environmental Law Resource Centre
ENVSEC	Environment and Security Initiative
FNI	Fridtjof Nansen Institute
IDPs	Internally displaced persons
IMF	International Monetary Fund
MEA	Multilateral environmental agreement
MFA	Ministry of Foreign Affairs
MNP	Ministry of Nature Protection of the Republic of Armenia
MoP	Meeting of Parties (to the Aarhus Convention)
NGO	Non-governmental organization
NORAD	Norwegian Agency for Development Cooperation
ODA	Official development assistance
OSCE	Organization for Security and Co-operation in Europe
PEIC	Public Environmental Information Centre
RA	Republic of Armenia
RAMSAR	Ramsar Convention on Wetlands
SAP	Structural adjustment programmes
STCI	Save Teghut Civic Initiative
UNDP	United Nations Development Programme
UNEP	United Nations Environment Programme
UNCCD	United Nations Convention to Combat Desertification
UNECE	United Nations Economic Commission for Europe
USSR	United Socialist Soviet Republics
YSU	Yerevan State University

Introduction

Armenia and several other post-Soviet republics such as Georgia receive more development aid per capita from state donors than traditional aid recipients in the Third World. At the same, proximity to Europe means that the republics in the South Caucasus are involved in various partnerships formed to align their systems of government and politics more closely with those of European countries. In analysing the Armenian case and issues related to environmentalism and development, this book seeks to broaden our understanding of this nexus of relations affecting several post-Soviet states. The ethnographic data comprise two tightly interwoven threads: environmental activism in Armenia – which is tied to European processes of what are called environmental rights – and a Norwegian-funded development cooperation project about environmental management aimed at Armenian authorities and organizations. The former relates to a European multilateral agreement called the Aarhus Convention[1] and the latter to bilateral relations and development policies directed at the post-Soviet Caucasus.

Although my principal locus is Armenia, the object of study lies at the point of convergence between sites in the world of international development projects and where their different offshoots have led (me), be it in Armenia, Moldova or Norway. I will argue that this international aid field exists not only in professional and social encounters but also in documents sent back and forth between activists, development consultants, government officials and transnational organizations. The common denominator, however, is that Armenia is the main locus and target of change in this ethnography, either from within or as a result of outsiders' influence and policies.

My argument is that 'the locals', who ostensibly are at the receiving end in Armenia, take an active part in forming, interpreting and making use of new entitlements by establishing networks and challenging authorities by connecting themselves to wider narratives and imaginaries of the global, the environment, development and Europe. I tie these elements together by applying the concept of assemblages insofar as it facilitates an analysis of how connections are made, claimed and conjured across time and place.

With regard to Armenia, my research touches on several fields, sites and 'global connections'.[2] Analysis of such connections should be based on concrete engagements rather than abstract principles of power and knowledge.[3] These engagements are situated in various places: Armenia as a political entity in the international arena as signatory and party to several multilateral environmental agreements, Armenia as an 'object' of and participant in bilateral development projects together with Norway, and fields and sites in Armenia where 'environmental rights' are contested. The book will explore issues pertaining to the Armenian natural environment and mining. Yet these issues in themselves are not dealt with substantially. I have rather chosen to discuss the environment as an object of contested political activity. I aim to understand the establishment, development and deployment of a multilateral environmental convention in its transnational context and in its Armenian context. The Aarhus Convention and the people and organizations surrounding it constitute a practice in and of itself to which various coalitions and groups attach themselves while availing themselves of the available compliance and arbitrary mechanisms to lodge protests and objections, thereby, in James Ferguson's words, making 'a hash of the vertical topography of power on which the legitimation of nation states has so long depended'.[4]

I use my experience as a project manager of one of the development projects in Armenia to analyse some central features within a 'scheme' to bring Armenia closer to Europe. Through the management of this project, I gradually became intrigued by how what I had done as project manager and the policies informing my work were legitimized in the donor office in Norway. Likewise, processes related to the Aarhus Convention somehow rested on a set of shared premises relating to development and 'the environment' as an object of political action, thereby Europeanizing Armenia from the inside as well as from the outside.

Much of what has been written on what is sometimes called 'western democracy export'[5] has revealed the ethnocentricity of outside interventions whose objective is to '[compel] them to be like our outdated image of "us"'[6] by exporting organizational categories and ideas such as 'civil society' and 'NGOs'. But what if 'they' are not interested in being compelled? What if 'they' want to attach themselves to an imaginary and outdated image of 'us'?

I was in Armenia as an agent of development change, something I found slightly problematic at the time and which this book is an attempt to resolve. I see my own participation as alternating between phases of hope, practical administration and critical understanding.[7] Development is imbued – I argue – with too much hope and inconsistent administration practices. I have no wish to protect myself; rather, I want to use this experience to ask questions pertaining to the development apparatus and advance research on issues I was involved in at first hand. My participation in webs of practices and policies tells a larger story related to international development aid and Europeanization and prompts several questions, such as how the management of Norwegian foreign aid in the Caucasus evolve and affect projects, and why Armenian activists claim adherence to a particular idea of Europe.

Let me briefly point to two different ways of framing and contextualizing Armenia. As a former Soviet republic, Armenia can be understood in light of its Soviet heritage or we can frame Armenia as an object for foreign aid. To me, both are well founded, yet the former is the most common within anthropology. In my view, both should function as an invitation to make use of the anthropological literature and insights from a wide variety of areas, in an effort to benefit from and contribute to post-socialist and post-colonial literatures in the post-Cold War world.[8]

Politics of the environment and development as anthropological problems

This book addresses issues of post-socialism, development and globality in a way I shall frame as an anthropological problem. The ethnography of Armenia's implementation of the Aarhus Convention, the foreign aid project and the role of local and international NGO networks are characterized in many ways by geographic and temporal dispersion. In this ethnography, projects, concepts, documents and networks have inherent flow capacities, yet they operate within a trajectory of post-Soviet 'transition' and development in Armenia, characterized by continuity and change. So, while acknowledging the abrupt change wrought by the dissolution of the Soviet Union, with the various democracy projects and concepts following in its wake, historical continuities and trajectories play an important role in understanding how such projects evolved on the ground, how they were negotiated and resisted. These processes, I suggest, take place within networks.

How can we conceive of a network in a way that encapsulates the multiple and flexible connections it contains? In a seminal paper to the development of ARPANET, the predecessor of the Internet, Paul Baran outlined three different types of network[9] (see Figure 0.1). The idea behind the third diagram is that in this context digital data could be moved across shared networks via multiple connections. The anthropologist Dominic Boyer extends the notion of distributed network to better understand news media in the digital age.[10]

The three diagrams can also work as an illustration of three different ways of conducting fieldwork and consequently of what we perceive as context. Whereas diagram A resembles traditional fieldwork within a confined social arena at the centre with outward-going connections and contexts, diagram B resembles a multisited ethnography and diagram C a form of ethnography where informants, ethnographers and contexts are connected in a multitude of ways with no apparent centre of gravity. As a heuristic device, this model is useful when considering how the

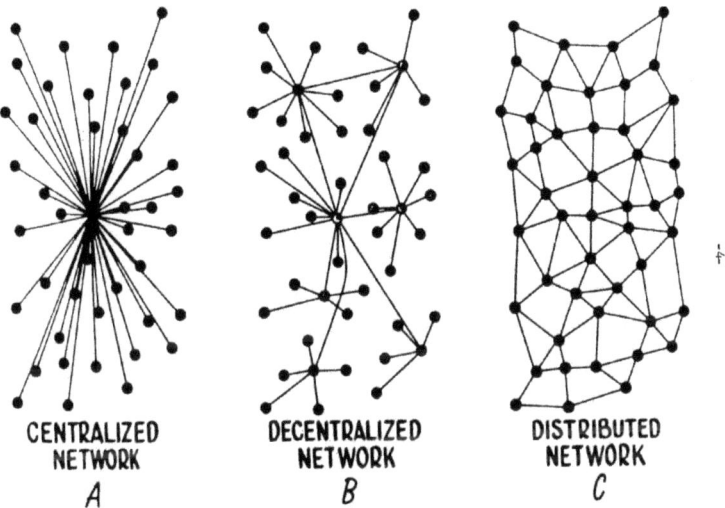

Figure 0.1 'Beating the vulnerability problem'. Copyright: RAND Corporation.
Source: Paul Baran, *Some Remarks on Digital Distributed Communications Networks* (Santa Monica, CA: RAND, 1967).

field in question is delineated, how the different positions within this distributed network can be understood and how I myself took part as a broker at several of the intersections within the network.

When studying the implementation of a multilateral environmental agreement such as the Aarhus Convention and a specific foreign aid project in Armenia with the distributed network it constitutes, it seems pertinent to ask what kind of contribution an anthropological analysis may make. This requires us not only to define the field as such (where and when) but also to discuss how what I encountered can be understood in terms of what Rabinow has labelled an 'anthropological problem'.[11] This particular field is pervaded by norms and jargon: human rights, environmental rights, democracy and development policies. We are perhaps used to thinking of multilateral agreements as a subject best left to political scientists, whereas anthropologists should study the effects of such agreements or international conservation initiatives in specific local contexts, for example the consequences of a new national park regime on Madagascar for local people's ability to continue their traditional way of life.[12] It is important to note that this presupposes separation of various levels such as the global and the local or what can be referred to as the 'vertical topography of power'.[13] I would suggest that the Aarhus Convention is first and foremost practised through networks that are imbued with practices, rules and policies that are not easily identified as either global or local. Rather, these practices actively crisscross these assumed levels to an extent that makes the divisions more confusing than enlightening. An anthropological contribution will thus be to analyse the networks and practices in their contested and complex interconnectedness within a distributed network.

One characteristic of development policies and neo-liberal reforms is their active dissemination of a 'grid of normativity into an expanding range of situations'.[14] We should investigate concepts and assumptions we normally take for granted through practices and performances since it is through them that concepts are made real. We need to investigate 'environmental rights', 'Europeanization' and 'development' in Armenia not as given entities or processes but as arbitrary, contingent and powerful.[15]

When I as an ethnographer placed myself in the midst of these relations, I found myself sited 'among anthropology's problems'.[16] As I was directly involved in the implementation of what I will call the Armenia project, this was where I found myself, in a tight, yet interesting spot. With this in mind, I set out to observe and analyse how norms and policies are assembled into contingent forms.[17] A problematization, then, is a kind of historical and social situation – saturated with power relations. I take the Europeanization of Armenia to be such a process, in which Armenian activists and project implementers play their part responding to mechanisms of international law and donor priorities.

Anthropological problems are not static or fixed; they constitute a historical place that is contingent on a more general situation comprising scientific knowledge and political actors, for example. Their distinctiveness resides in how they are 'simultaneously the object, the site and ultimately the substance, of thinking'.[18] Armenia's environmental politics and practices are the object and site, as is also the development project. As I am part of the project, I am also part of the thinking behind it and its legitimization. That was *my* problem. In order for something to be a problematization, it needs to contain 'sanctioned seriousness' or truth claims legitimated by institutions.[19] In addition, problematizations do not rely on dichotomies (such as insider/outsider, participant/observer, local/global) but rather on a *relationship* between a given (problematized) situation and the analyst (observer).[20] The relationship for me was problematic insofar as I had to navigate between different truth claims (sometimes overlapping, sometimes at odds) concerning the situation in Armenia, corruption, the need to improve their environmental management and my institutional affiliation as a research fellow at an institute dependent on research grants but also on sources of funding and project management assignments of the type I was involved in. In addition to establishing a project network, we also participated in existing networks inside and outside Armenia (using them as hubs to gain access). I actively participated, legitimated and designed the network(s) in question in a situation similar to what has been described elsewhere, where we as academics are somehow insiders and participants in policy networks as well as skilled workers in project acquisition.[21] I direct attention to this challenge because the ethnography set out in the subsequent chapters highlights these connections, fluidities and networking efforts between different practices of different organizations, institutions, documents and localities.

In the present ethnography, we have projects, seminars, environmental activism, networks, documents and project proposals that respond to and legitimate practices and policies. In *Post-Soviet Social*, Stephen J. Collier asks 'how certain practices associated with ethnography can fit into a toolkit for contemporary anthropological inquiry'.[22] The rationale for writing traditional ethnography originated in specific circumstances in which the culture or ethnos constituted the object par excellence of anthropology.[23] Anthropology, with its emphasis on participant observation in a relatively confined space – and in parallel with the colonial encounter – relied on an 'isomorphism of space, place and culture'.[24] But other kinds of objects, Collier argues, are just as interesting for anthropologists even though we still tend to start our inquiries in a certain place and even if we are led to new sites later on.[25] The present project bore such traits. What from the start looked like an Armenian 'problem' located within Armenia proved instead to be an assembly of networks, affiliations, projects and funding opportunities that not only transcended Armenia as a site but were also spread across many different places, in some of which I was actively taking part myself.

I take spaces to be hierarchically interconnected rather than naturally disconnected, where 'cultural and social change becomes not a matter of cultural contact and articulation but one of rethinking difference *through* connection'.[26] These two authors urge us to enquire into the unity of 'us' as well as the otherness of the 'other'.[27] Who are 'we' who, for various reasons and from various platforms, have tried to develop Armenia and other post-Soviet states? Where do 'we' come from? If the world consists of 'culturally, socially and economically interconnected and interdependent spaces' that essentially produce difference,[28] should we not then turn our attention to how different locations take part in various differentiating encounters with one another? In the European context of the Aarhus Convention and of the Norwegian-funded project, Armenia is but one such place where differences are produced.

Writing a thick description has been regarded – I believe rightly – as *the* anthropological endeavour. Anna Tsing, however, has shown how globalization through global connections is fragmented: 'Through fragments, ethnographers can immerse themselves in the contests and engagements of the present.'[29] This way of doing, contextualizing and writing up ethnography has several implications and I will attempt to identify those with most immediate bearing on my research.

The first implication is that we as anthropologists end up exploring sites other than those 'close' to the field. The second is that we as anthropologists have an obligation to account for the way in which we make these connections. The third is that our informants (and I) are themselves the makers of context. In my case, Armenian civil society activists can identify as such as long as their work is a continual reminder of their attempts to belong to civil society. Civil society is not something to which these activists belong per se; it is something to which they strive to belong by making claims concerning 'environmental rights', 'democracy' and so on by various means such as protests, petitions and routine NGO management. They make claims about human rights, environmental rights, about acting on behalf of a wider population as well as by referring to the Aarhus Convention.

The two projects: Environmental rights and foreign aid

Two concerted efforts to enhance environmental governance in the Republic of Armenia are discussed in this book. Rather than inquiring into how they performed (results and shortcomings), I approach them as 'projects' that are invented, contested, renegotiated and made use of in other ways. These two projects operate in several areas and in an overlapping manner. 'Project' here has a double meaning: as a singular project with a limited lifetime and available funding and as a kind of scheme, endeavour, a more or less concerted undertaking involving multiple actors. The participants in my ethnography are foreign ministries, UN agencies, the Organization for Security and Cooperation in Europe (OSCE), development consultants, researchers, local authorities and activists. Broadly speaking, the incidents I discuss took place under the umbrella of wider initiatives to turn Armenia into a state operating in accordance with European governance standards and agreements on environmental management.

Although increased transparency and participation in this field are, as in others, usually regarded as inherently 'good', one may ask how such projects and procedures are used. I am interested not because the various claims to development and democracy *are* universal and the anthropologist's task is merely to gather ethnographies on their effects in various contexts. Rather, universals are interesting as enactments to which someone, somewhere, for specific (or perhaps often unclear) reasons lays claim. Moreover, claims to the same universal may be used by different actors for competing purposes. In other words, the question is how these claims are applied in practice[30] and how they are embedded in practices that cross local, regional and global arenas.

The two different 'projects' are the Aarhus Convention and a Norwegian foreign aid project. The first I understand to be a modernization project as described by Scott[31] and Li[32] and what Tsing has coined 'bundles of ideas and practices'.[33] The Aarhus Convention and practices following its implementation in Armenia are part of a wider assemblage of environmental rights and Europeanization. Although the Aarhus Convention is institutionalized through various mechanisms we will get to know later on, it makes sense here to consider the convention and the proliferation of institutions and practices it spurs as a modernization scheme and a bundle of ideas. This approach is useful as it directs attention towards the performative and claimed aspects of the projects rather than their institutionalization and policies.

I understand the Aarhus Convention as a 'project of scale-making';[34] its applicability to Armenia is not simply a matter of effective implementation (or even resistance) but rather a process of ongoing negotiation and arbitration. I will focus on the implementation of the Aarhus Convention in the Republic of Armenia and how it spurs the creation and development of practices and affiliations in Armenian civil society domestically and internationally as well as claims of 'belonging to Europe'.

In a more conventional understanding, the 'project' here is a specific development project funded by the Norwegian Ministry of Foreign Affairs and implemented by the Fridtjof Nansen Institute (FNI). It will be referred to as 'the Armenia project'. As we will see, although it was a small-scale project with limited ramifications, it can also be understood as unfolding within a wider assemblage of foreign aid in post-Soviet states. The partnership between various Armenian ministries and the FNI proceeded in the form of seminars and 'capacity-building' efforts and lasted for five consecutive years.

The grant mechanism is managed by the Ministry of Foreign Affairs (MFA) and filed as 'ODA' in the NORAD database.[35] The name of the project mechanism has varied over the years; during the implementation period, it was called 'Project cooperation in the South Caucasus, Central Asia, Ukraine, Belarus and Moldova' on the ministry's website.[36] I was involved in this project as project manager and my interest in using my own experience grew from idea into research topic a couple of years after the Armenia project came to an end in 2010. Many of the evaluations and considerations in this book did not feed into the project cycle. In hindsight, I personally regard the Armenia project to have been of limited practical value to Armenia, whereas the focus during the implementation stage was on practical measures and acquisition of financial support. By 2010, I was advising the FNI not to request more project funding. The analysis of the project in Chapters 4 and 5 will deal with how a project that started out and remained couched within the project proposals in a language of hope increasingly became a project of management and technicalities that eventually led the project astray. Yet it was not a failure in conventional terms insofar as it secured renewed financial support year after year.[37] Norway's development cooperation policy is perhaps – as has been noted in general by Mosse – not the best guide 'to understanding the practices, events and effects of development actors, which are shaped by the relationships and interests and cultures of specific organizational settings'.[38] I will nevertheless argue that policy models and formal requirements, such as the Logical Framework (LOG frame) approach, have a huge effect.

Together with the processes related to the Aarhus Convention, the Armenia project constitutes a particular fabric of post-Soviet change and international foreign aid practices in Armenia. Taken together, these two 'projects' direct attention at processes that went on at several sites: project management at the FNI with reporting and application cycles to the Norwegian MFA, project implementation in Armenia, environmentalism in Armenia and communication with the Aarhus Compliance Committee.

One of the 'makeshift links' across diverse places that make projects seem coherent is the forging and invocation of networks and alliances.[39] How do networks come into being and what does it take to 'claim' ownership to them? By network, I mean 'a set of institutions, knowledge practices and artefacts thereof that internally generate the effects of their own reality by reflecting on themselves'.[40] I was part of such a distributed network. My empirical material is not something that is easily confined and limited to a given social field and physical entity like a village. Rather, my object of study is as mentioned characterized by being located in different places (most prominently Armenia and Norway but also Azerbaijan, Georgia and Moldova at certain points). The field exists not only in social encounters but also within documents sent back and forth between the actors.

Data collection and fieldwork

The empirical data in this book have three main strands. First, much of the data collected for this book stem from my work as project manager of the Armenia project, in the period 2006–10. The bulk of this material will be discussed in Chapters 4 and 5. Even though I was not a member of the project management team when the early 'pilot project' started in 2005, I was involved in all of its main activities. I became project manager in late 2006 just after the project's first seminar in Armenia and remained in this position until the project was concluded in 2010.

From 2006 to the end of 2009, I spent around three to four weeks in Armenia each year managing the project and four to seven months managing it from Norway. Gathering data by using my own experience as project manager in a small-scale development project is inspired by the work of David Mosse.[41] The approach allows me to analyse how policy and practices coexist in development projects and how they are negotiated by project partners (Norwegian and Armenian) and in dialogue between the implementer and donor, for example, between FNI and the Norwegian MFA.

Second, I conducted anthropological fieldwork in Armenia throughout 2010. At the time, I lived in Yerevan, Armenia's capital. While there, I managed the Armenia project in close collaboration with our Armenian partners. I regularly met with my informants, and I also conducted interviews and took part in different meetings, conferences and demonstrations.[42] During fieldwork in 2010, I followed processes and claims related to environmental rights, especially mining issues with which civil society representatives and the environmental management sector were concerned.

Third, the empirical material also consists of documents and communication between Armenian activists and the Compliance Committee of the Aarhus Convention on cases brought before it for adjudication. I monitored the progression and outcome of these issues, which were decided in 2011 and 2014, respectively. Attending the Meeting of Parties to the Aarhus Convention in Chisinau, Moldova, June 2011, where Armenian NGOs took the issue of Armenia's (non-) compliance up with the committee, gave me an insight into the processes at the international level and how Armenian environmentalists and government officials negotiate in the international arena.

These three strands of data may seem full of discontinuities insofar as the Armenia project lasted from 2005 to 2010, my Yerevan-based fieldwork took place in 2010 and the main phases of the convention-related communications occurred in 2011 and 2014. Apart from their thematic interrelatedness, these issues are more temporally parallel than might appear at first glance. While the Armenia project ended in 2010, communications with the donor continued into 2012. The material covered in the Aarhus case extends back to 2006 and the court cases in Armenia largely took place in 2009 and 2010. Communication between the Armenian activists and the Compliance Committee started in 2009. Hence, while I was on fieldwork in 2010, significant events occurred that extended backwards in time (and hence were more aligned with the Armenia project's timeframe). They also involved some of the people who were also involved in the Armenia project and I discussed the ongoing compliance case and court cases with my informants and in additional interviews with other relevant people.

My extensive involvement in parts of the field as project manager and how the job should be tackled analytically and ethically calls for some methodological considerations. As others have observed, it is 'impossible to speak of ethnographic "data" independent of their collector and analyst'.[43] This obviously applies to me as well. I am part and parcel of the ethnography set out in the following chapters to the extent that the field is both within and without myself.[44] My aim is therefore to turn what is familiar to me as a project manager inside out so as to 'render it accessible ethnographically'.[45] The ethnography of the Armenia project places the ethnographer at its core, since I as its project manager was in charge of running it. The empirical material in these chapters is therefore constituted by personal project experiences, project documents (applications, reports and support letters) produced largely as a result of plans and ideas originating in the anthropologist's own office.[46]

One important feature here is that anthropologists working in development projects do not necessarily conduct themselves and act as anthropologists.[47] That was probably the case with me. Even though I am employed as a researcher at FNI in my capacity as a social anthropologist, in the Armenia project I was not deploying my anthropological knowledge and practices per se. Rather, I managed the project and adapted myself to meet the various requirements stipulated by the donor. My scepticism – stemming from my training as an anthropologist – was not something that could be easily and constructively translated and utilized within the project framework. Does my involvement imply that I am a development (or applied) anthropologist? Apart from marketing our background as social scientists at a research institute, FNI staff did not really emphasize our particular academic qualifications when we applied to run this project, as opposed to when we apply for research grants otherwise, the institute's main source of financing. The project can be better understood as one that by chance was led by an anthropologist rather than one in which the intention was to use anthropological knowledge. My anthropological knowledge is not amenable to grids, LOG frames and so on,[48] management tools the Armenia project had to apply and utilize. If I had refused to use these managerial tools, the project, I believe, would have collapsed. If I had written the project proposal based on anthropological knowledge, we would not have received funding.

What I did as project manager was in significant ways intertwined with Aarhus-related processes in Armenia and unfolded within the institutional Convention set-up. And what if my ability to manoeuvre the project had more to do with how I could align and harmonize it with related processes – however far-fetched, arbitrary or non-committal these connections actually were? Pursuing ethnographic fieldwork in a place where I myself was situated as project manager means that my position is well defined; I do not pretend to be 'standing above the fray or of suppressing subjectivity'.[49] My own involvement as project manager is at the same time challenging for the exact same reason: subjectivity. A proposition to resolve some of the dilemma is based on an argument for reinstating ethical thinking in development. In *A Moral Critique of Development*,[50] the contributors set out to explore and forge links between development anthropology and moral philosophy or in other words between understanding and responsibility.[51] One particularly interesting feature is the argument that development could be understood as going through phases of hope, administration and critical reflection.[52] The authors claim that not only has development gone through these phases historically, but they are also present within singular development projects: thus it is important to take into account the moral imperative of developmental utopias, practical concerns when *doing development* and critical questions about whether development proved more of a mess than a must also within singular development projects.[53]

To me, it is clear that these tendencies not only reflect historical phases but also aspects of specific projects such as the Armenia project and the distributed network which I helped construct and belonged to. In the trajectory of the project discussed by Mosse,[54] it started as hope, became more and more a matter of administration, which in the end led the author to think critically about what he was doing.[55] I believe that development as hope, politics and critical understanding is best understood as a triangle in which the three aspects are not treated as being mutually antithetical but as different aspects of project life. This is in line with what the authors suggest, that the three aspects presuppose each other.[56] An interesting feature of these three aspects – hope, administration and critical understanding – is that the terms provide a way of delineating the phases I myself went through with regard to the Armenia project.

Developing and extending this point for the purpose of my analysis could imply that in order to locate western 'do-gooders' and post-Soviet 'recipients' – as the post-socialist literature tends to do – within a common framework, it could be argued that both are adhering to the same assemblages and participating in the same networks. Despite originating from different strands, claims of adherence to global values of democracy, transparency and participation are rife. Thus, scales that are conjured from both sides are where we find common ground when we meet in the manageable slices of reality projects construct.[57] Rather than regarding us as located at opposite ends of the 'development encounter', it is perhaps better to think of us as occupying a common framework of 'developers and the developed, self and other'.[58]

As a heuristic device to organize the material around, I find the notion of development as hope, politics and critical understanding fruitful. Discussing various phases and aspects of environmental activism in Armenia and analysing them in relation to these three categories allows me to escape the often uncomfortable premise of cynicism, passivity or mere adaptation.

One of the purposes of this study is to discuss and enlarge on what we know about various manifestations and legitimizations of environmental policies, development policies, environmental activism and project implementation and claims to them. I try to show that the field of project cooperation is open for, if not naked manipulation, at least tacit adjustments and misrepresentations by actors like me. I, like many others I assume, treated project acquisition, management and reporting as a practice where adherence to policy changes in a beneficial way was crucial. In so doing, I am not much different from those NGOs and activists in the post-Soviet areas that depend on foreign aid and whose most important connection is with the donor.[59] A better understanding of these processes can be reached with the use of post-colonial literature, thereby combining post-socialist and post-colonial literature as has been called for in the post-Cold War era.[60]

Structure of the book

The following questions are addressed in this book, especially in the four empirically oriented chapters:

1. How can we understand the Aarhus Convention as a social and political process of scale making and how it plays out in Armenia? (Chapter 2)
2. In what ways and where (in the streets, in documents?) does Armenian civil society use domestic and international mechanisms in order to make its networks real? (Chapter 3)
3. How do project reporting cycles and adjustments affect, legitimate and alter project implementation? (Chapter 4)
4. In what ways are networks and project spaces made and maintained through development projects? (Chapter 5)

The next chapter will provide the contextual and historical background within Armenia and in relation to the Aarhus Convention. Armenia is the site and object – with the active consent and participation of Armenia and Armenians – of a range of projects, developmental and otherwise, that interpret Armenia as being in a process of Europeanization. In the rest of Chapter 1, I develop a conceptual framework suited to the forthcoming analysis.

The Aarhus Convention and the fashion in which it came about, the institutional set-up it spurred in Armenia (and elsewhere), are indicative of a neo-liberal approach to governance with a global reach, to which governments and environmentalists are eager to subject themselves but also to challenge and subvert. Chapter 2 elaborates on how this takes place at the international level and through efforts to develop a pan-European legal framework for environmental rights and the kind of institutional proliferation it has caused in Armenia. The chapter also analyses how European values are touted in and with regard to Armenia. In Chapter 3, the focus is on how and where (in the streets, in documents) Armenian civil society uses domestic and international mechanisms to make their networks real. This is the second version of how Europe is performed with regard to Armenia, for example, how activists make use of domestic and international mechanisms.

The entire process of reporting, applying for and, in effect, negotiating project support from the Norwegian MFA shows how the practice of latching minor projects onto ambitious (albeit fairly superficial) development policies is an endeavour in the technicalities of benchmarking, identification of risks, inputs, outputs and impacts to apply 'management by objectives' jargon. Chapter 4 addresses this issue in terms of Norwegian foreign aid efforts in Armenia and the Caucasus and the ways in which donors apply projects of scale in Armenia. It also includes how the project mechanism's reporting cycles and adjustments affect, legitimate and alter project implementation. These issues will be analysed largely by depicting the relationship between donor and implementer in the Armenia project. It is discussed with regard to how the project management tool – the LOG frame – and other development-related administrative practices affected the project. In Chapter 5, I ask in what ways networks are made and maintained through development projects and how they constitute professional and social project spaces. It can be understood as a process of enacting 'Europe' through seminars and repeated behaviours at east/west crossroads. This ethnography tells fascinating as well as revealing stories of participation, collusion and cooperation in the world of development and environmental projects.

The final chapter wraps up the ethnography and discussion and points to possible avenues for future research in the field, calling at the same time for concerted efforts to bring the anthropology of post-socialism and development together, as attempted in this book.

It is worth noting here that the reader will see how the vertical structure of the ethnography, starting in Chapter 2 at the international level and with Armenian activists campaigning at home and abroad in Chapter 3, through Chapter 4 on donor organizations and project management and Chapter 5 on project implementation with Armenian partners, is just a heuristic device for organizing the material. This vertical dimension is gradually subverted by the activities of the involved actors through various claims pertaining to the world of international development and environmentalism through the distributed networks which I and my informants helped create, were members of and participated in.

1

Development and 'transition' in Armenia: Contexts and concepts

I was introduced to Armenia in September 2006, when I found myself at a holiday resort in the Armenian mountains participating at a seminar discussing how Armenia could honour its 'international obligations' in its management of the environment. The project was funded by the Norwegian Ministry of Foreign Affairs (MFA), while the FNI was the implementing party. During the five-day seminar, lectures were given on topics related to the various multilateral environmental agreements (MEAs) Armenia had ratified, lessons Norway had learned from implementing MEAs and an international perspective on implementation practices and experiences. The role civil society might have in this process was also discussed.

Three days earlier, I had arrived in Armenia on my first ever visit to the country. On the flight from Moscow, passengers clapped as we landed at Zvartnots International Airport and I soon discovered that this small, landlocked country is quite different from Russia, although they share a common Soviet past. After checking in at the university guest house, I decided to have a look at the city. I went down the main boulevard Mesrop Mashtots Street – and found a street café opposite the opera. While waiting for a bottle of the local Erebuni beer and barbeque – *khorovats* – I looked out on the bustling street with its congested traffic. Soviet-era cars such as Volgas and Zhigulis were nearly outnumbered by European SUVs and the occasional Iranian-made Khodro. Looking up the climbing street, I saw a statue in front of an impressive building and on the hilltop behind a giant statue of a woman holding a sword in her hands.

I did not know it then, but the first of these statues was of Mesrop Mashtot, the inventor of the Armenian and Georgian alphabets. The Armenian alphabet was created in AD 405, making Armenian one of the first languages the Bible was translated into. Preceding this, Armenia was the first state to adopt Christianity and the Armenian Apostolic Church thus traces its history back to 301. The building behind the statue of Mashtot is the Matenadaran, a museum of old Armenian manuscripts built during the Khrushchev-era thaw when Armenia was a Soviet republic. The statue on the hilltop is of Mother Armenia, erected in 1967, replacing a statue of Josef Stalin that stood on the same spot until 1962. Had it not been for the opera building and the smog, I would have been able to see Mount Ararat in the distance where, according to biblical legend, Noah's ark came to rest. One of his sons – Hayk – is considered by Armenians to be their forefather. Hence, Armenians call their land Hayastan – land of Hayk.

Hayastan

Armenia – or Hayastan – is geographically located at the very fringes of Europe. As a modern-day political entity, its official name is the Republic of Armenia and it gained its independence on 21 September 1991, after some seventy years of Soviet rule, which obviously left its mark politically, economically, structurally, socially and culturally. Armenia is a mountainous, landlocked republic located in the South Caucasus, with 2.94 million inhabitants.[1] The map in Figure 1.1 shows the internationally recognized political entities and borders in the region.

Armenia covers approximately 30,000 square kilometres and has a continental highland climate with fairly harsh and cold winters and hot summers. No point is below 390 metres above sea level and at its highest point – Mount Aragats in the Aragatson province north-east of the capital Yerevan – it rises 4,090 metres above sea level. Yerevan is approximately 1,000 metres above sea level, with the fertile Ararat

Figure 1.1 Map of Armenia. Copyright: Library of Congress, Geography and Map Division.
Source: US Central Intelligence Agency. Armenia. (Washington, DC: Central Intelligence Agency, 2002) Map. Retrieved from the Library of Congress, https://www.loc.gov/item/2002625531/ (accessed 15 February 2018).

valley sloping south-eastwards to the Arax river, the border with Turkey.

When the Soviet Union was formed in 1922, Armenia was one of the three founding members of the Transcaucasian Socialist Federative Soviet Republic (TSFSR), together with Azerbaijan and Georgia. That republic lasted until 1936, when it was split into three separate Soviet republics.

Independence and crisis in Armenia

The first post-Soviet years were extremely traumatic for the Armenian population with Armenia warring with Azerbaijan over the Armenian-dominated autonomous republic of Nagorny Karabakh, situated within Azerbaijan. The war led to the 1993 blockade by Azerbaijan and Turkey, hindering the direct import of most goods into Armenia, including gas for heating. Most of the armed conflicts that followed the collapse of the Soviet Union took place in the Caucasus and of them the war over Nagorny Karabakh was definitely the bloodiest.[2] The actual number of casualties is hard to verify since both sides tend to exaggerate their own losses and downplay those of their opponents. According to different sources, however, casualties range between 17,000 and 25,000, with roughly two-thirds on the Azerbaijani side. The number of internally displaced persons (IDPs) in Azerbaijan is around 750,000 and around 350,000 Armenians fled Azerbaijan.[3]

In 1994, a fragile ceasefire came into force in Nagorny Karabakh. Armenian forces and freedom fighters (*fedayehin*) now controlled most of the former autonomous republic Nagorny Karabakh and the Azerbaijani provinces situated between it and Armenia proper. Due to the conflict – which prompted Azeris living in Armenia to flee for Azerbaijan – Armenia is now an ethnically homogeneous state; 98 per cent of the population is Armenians. Armenia has never formally recognized the Republic of Nagorny Karabakh despite it being the quasi-republic's only trading partner. The frozen conflict casts a long,[4] dark shadow over Armenian political discourse. The political climate in both countries is at such a low ebb that any sign of willingness to compromise by either part would be seen as betrayal, even though the political elites in both countries doubtless realize the necessity of doing so. The wars have benefited key political and economic figures in the various conflicts in the post-Soviet area.[5] In Armenia, the separatists of the 1990s became state builders and the mother republic's heads of state and 'state-like entities'[6] like Nagorny Karabakh gained legitimacy and influence as functioning de facto republics.⁷ The hold of the 'Karabakh clan' on Armenian politics is evident: two former presidents are originally Karabakh Armenians and both held senior positions in Karabakh during the war: Robert Kocharyan (1998–2008) led the separatist Arthsakh movement and was the first president of Nagorny Karabakh (1994–7). Like Kocharyan, president Serzh Sargsyan (2008–18) was born in Stepanaekert, Nagorny Karabakh, and fought in the war over Nagorny Karabakh. He became minister of defence in Armenia in 1993, prior to the 1994 ceasefire. In addition, Kocharyan's predecessor and Armenia's first president, Levon Ter-Petrosyan (1991–8), led the Karabakh movement from Yerevan.

When Armenia gained independence in 1991, it was still struggling with the aftermath of the severe 1988 magnitude 7.0 earthquake in north-western Armenia whose epicentre was close to the town of Spitak. The hardest hit city was the second largest in the country, Gyumri (at the time known as Leninakan), where more than half of the taller-frame stone buildings collapsed, leaving half a million people homeless. Around 24,000 people are estimated to have died following the earthquake and as of 2015, around 1,000 families are still living in the 'temporary' shipping containers set up after the earthquake in Gyumri. Yet another 1,000 families are living in severely damaged buildings.⁸ Another consequence of the earthquake is that Armenia's only nuclear power plant – Metsamor some 50 kilometres from Gyumri – was closed for security reasons from early 1989 to 1993. It was restarted to compensate the loss of fuel caused by the Azerbaijani and Turkish blockade.

As in most other post-Soviet republics, Armenia saw the establishment of many non-governmental organizations (NGOs) following independence. Many of them came as a response to the many aid programmes funded by the West. The first environmental NGO in Armenia was reportedly the *perestroika*-era Green Union of Armenia, established as Goyapahpanutyun in 1985.⁹ For the most part, these NGOs are limited in size and impact mostly because their most important connections are with their international donors. They therefore have few incentives to work together at the local level.¹⁰

Literature on civil society in the post-Soviet area often focuses on the unwanted or unintended effects of democratization initiatives funded by western donor agencies and governments.[11] According to Armenians, there are three types of NGOs in Armenia: genuine, 'grant-eaters' (*grantagerner*) and pocket (*grbanayin*) NGOs.[12] The popular impression in Armenia is that many NGOs are established by the political elite for their own economic benefit. The sheer volume of western development interventions in Armenian civil society may in fact have 'turned democracy into a project and civil society into NGOs'.[13] The growth of NGOs following the dismantling of the Soviet Union was largely a response to western donor priorities such as fostering civil society in the wake of the Soviet collapse. Whereas Armenia had 44 registered NGOs in 1994, it only took two more years to bring the number up to 1,500. At the time of fieldwork, Armenia had more than 3,300 registered NGOs.[14] Civil society and NGOs were held to be the 'magic bullet'[15] or 'connective tissue'[16] between state and society. The result, well documented with regard to Russia,[17] was a proliferation of NGOs mainly preoccupied maintaining a 'special relationship' with their donors and their donor priorities in a fashion that did not foster domestic cooperation within civil society. Further, the proliferation of this kind of organization, mostly small set-ups run by 'NGO professionals', inspired a view of NGOs as mostly concerned about taking care of themselves.

Making Armenia European

The various processes in the field of environmental management and international development in Armenia can be understood as a (post-Soviet) process of Europeanization. By Europeanization I mean processes that in different ways are intended to bring Armenia and other former Soviet republics closer to Europe via institutional set-ups, changes in governance and law. They take place under umbrellas such as the Eastern Partnership (EaP), a joint initiative involving the European Union, Armenia, Azerbaijan, Belarus, Georgia, the Republic of Moldova and Ukraine. Negotiations on a new agreement between Armenia and the EU were opened in 2015, to replace the old 1999 EU–Armenia Partnership and Cooperation Agreement despite Armenia's decision in 2013 not to sign the Association Agreement with the EU.[18] Another collaborative forum is the United Nations Economic Commission for Europe (UNECE). Seen in this light, Europeanization is a loosely defined package of processes of European semi-integration, not to be confused with the tighter integration envisaged by EU member states. In fact, for those who nourish a hope, EU membership for Armenia is not on the table. These processes are nevertheless important, especially considering the uncertainties stemming from Armenia's 2013 membership of the Eurasian Union. Armenia, together with Belarus, is also a member of the Collective Security Treaty Organization, an offshoot of the Commonwealth of Independent States.

An important question is what 'Europe' constitutes in Armenian and international political discourse. 'Europe' can have (at least) two different meanings, as a place and as an idea.[19] Armenia, it is argued, has to choose between Europe and Russia as its foremost strategic ally.[20] 'Europe', however, features most prominently in Armenia as an idea, rather than as an economic or strategic ally.[21] The Russian Federation is Armenia's main trading as well as strategic partner. Evidence of the efforts Armenia is making to tie itself closer to Europe can be found in the European conventions and governance instruments that are (potentially) changing Armenian environmental law and management, including the Aarhus Convention of course. The convention offers an interesting case since one of its aims is to help 'countries of Eastern Europe, Caucasus and Central Asia and of South-Eastern Europe to improve their environmental standards'.[22] Europe as idea is projected onto former socialist republics. My material suggests that this could be studied not merely as an Armenian response to external influence or impositions but also reflexively in a way that highlights the interconnectedness between international actors (donors, project implementers), Armenian activists and bureaucrats, between small-scale development projects and larger-scale political processes, networks and practices. This book studies processes related to what for now may be loosely termed the Europeanization in Armenia, even though it will not disregard the counter-European tendencies in the post-Soviet area such as the Eurasian Union.

UNECE and the environment for Europe process

It is useful to revisit processes on the European stage after the fall of the Iron Curtain because they enabled the creation of the Aarhus Convention, whose precursor was within the UNECE framework. The United Nations has five regional commissions, of which UNECE is the European branch. Its full name is the United Nations Economic Commission for Europe. UNECE has fifty-six member states: all the European states, Canada, the United States, Israel and the entire area of the former Soviet Union including the post-Soviet republics in the South Caucasus and Central Asia. Immediately following the fall of the Iron Curtain, sixteen newly independent states joined UNECE, countries that 'at least symbolically, were keen to embrace democratic values'.[23]

UNECE hosts various committees, one of which is the Committee on Environmental Policy. The Aarhus Convention and other environmental instruments fall under the umbrella of this committee. The UNECE secretariat is based in Geneva, Switzerland. Under this framework, Josef Vavrousek, former minister of the environment in the former Czechoslovakia, initiated the 'Environment for Europe' process, whose first conference was held in 1991 in Prague. Following the 1995 publication of *Guidelines on Access to Environmental Information and Public Participation in Environmental Decision-Making*, the broadened membership base provided the momentum UNECE needed to promote a governance agenda that combined norms of environmental protection with democratic entitlements.[24] This was embraced within UNECE as having a transformative potential in forging a new social contract between citizens and governments in the former socialist countries.[25]

UNECE's promotion of environmental information disclosure, however, 'cannot be divorced from its democracy promotion efforts in Central and Eastern Europe'.[26]

The specific historical and ideological context of the Aarhus Convention should therefore be taken into consideration. As an ideological vehicle, the Aarhus Convention is clearly *liberal* in the way 'environmental democracy' was largely defined by US and Western European models of market liberalism.[27] Private companies have considerable discretion, they are exempt from public accountability and public authorities can refuse to disseminate environmental information if deemed commercially sensitive.

It was at the Fourth Environment for Europe Conference – in Aarhus in 1998 – that the Aarhus Convention was adopted and opened for signature. In the minutes from the Third Conference in Sofia, Bulgaria, it was stated that a 'regional Convention on Public Participation should be developed with appropriate involvement of NGOs'.[28] One of the aims of the entire process was to help 'countries of Eastern Europe, Caucasus and Central Asia and of South-Eastern Europe to improve their environmental standards'.[29] It is a rather obvious example of a scale-making project and Norwegian policies on supporting projects in the region are, as we will see, in line with this.

As said, the Convention rests on liberal democratic premises and leaves the parties with significant interpretative discretion; but it also introduces an original connection between the environment and human rights. Information can be understood by activists and NGOs as a means to reach a political end; if they can get hold of the information, they can more easily hold governments to account. Although the Aarhus Convention made 'the greatest legal progress in ensuring transnational public entitlements', convention parties have repeatedly put procedural difficulties in the way when handling public information requests.[30] Governments often justify these blockages precisely with reference to their ample discretion under the Convention,[31] for example, governments can interpret Convention provisions in a way that fits their existing legal and regulatory frameworks.

UNECE oversees a total of five environmental conventions and eleven protocols, regulating air pollution, environmental impact assessments, industrial accidents, transboundary waters and public participation. 'These treaties', UNECE states, 'are concrete and effective instruments to bridge the former dividing line between East and West and to integrate countries with economies in transition into a pan-European legal and economic space'.[32]

This is a clear example of UNECE's ambitious politics of scale and also a triumphant[33] perspective on a post-Cold War process of transition that at the time was both fashionable and naïve.[34] Although the end of the Cold War is referred to as a 'former dividing line',[35] it persists in many ways in a different guise: 'economies in transition' are welcomed into a pan-European community. It could very well be argued that the reason attempts are made to persuade these countries to join the pan-European project is to make them 'western' in form and get them to change their affiliation from 'them' to 'us'. The tools to be employed, which reveal it as a scale-making project, are various standardized norms and procedures under the conventions and protocols. Armenia thus endeavours to become truly European, and it is a fairly commonly held view that the Aarhus Convention and similar instruments can be regarded as a form of entry ticket to the 'club of civilized, democratic societies'.[36]

European standards through the Aarhus Convention

The Aarhus Convention – its full name is the United Nations Economic Commission for Europe (UNECE) Convention on Access to Information, Public Participation in Decision Making and Access to Justice in Environmental Matters – will be put under special scrutiny in this book. The practices it leads to in Armenia will be treated as empirical data. The Convention will not be understood as a given, or Armenia's implementation of it and its mechanisms as matters of effectiveness, compliance or success.

The Aarhus Convention, as the long version of its name suggests, is a 'pan-European' environmental convention covering issues related to public participation in decision making and access to information on environmental issues. It was adopted in 1998 at the Fourth Ministerial Conference in the 'Environment for Europe' process and entered into force in October 2001, when it became a legally binding instrument in those countries that had ratified it. As of August 2015, forty-eight countries have ratified the Convention. Out of these, ten were not among the original signatories, but acceded later, including the Republic of Armenia in 2001. The most notable non-participating country in Europe is the Russian Federation. The secretariat of the Convention is located in Geneva at the headquarters of the UNECE. Every third year, the parties to the convention (the countries that have ratified it) convene at what is called a Meeting of Parties (MoP).[37]

In general terms, the Aarhus Convention seeks to combine human rights with protection of the environment. Rules and procedures on access to information, decision making and justice are defined in the legally binding text and make up what are commonly referred to as the 'three pillars' in the discourse on environmental rights. A basic premise of the Convention is that sustainable development can only be reached through the involvement of all relevant stakeholders. Given that the Convention seeks to 'promote environmental democracy' through 'a set of standards that are designed to be achievable across a large and politically diverse region,[38] there appears to be an implicit belief in a universal (or at least European) standard of democratic environmental practices and how they can be best achieved. In short then, according to the UNECE, the Convention seeks to strengthen 'environmental democracy' by providing parties to the Convention with rules and obligations, which for many countries requires a completely new approach to management as well as changing the environmental discourse. Among the parties to the Convention, status and means of implementation obviously vary. In Norway, for instance, ratification led to a new act, regulating access to environmental information and decision making. In Armenia, the rights under the Convention are formally warranted under the constitution of the Republic of Armenia. Armenia is further obliged to ensure that its existing legal acts and regulatory framework are updated to accommodate the Convention principles. This can be done either by amending existing legal acts or introducing new laws. Here, much remains to be done, also because although formal democratic institutions are established in Armenia, Armenia has a long way to go before it becomes a democracy in the conventional meaning of the term.[39]

The above has placed Armenia within its post-Soviet, developmental and European context. Analytically, it can be situated within literatures focusing on post-socialism, development practices and the role of regional and global mechanisms and how they operate in various contexts. In the remainder of this chapter, I shall deal with these issues and subsequently argue for a combination of the various analytical frameworks.

Post-Soviet transition or development?

Armenia's past as the Armenian Socialist Soviet Republic (ASSR) implies that studies of Armenia largely proceed from within the realm of post-socialist studies. Within the study of post-socialism, there is a substantial literature on the exaggerated optimism of 'transitology' of the 1990s,[40] the ethnocentricity of western democracy exports,[41] the focus on NGOs and civil society as vehicles of democratic change[42] and more specifically their impact in Armenia.[43] Differences aside, this literature often emphasizes our need to consider not only the specific historical setting following the collapse of the Soviet Union but also to acknowledge that several aspects of 'actually existing socialism' were seen as legitimate by large swathes of the population as long as the states managed to provide job security and welfare.[44] Legacies of corruption, network practices, property regimes and public infrastructure also need to be taken into consideration.[45]

On a more general note, from the micro level of implementing a development project to the larger east–west discourse, the same narrative emanates from the perceived fact that the West 'won' the Cold War: the East needs now to learn from the West through the transfer of expertise, 'capacity building' and 'democratization'. Unlike the Third World, however, the Second World was perceived to be like us and therefore able to 'recover'.

Following the collapse of the Soviet Union, it was generally anticipated in the West – by governments, economists and NGOs – that the former Soviet republics would 'transition' into liberal democracies and market economies. It did not take long before this naïve and even 'triumphant' attitude was replaced with 'disillusionment' and 'adjustment'.[46] Yet contacts, alliances, projects and networks were established across the former political divide: western fly-in experts touted the virtues of democracy and a 'vibrant civil society' and participants from both sides took part in what has been dubbed a 'game of co-operation'.[47] In this game, it is probably fair to say that both sides played an equal part, although the prevailing power relations enabled western donors to set the stage, leaving the recipients to accommodate and adjust to changing donor policies.[48]

Governments in the newly formed independent states were eager to sign international agreements regulating environmental politics, since it indicated membership of the international community. Whereas many western European countries normally ratify an international instrument after EU and national laws and regulations have been brought into compliance, many former socialist countries went the opposite way, ratifying the international instrument in question and then beginning the (slow) process of aligning domestic laws with the ratified convention.[49] By implication, one might say, this puts the emphasis on the intention to change rather than its actual implementation, a process a good few of my informants claimed got nowhere at all in Armenia. On the same note, newly established local environmental organizations were eager to forge alliances with environmental NGOs in the West. In many instances, these organizations were in fact established with the support of western donors, suggesting that NGOs, transnational institutions, development organizations, governments and academia were forging global connections in the post-Soviet area. These connections can be analysed via the concrete engagements and practices they gave rise to, rather than by taking the ideology of 'democratization', 'civil society', 'capacity building' and 'environmentalism' at face value. For instance, 'civil society' should not be taken as a neutral concept we can employ analytically in a given field; rather, we should look for ways in which the concept is used, employed and embedded in practices.[50]

'Environmental governance' is one such phrase, which in various ways permeates the field of post-socialist change and the efforts of newly independent states to become truly 'European'. Armenia is one of several countries impatient to create closer ties with Europe by signing and ratifying international environmental agreements. 'Environmental governance' can simply be understood to mean formal and informal rules and procedures by which a society manages its natural resources. One way in which Armenia does this is by concluding various agreements with other states. These mechanisms are usually referred to as MEAs and regulate, for instance, the management of wetlands[51] and responses to desertification.[52] The Aarhus Convention relates to procedural issues concerning the right of citizens to have and demand access to information and participation in decision making, to be discussed in the following chapters. These procedural issues have spurred institutional proliferation and been decisive to the emergence of new practices among environmentalists in Armenia. Environmental governance seen thus is a set of internationally sanctioned rules and practices. In the case of Armenia, it involves a complex web of local organizations, international donors and institutions.

Another take on Armenia is to analyse it in terms of foreign aid and development. Over the past twenty-five years, Armenia has been caught up in convergent streams of conflict, post-socialist transition programmes, neo-liberal governance efforts and development projects. Armenia, Georgia, Moldova and Kyrgyzstan are the largest recipients of foreign aid per capita among the former Soviet republics. In 2016 Armenia received $111.6 per capita, whereas Georgia received the highest figure, $124.4 per capita.[53] To compare, the Armenian figure is above that of countries such as Kenya, Malawi, Mozambique, Tanzania and many of the other 'traditional' recipients in Africa and elsewhere. Insofar as these numbers are per capita only and these African nations receive much more foreign aid than Armenia in absolute terms (Armenia received $408 million in gross total compared to Kenya's $2.593 million),[54] the figures still indicate a substantial effort to develop various former Soviet republics. There is a multitude of development projects aimed at 'democratizing' Armenia, facilitating 'capacity building' and so on.

In many ways then, the case of Armenia should contribute to the scholarly discourse both on post-socialism as well as development and especially on the linkages between them and the continuing effects of the Cold War rhetoric.[55] In the analysis of my ethnographic data, I therefore make use of insights from post-socialist studies and post-colonial literature on development comparatively, hoping thereby to contribute to the dialogue between post-socialist and post-colonial studies while refusing to accept the intellectual division of labour in the social sciences inherited from the Cold War.[56] Especially when considering the inner workings of development projects and the relationship between policy, practice, donor and recipient, I will argue that we have much to gain from engaging with the literature of the post-colonial area. Indeed, I believe a better understanding of especially the Armenians' own participation in the projects may be reached this way.

Post-socialism

Its discussion of these processes of transition, transformation and change in the post-socialist world and their warranted and unwarranted consequences on people's everyday life is probably the main contribution so far of the anthropology of post-socialism. It includes works on legitimacy, privatization and transition,[57] economic reforms,[58] with several on post-socialism,[59] civil society,[60] value transformation and property,[61] urban life[62] and, speaking perhaps most clearly to the point of this discussion, Burawoy and Verdery in the edited volume *Uncertain Transition*.[63]

Burawoy and Verdery claim that certain 'conventional metaphors' haunt theories of modernization, marketization, democratization and thus transition.[64] A characteristic hallmark of modernization theories is their focus on macro structures rather than the micro level of everyday practices[65] and although transition should imply a process connecting past and future, it is often 'committed to some pre-given future or rooted in an unyielding past'.[66] Transition theories are often teleological and lack sensibility towards everyday life.[67]

'Transition' can be understood as a period of 'suspension' between past and future.[68] As regards my ethnography, I take this to cover not only a wide range of practices but also attempts to compel nation states to affiliate with Europe. The connective tissue here is how these attempts are made from both sides – obviously not from past and future – but from east and west, from the 'subject' of development and from the agent of development. We also need to take into account how conflicting social imaginaries can co-exist, since the process of transformation in effect replaces socialist modernity's portrayal of capitalism as erroneous with capitalist modernity's portrayal of socialism as flawed.[69]

Within anthropology there has been a debate on post-socialism's contribution to the development of anthropological theory, the persistence of Cold War imageries[70] and whether western anthropologists have leaned towards 'ambivalent Orientalism':[71]

> Rarely has social change been so dramatic and simultaneously so accessible to scientific research as in the case of the unexpected collapse of socialism in the former Soviet sphere of influence in Europe. However, early hopes of anthropological theory building soon gave way to disillusionment.[72]

The assertion that post-socialist anthropology has contributed less than what one might have hoped for is perhaps a bit exaggerated, yet theories from other strands of anthropology could be given a freer rein within post-socialist studies.[73]

Rather, the contributions examining post-socialist change have shown among other things that western interventions such as market reforms and participatory cooperation schemes have often been rather naïve, and their results varied, something connected with various historical and political trajectories of the post-socialist states.[74]

Exactly this capacity and willingness to critically question western efforts at 'democratizing' the former socialist countries is a significant contribution. Where the 'fashionable transitology' was imbued with normativity and change was considered something that just happens by necessity, anthropologists have been able to reveal the workings of the socialist system with its emphasis on informal networks such as *blat*,[75] legitimacy through the 'benevolent Father party',[76] the production of mistrust[77] and how 'talk' is constituted around 'litanies' about everything that does not work as it should.[78] There is also a vast literature on property rights, changing dynamics in cities and so on.[79]

The consequences of the economic shock doctrine have reportedly gone through phases such as 'triumphalism', 'disillusionment', and 'adjustment',[80] where societies are often mistakenly perceived as blank slates ready to adjust and adopt democratic practices. It resembles development aid in Africa where it is seen as 'hooking citizens up into a national – and ultimately universal – grid of modernity'.[81] There are also several relevant contributions on civil society and the emergence of NGOs, showing how problematic the western export of the concept of civil society as if it really existed in its ideal form in the West.[82] It has created a sector dependent on foreign aid,[83] a game of cooperation with 'ritual lip-service'[84] and project-speak.[85] The cited literature largely stems from ethnographies of east and central Europe, the Balkans and Russia. With regard to Armenia, there is a substantial literature on NGOs, civil society and social movements[86] showing the dependence of Armenian civil society on foreign funds insofar as 'democracy has become a project'.[87] It also describes how new social movements emerge both in collusion with and in opposition to NGOs,[88] which, it is argued by activists, sought to 'mitigat[e] the damage rather than oppos[e]' it.[89]

Ishkanian argues that the activists she writes about (which to some extent comprise the same activists, NGOs and networks I write about) challenged the 'gospel of neo-liberalism'.[90] I, on the other hand, want to discuss how these activists attach themselves to neo-liberal artefacts such as the Aarhus Convention.

From my own experience of studying exports of western democracy to Russia and especially Norwegian project collaboration programmes there[91] and also to some extent in Azerbaijan, Belarus, Georgia and Ukraine,[92] the situation is strikingly similar to what I observed in Armenia, although the various countries have definitely followed different political and historical trajectories. Civil society – or at least those parts of civil society I am familiar with – is utterly dependent on foreign funds in a situation where the legal frameworks regarding NGOs have been tightened by lawmakers over the years in several countries, most notably perhaps in Armenia, Azerbaijan and Russia. At the same time, although the public's trust in NGOs is limited, ad hoc networks flourish in many places in the former Soviet Union. With regard to Armenia, there are descriptions of how these networks coexist and nourish themselves on established NGOs in a 'surreptitious symbiosis'.[93] But I think what is often missing in these contributions are relevant anthropological studies of the nexus of policy and practice in development aid and the participation of the 'locals'. This, I hold, can be better accounted for by employing a focus on how claims to belonging to Europe are made real by invoking assemblages.

If I had chosen to stay more or less comfortably within the confines of post-socialist anthropology, I certainly would have had relevant theories to draw on. There is an abundance of literature on various practices and effects pertaining to developments within post-Soviet, Russian and Armenian civil society, the relationship between donor and recipient and so on.[94] Where post-socialist anthropology has various perspectives related to state socialism's legacies,[95] post-colonial studies focus on the interconnection of policies and practices and their mutual legitimation.[96]

Development

Research literature on foreign aid and development often follows two distinct tracks. Aid and development can be understood as instrumental terms, where project success or failure is consequently seen as inherent to the initial project design. Aid and development can also be seen as a form of dominance in which aid recipients are perceived as passive/cynical/adaptive bystanders to the technicalities of project implementation, depoliticizing the entire field.[97] Whether development is seen as a given, linear path or just another form of domination depends on more than the perspective applied. The most radical, discursive approach sees the poor as a result of the discourse itself, since that is what produced the 'massive underdevelopment and impoverishment, untold exploitation and oppression' in the first place.[98] This is an example of seeing development in the light of metanarratives or grand narratives. While this certainly makes for insights, it is often fairly general. My focus will rather be on the miniscule practices pertaining to a specific development project. Thus, other perspectives are needed.

In a developmental logic that has largely been based on the presumption of linear development, a necessary premise is that all countries want to achieve the same goals and head in the same direction, for example, along the same path of development. The only difference between them and the donor is that the latter has come further than the former. This is inherent also in Norwegian development policy (democratization, increased European integration, etc.), which in one sense is to pathologize the perceived underdeveloped.[99] This happens because the recipient countries are evaluated according to ostensibly objective criteria such as 'democracy', 'human rights' and 'civil society'.[100] The relationship is further characterized by asymmetrical access to financial means. Here, development aid can be understood as a form of domination through the prescription of new remedies, remedies only the donor can prescribe. Considering the various aid programmes targeting countries in the former socialist bloc, several analysts have observed how western donors want them to develop according to democratic and neo-liberal principles – and that this is a 'fixed identity' – whereas the identity of the recipients is understood to be fluid and confused and in need of shaping.[101] To trace the trajectories of international aid programmes in Armenia would exceed the scope of this book, but I want to investigate what Armenian activists think of the Aarhus Convention (Chapters 2 and 3), how they make use of it and also how ideas of transition and Europeanization permeate the Armenia project (Chapters 4 and 5).

I suggest looking at the interconnectedness of policy and practice in the world of development because, it can be argued, aid policy does not necessarily work as a compass for practice, although it may legitimize practice.[102] Projects – as my ethnography will show – have a social life of their own, involving donors, implementing partners, target groups and others,[103] with alliances, project narratives, shifting priorities and possibly organizations needing to maintain relationships because they can affect how outcomes and results are reported.[104]

Let me reiterate the arguments of David Mosse regarding the workings of policy and practice in the world of development aid because they offer useful insights for the forthcoming analysis.[105] Regarding the relationship between policy and practice in development projects, Mosse has argued that (1) policy (development models, strategies and project designs) primarily functions to mobilize and maintain political support, that is, to legitimize rather than guide practice; (2) development interventions are driven not by policy but also by the exigencies of organizations and the need to maintain relationships; (3) development projects work to maintain themselves as coherent policy ideas, as systems of representation as well as operational systems; (4) projects do not fail; they are failed by wider networks of support and validation; and finally, (5) 'success' and 'failure' are policy-oriented judgements that obscure project effects.[106] Not only do they obscure outcomes, failures have to be managed through 'adjustment and compromise … critical to holding assemblages together'.[107] Policy in this regard is to be taken as an institutional practice stemming from the social life and politics of development organizations.[108]

Success and failure may be instrumental in the evaluation of a given project's results and shortcomings. But more often than not – especially when ambitions are abstract and because the world is a messy place – it is hard to pin down the effect of a given project. Another way of judging success or failure is to identify the project's actual support network, as Mosse argues for. The puzzle is that you do not always know what kind of judgement is being passed, what the project outcomes are or the nature of the network support.

An indication of how this understanding of the inner workings of development policies and projects may be linked to practices can be found in Gould's description of the perpetuation of aid dependency and global inequality where he uses the example of Tanzania.[109] Through participation, the aid domain is a self-referential order, he suggests,[110] resting on governance practices that serve 'to perpetuate the aid relationship'.[111] Aid is moreover imbued with concepts such as 'capacity building' and 'civil society'. The performative aspects are rather clear inasmuch as project management 'implies a certain professional habitus, a certain mode of utilitarian calculation, one for which rhetoric is substance; presentation is output; quantity (of funding) is quality etc'.[112] Within this argument, the skilled professional – both developer and recipient I assume – can adapt to the 'rules of the aid game' in both creative and subversive ways.[113] I take this to imply that disguised within the virtuous, donative and promissory language of aid,[114] 'co-operation' and participation entail practices and performances that smooth over differences, domination and, at worst, disingenuous motivations: '"community" (and "participation") are other sure-fire winning words (again governmental and non-governmental organizations differ very little in recourse to them), living blameless lives of their own in language, policy and analysis.'[115]

Claims, universals and assemblages

To recapitulate, this book will discuss and analyse empirical data and observations from different fields and sites. The practices related to the

Arhus Convention in Armenia can be divided into two categories: the creation and legitimization of the Arhus Convention and its institutional proliferation in Armenia and the streetwise and document-wise practices of concerned citizens and coalitions of Armenian NGOs in making use of the Aarhus Convention's provisions and mechanisms to launch protests and campaigns against mining projects and other issues. Likewise, the implementation of the Armenia project funded by Norwegian authorities entailed two dimensions: reporting practices and dialogue between donor and implementer in Norway, on the one hand, and specific project practices in Armenia, on the other.

An assemblage is understood here as a configuration through which various forms of technoscience, economic rationalism and other expert systems gain significance.[116] Assemblages can be local or global in scale but are based on a set of 'impersonal principles, which can be set out and developed without regard to context'.[117] Although the phrase 'without regard to context' will doubtless sound alarm bells among anthropologists, the point is that assemblages have an abstract, fluid character allowing them to be fixed onto very specific social and political settings. Assemblage is an alternative to the categories of global and local. This process of attachment, obviously, has to be carried out by someone who, for example, adopts a certain value, ideal or standard as their benchmark. In a world where civil society forges links in the international arena, the notion of assemblage seems very relevant.[118]

When working with the term 'global assemblage', certain phenomena are assumed to exist that are 'abstractable, mobile and dynamic, moving across and reconstituting "society", "culture" and "economy" '.[119] These 'global phenomena' have a 'distinctive capacity for decontextualization and recontextualization, abstractability and movement across diverse social and cultural situations'.[120] Global forms are thus able to assimilate new environments. The difference between global forms and kinship systems or the *kula* exchange is that the two latter rely on shared understandings and meanings.[121] Global forms, on the other hand, do not rely on a shared understanding to make them intelligible,

Collier and Ong argue, but can fix themselves onto a range of different situations and contexts. This capacity of global forms is moderated by 'specific technical infrastructures, administrative apparatuses, or value regimes'.[122] This is an important point and examples furnished by Collier and Ong include structural adjustment programmes (SAPs) enforced by the International Monetary Fund (IMF), along with other plans and programmes spiralling out of the Bretton Woods institutions. Arguments related to promoting and ensuring human rights supported by international human rights' organizations make up another field in which one kind of abstract idea is projected onto quite different locations and contexts.

An important issue to do with the concept of assemblage is whether it implies a sense of stability or not. According to Collier and Ong, the composite term 'global assemblage' has inherent tensions: 'global' suggests flow, seamlessness and one-size-fits-all, whereas 'assemblage' implies heterogeneity, instability and situated practice.[123] In other words, global assemblages are constantly in the making, their temporality emergent. Assemblages are not 'reducible to a single logic'.[124] But again, we need to consider the situated practice in which these assemblages work. How should we understand the notion of global form and whether assemblages can eventually change a given global form? If we consider abstract claims such as those derived from human rights, for instance, as things someone (international and domestic NGOs, politicians, or others) projects onto a specific context (Armenia or wherever), we may conceive of human rights as making up a fixed entity, a global form. But understanding them as fixed is, I would say, to oversimplify the case. The perceived relationship between assemblages and global forms is that the latter are general and abstract, whereas assemblages take place in specific settings. As global forms have the capacity to decontextualize and recontextualize into different social, cultural and political settings,[125] assemblages are the particular articulations of these global forms.

First and foremost, I intend to interpret and analyse the two-way relational, co-dependent and reflexive bond between a 'global form' and its local deployment or usage. But it is also imperative to acknowledge the networks and institutional and financial co-dependencies that arise. They are co-dependencies in which legitimization hinges not so much on the international arena's capacity and willingness to foster local change where change is needed, as one often thinks, but also on how local projects legitimize policy frameworks in faraway development agencies and ministries. This last point is obviously in line with the argument that development projects work to maintain themselves as coherent policy ideas, as systems of representation as well as operational systems.[126]

It is on the various sites, projects, seminars, organizations and in policies and documents, where these claims are made and assemblages negotiated, I focus my analysis. Tsing invites us to look at how globalist projects such as the Aarhus Convention evolve as they are articulated in sometimes overlapping hegemonic scales. One such scale is the claim that Armenia belongs to Europe, hence Europeanization as a scale. Another is the focus on MEAs (voiced by FNI and the MFA).

Conclusion

In this chapter, I have discussed and fleshed out different Armenian and European contexts as well as theoretical perspectives that can shed light on the empirical material to follow. My research field is spread across different locations that are interconnected by networks extending across borders of nation states. At the same time, the non-place of project management is characterized by a confused relationship between practices and the policy frameworks intended to give them direction.

The conceptual framework has one overarching perspective, the notion of global assemblages as an anthropological problem. This is a crucial analytical insight and necessary in order to understand how 'global', abstract principles may attach themselves to local specific settings and how they come to signify and 'mean' so much for so many in different places. Yet we need to acknowledge that such universals do not exist outside or independently of practices; they are articulated and given substance through performance. Environmental rights, transparency and other scalable concepts gain traction and meaning through being practised.

Taking up the stance of Chari and Verdery,[127] who believe it is about time to leave the intellectual divide between post-colonial and post-socialist scholarly traditions behind, I have argued that Armenia, as a post-Soviet state that is also a major development aid recipient per capita, is a suitable ethnographic starting point of a study aiming to contribute to post-Cold War ethnography. More specifically, it has persuaded me to devote considerable space to theoretical insights from the world of aid and development, with the intention of applying them to (parts of) the following ethnography. And while it is true that the achievements of post-socialist anthropology are great and have shed light on various processes of change and continuity in the post-socialist world, I have also argued that when analysing the nexus of policy and practice, it is, in my opinion, better covered in the post-colonial development literature. One of the most useful contributions I have discussed is the analytical toolkit for understanding the complex relationship between development policy, practices and networks.[128]

Assemblage theory is useful in understanding how connections are made, claimed and conjured across time and place. Abstract ideas and concepts hit the ground in sticky engagements, between NGOs, development projects, the Aarhus compliance mechanism and so forth. I argue that we need to acknowledge that although these abstract principles are put to use in specific localities, their interconnectedness with other parts of a fluid network of global connections and legitimizations is in many ways as important as the place-specific context. Thus, although the main parts of the previous chapter situated and contextualized Armenia in its post-Soviet situation, the bulk of my ethnography resides at a somewhat less localized level, in documents, networks, at international meetings, in transnational organizations, in Armenian courts and streets. My concern has been to facilitate a better understanding of how these sticky engagements unfold, become potential resources and risks, all relying on the possibility and ability to legitimize and foster networks.

Ever since I started studying NGO activists, I have grappled with how their agency should be understood. Even though there is a vast literature on the flourishing NGO sector, third sector, civil society, social movements or whatever we would like to call it, I find that it often tends to treat activists themselves as either cynical players supremely capable of adapting to shifting donor priorities or as fatigued, passive bystanders dominated by those same western donors. When we try to dig deeper, we risk diverting our attention to a search for 'ulterior motives' and so on. We cannot know what those motives are. But we can see what is actually done and how those actions are claimed to stand in relation to wider networks of practices, concepts, laws and donor priorities.

Part One

Environmental rights and politics in the post-Soviet Caucasus

2

Transparent environment: 'Helping' countries into a 'pan-European' legal space

This chapter takes a closer look at how the Aarhus Convention, as a common legal and normative framework for environmental management, instigated new practices and institutions in Armenia. I want to show and argue here that 'transition' is a multifaceted and complicated process which needs to be approached with care in our analysis. The key questions are the following: What kinds of practices does the Aarhus Convention evoke? How do states, political entities and non-governmental organizations (NGOs) confirm, validate, uphold or even disregard the convention?

In this chapter, I make use of three empirical cases to discuss the proliferation of the Aarhus Convention in Armenia and its international dimension and scalable premises. They are, first, an international meeting of the Convention parties in Moldova in 2011; second, the role of the government-appointed focal point in Armenia; and third, how the Aarhus centres work in Armenia. These cases, I will argue, reveal the grid of normativity the Convention casts over Armenia; but more importantly, they show the involvement of Armenian activists and government-appointed officials in conjuring and claiming Europe and the Aarhus Convention 'as their own'. This is done partly by inventing and using networks that are precarious and volatile. Crossing through these empirical levels is an analysis of how certain phenomena such as human rights, transparency, participation, access and democratization are claimed and acted upon. For this task, I employ anthropological treatments of the concept of 'transition'. Whereas transition is a much debated issue,[1] it is often applied, I find, in ways that fail to take sufficient account of the interconnectedness and participation of 'our informants'. The ethnography in this book offers one example of a programme of transition of the former communist bloc in Europe.

Global entities are not given, such that local reactions, resistance and implementation can simply be treated as responses and variables. What is needed instead is a more open-ended perspective where the various interconnections between global and local levels can be traced and subjected to analysis. The Aarhus Convention seeks to develop the same principles and mechanisms from Reykjavik to Bishkek. While the following chapters discuss these elements in turn, let me quote Tsing on the processes entailing what she calls 'encounters across difference':

> Attention to friction opens up the possibility of an ethnographic account of global interconnection. Abstract claims about the globe can be studied as they operate in the world. We might thus ask about universals not as truths or lies but as sticky engagements.[2]

In development studies as much as in post-socialist anthropology, we risk analysing our data merely in terms of resistance, adaptation or consumption. Tsing's coining of the term 'friction' offers something different; it is 'not a synonym for resistance',[3] although it may be associated with it. The implication of understanding universals as 'sticky engagements' is that they are better understood as unfinished aspirations rather than preordained entities. With this in mind, let us have a look at the Aarhus Convention and its manifestations in Armenia and beyond.

Palace of the Republic, Chisinau, Moldova

It is 2011, and I am on my way to a palatial congress hall of late-Soviet design, in Chisinau, Moldova. Upon receiving accreditation and passing the security check, I enter the conference room where a meeting is under way. Several closed meetings have been held in advance, where the different parties have deliberated and adjusted details of the findings to be presented to the participants. In the hall, I immediately spot several people I know from Armenia: Anush, Hermine and Tigran were sitting together. I joined them, and we exchanged greetings in hushed voices so as not to disturb anyone; we also briefed each other on the latest news about 'the Armenian case'. What we were about to take part in was the fourth Meeting of Parties (MoP) to the Aarhus Convention. The chairperson and his assistants are seated on the podium; the parties' delegations (government representatives) were seated at several long tables extending from the podium. At the back of the hall, several NGOs were gathered at another long table facing the podium. On either side of the official delegation tables, chairs are placed in rows for people like my Armenian friends and me. Sitting in a corner behind glass walls, interpreters are busy providing simultaneous translations into the Convention's official languages, English, French and Russian. I spot the Armenian delegation consisting of the national focal point Hasmik and a government official from the Ministry of Nature Protection. Several chairs are empty; many delegates are outside making phone calls or simply stretching their legs. At times, it seems as if no one is paying much attention to what is being said on the podium. According to Anush and Hermine, most of the substantive issues have already been dealt with and settled behind closed doors in the preceding days; what remains is to have these decisions adopted in the formally prescribed manner and round the whole thing off.

What was it that caused the Armenian activists to bring their case against mining in Armenia for adjudication at this meeting and what kind of processes had preceded it in Armenia? The remainder of this chapter will try to explore the roots and practices of which the Chisinau meeting was merely one expression. As a triennial ritual, it seems as if the MoP largely serves to recommit the parties to the Convention. If we consider the participating states, the NGOs and transnational organizations as a network of sorts, the MoP can clearly be regarded as an event in which the various intentions are collectively shared, common ground is emphasized and disagreements ironed out. Although a decision by the meeting to reprimand a country for failing to uphold

Convention principles is essentially meant to foster change, it would be to miss the point if one ignored its purpose as a vital reminder of the common understanding supposedly shared by the different countries.

If none of the implementing countries is found to be in breach of Convention principles, the MoPs could arguably be accused lacking teeth and having subsided into irrelevance. The way the MoP works and how its practices such as the 'decisions on compliance' are taken with regard to nine individual countries on the final day of the Chisinau MoP are a matter to which I return in Chapter 3. In addition to Armenia,[4] decisions were taken on the compliance of Belarus, Kazakhstan, Republic of Moldova, Slovakia, Spain, Turkmenistan, Ukraine and the UK. If none of these countries had been in the dock in this rite of passage, then less would have been at stake at the MoP, rendering the entire process somewhat irrelevant. In passing judgement on the compliance of such a significant number of countries, the MoP was highlighting and indeed instigating future reporting cycles, meetings and procedures. I consider these offshoots as practices spinning out of the Aarhus Convention. Let us dig deeper back in time to identify the characteristics of this convention.

What anthropological readings and analyses of international law suggest is an understanding of international law as a process and how it actually works in 'the corridors of international tribunals' and particular settings.[5] Legal texts, such as the Aarhus Convention, are documents that are open to interpretation and diverse uses;[6] they are full of intentions and normative bearings insofar as they are not entities in their own right 'but a collective patterning of intention'.[7] International law, I would suggest, is therefore also a practice. But with regards to the Aarhus Convention, it is crucial to look at the provisions entailed in the convention text.

The three pillars of the Aarhus Convention

The Aarhus Convention has spurred much activity in Armenia involving transnational organizations and funding. From its Yerevan office, the Organization for Security and Co-operation in Europe (OSCE) has overseen the establishment of what are called Aarhus Centres throughout Armenia. This OSCE activity has been financed by a project under the auspices of the Environment and Security Initiative (ENVSEC), a joint project involving OSCE, NATO, United Nations Environmental Programme (UNEP) and United Nations Development Programme (UNDP). The Armenian Ministries of Nature Protection and Territorial Administration have represented the Armenian government in this process. At the time of my fieldwork (2010), eleven such centres were up and running and four more were under way. The centres are supposed to 'promote public access to environmental information and participation in decision making in Armenia and are also expected to help create a public climate of transparency in environmental affairs and thus to the general democratization and good governance of the country'.[8] Although these centres do not in any way guarantee actual changes on the ground, their existence arguably creates a new arena for Armenian environmentalists and concerned citizens. This international institutional set-up gives Armenian activists (and others) an opportunity to address domestic issues – for example, by making claims – at the international level. For instance, when an Armenian NGO filed a complaint with the Compliance Committee of the Aarhus Convention, the committee concluded in 2008 that Armenia had failed to 'be in compliance' with all of the three pillars of the convention.[9] In order to understand this better, we need to dig somewhat deeper into the three pillars as they appear in the convention text.

Access to information

Under the articles on information, it is stated that public authorities 'in response to a request for environmental information' shall 'make such information available to the public'.[10] This information shall be made available within one month and in the form requested unless the public authority deems it reasonable to issue the information in another form. The request does not need to be followed by an explicitly stated interest, but the request cannot be unreasonable or too generally formulated.[11] Disclosure can be denied if it adversely affects the confidentiality of commercial interests, national defence or public security.[12] Public authorities are further obligated to 'possess and update environmental information relevant to their functions'.[13] Article 5 also lists the obligations of public authorities to ensure that environmental information is 'progressively' made electronically available and at 'regular intervals … disseminate a national report on the state of the environment'.[14] Even though the Convention is limited to the responsibilities of public authorities, the ratifying countries ('the Parties' to the Convention) should encourage 'operators whose activities have a significant impact on the environment' to inform the public regularly and sufficiently.[15] The Convention grants the concerned public ample rights to request and receive environmental information, while giving the state certain discretionary powers to interpret the requirements according to their own laws and practices.

Access to participation

The second pillar is divided into provisions on public participation in 'specific activities',[16] public participation 'concerning plans and programmes relating to the environment'[17] and public participation in 'preparation of executive regulations'.[18] Whereas the two latter concern the legal, regulative and administrative ordering and management of the environment, the former deals with specific licenses and cases and is of most relevance to the case discussed in Chapter 3. 'Early public participation' should be provided for – commonly through notifications and public hearings – and the public should be informed of proposed activities, the application prompting the decision to be taken and how the public can participate. Applicants are also encouraged to enter into a discussion with affected members of the public.[19] Each party is committed to facilitating public participation at public hearings or to allowing the public to submit written comments and opinions.[20]

In practice, the right of participation is the right of affected members of the public (environmental organizations, affected communities and others) to be informed about commercial activities in a designated area for which plans have been prepared or applications submitted. This includes the right to participate at public hearings and express opinions orally or in writing to relevant public authorities. The right to participation does not, however, include the right to take part in the final decision by the government or public authority.

Access to justice

Under article 9, parties to the Aarhus Convention are urged to ensure within the framework of national legislation that persons or the 'public concerned' have access to a review procedure before a court of law or 'another independent and impartial body established by law'.[21] This procedure shall be 'expeditious' and 'free of charge'.[22] The Aarhus Convention defines 'the public concerned' as

> the public affected or likely to be affected by, or having an interest in, the environmental decision-making; for the purposes of this definition, non-governmental organizations promoting environmental protection and meeting any requirements under national law shall be deemed to have an interest.[23]

This is obviously an important feature for concerned NGOs and, as we shall see in Chapter 3, a contested one for Armenian organizations. But while the three pillars of the Aarhus Convention represent fundamental and substantial values, if its implementation is superficial or fails to change practices where needed, these provisions risk being reduced to a set of pro forma rights of little practical application. As the same rights also legitimize government decisions in environmental matters, there is a 'risk that governments may abuse them, without providing members of the public with meaningful ways to voice their concerns'.[24] This could very well be the case in Armenia where ratification of multilateral environmental agreements is in many ways part and parcel of the Armenian government's effort at 'Europeanization'. Whether the apparent failure to grant substantive rights *in practice* can be attributed to governmental indolence, corruption, inefficiency or merely lack of political will is beyond the scope of this book to determine. What is within its scope, however, is to discuss how a coalition of Armenian NGOs makes use of the provisions of the Aarhus Convention to argue that they have certain rights which the government seems unwilling to recognize.

It is worth noting that the very enjoyment of the substantive rights granted by the convention relies on the definitions, practices and norms stipulated in all the other articles. Take article 20-1, for example, on the Convention's date of entry into force: 'This Convention shall enter into force on the ninetieth day after the date of deposit of the sixteenth instrument of ratification, acceptance, approval or accession.'[25] The Convention came into force, for example, became a legally binding instrument, ninety days after the Republic of Armenia became the sixteenth state to ratify it. Armenian ratification occurred on 1 August 2001 and the Convention 'entered into force' 30 October of the same year.

This leads us to the ratifying partners. They have agreed to adopt the Aarhus Convention as a common and binding legal instrument or what is usually referred to as *lex superior*. The Convention text is legally binding on each and every country that has ratified it and national legislation shall – where necessary – be changed and/or introduced to enact the general norms stipulated in the Convention.

Between 1998 (date of signature) and the end of October 2001 ('entry into force'), the Convention remained a non-binding text. However, as it was expected to become binding sooner or later, several countries started reviewing domestic legislation in light of the Aarhus Convention. Among them was Norway, where the 'Environmental Information Act' came into effect in 2005. This act is one of the essential premises of the design of the Armenia project to be discussed in Chapters 4 and 5, as Norwegian 'comparative advantages' and experience legitimated the Armenia project.[26]

The Convention text requires the parties to 'be convened no later than one year after the date of the entry into force of this Convention.'[27] This is what is referred to as the MoP, to which each and every participating government should send representatives and where further agreements on the implementation of the Convention shall be decided upon. The first session of the MoP was convened in Lucca, Italy, in October 2002.

The Aarhus Convention and its compliance mechanism

In this section, I focus on an important detail of the Convention text, namely the compliance mechanism. This is a legally non-binding yet important instrument that enables concerned citizens and organizations to make cases known to the Convention parties for arbitration and interpretation.

According to article 15 of the Aarhus Convention, the MoP is required to find 'optional arrangements of a non-confrontational, non-judicial and consultative nature for reviewing compliance with the provisions of the Convention' in a way that allows for public involvement.[28] A working group was therefore established at the Meeting of the Signatories, leading the MoP at its first session at Lucca, Italy, to adopt decision I/7 on review of compliance and also to elect the first Compliance Committee.[29] The Compliance Committee addresses issues of compliance and reports to the MoPs, whereupon the parties adopt decisions on compliance. The compliance mechanism can be triggered by (1) a party addressing compliance by another party; (2) a party addressing its own compliance; (3) the secretariat referring a case to the committee; and (4) members of the public addressing the compliance of a party. In addition, the Compliance Committee may itself initiate compliance proceedings against one or several parties.[30] The committee consists of nine individuals with expertise of relevance to the Convention. Committee members have to be nationals of signatory states or parties to the Convention. Since 2011, a junior scholar in Armenian law has been a member of the committee. In Armenia, she works together with Hasmik, Armenia's national focal point for the Aarhus Convention, at an environmental law centre at Yerevan State University (YSU). She is also a member of an NGO established by Hasmik. Her qualifications were questioned by some of my informants, as were her relations with the Armenian government-appointed focal point. As party to the Aarhus Convention, Armenia is obliged to respect the spirit and wording of the Convention and translate it into domestic law. Herein lies Armenia's legal obligation regarding the Aarhus Convention, even though there is no binding enforcement mechanism directly related to it.

So what has Armenia done to become European in this respect? At the third MoP in Riga, Latvia, in June 2008, Armenia's implementation was put under scrutiny; Armenian environmentalists had filed a complaint over an issue of land use outside Yerevan. The decision and statement issued by the MoP regarding Armenia's implementation were fairly damning of Armenian authorities:

> By failing to ensure that bodies performing public functions implement the provisions of article 4, paragraphs 1 and 2, of the Convention, Armenia was not in compliance with that article. ... By failing to provide for public participation in decision-making processes for the designation of land use, the Government of Armenia was not in compliance with article 7 of the Convention ... By failing to ensure that members of the public concerned had access to a review procedure and to provide adequate and effective remedies, the Government of Armenia was not in compliance with article 9, paragraphs 2 to 4, of the Convention.[31]

What this in effect meant was that the MoP considered Armenia to be in non-compliance with all three pillars of the Convention. The severity of the case allowed the MoP to argue that it was not an isolated incident and serious doubts were raised about the republic's overall implementation of the Aarhus Convention. The Compliance Committee encouraged the Armenian authorities to report annually on progress.[32] At the same time, the Compliance Committee asked

> relevant international and regional organizations and financial institutions, to provide advice and assistance to the Party concerned as necessary in the implementation of these measures, in particular measures being undertaken with regard to implementation of articles

6 and 7 of the Convention and capacity-building measures for public officials and the judiciary.³³

At the two following MoPs in 2011 and 2014, Armenia's implementation of the Aarhus Convention was still under scrutiny, although the issue by this time was mainly to do with access to participation (2011) and access to justice (2011 and 2014).

In the remaining part of this chapter, I analyse different aspects of the institutional proliferation spurred by the Aarhus Convention in Armenia. First, I discuss the role of Armenia's government-appointed focal point to the Aarhus Convention before looking at the Aarhus Centres. These bodies show, I will argue, how Europe and European values are claimed in Armenia.

Unpacking the Aarhus Convention

Under the Aarhus Convention, the procedures stipulate how 'concerned citizens' obtain rights to access to information, participation and justice. In the following, I argue that the Aarhus Convention text can be perceived as the result of what Riles has called patterned intention.³⁴

International law is a work of practice, where legal obligations refer to more than fixed rules. The Aarhus Convention hit the ground running by being affirmed and contested by groups and communities that communicate through its norms and procedures.³⁵ It is these practices anthropology can help us understand better. Environmental activists and their opponents all take part in this community by promoting, applying and interpreting international norms and legal obligations. How did this Convention come about, and what kind of premises is it based upon?

As a text, what has become known as the Aarhus Convention exists in what is called 'authentic versions' in three languages, English, French and Russian. There are an additional three official UN translations in Arabic, Chinese and Spanish. On the Convention website is a list of unofficial translations in twenty-six different languages. For the most part, the translation languages are those of ratifying states, although some (including two of the official UN translations, Arabic and Chinese) are languages outside the UNECE member state area, which covers Europe, all of the former Soviet republics, the United States and Canada. The English version of the Convention covers twenty-five pages divided into twenty-two articles and two annexes. The Convention is legally binding on the countries that have ratified it, although measures to get non-compliant countries to mend their ways are rather weak. In these cases, it may be argued, continuous practice is all the more important, of which the MoPs serve as (ritual) reminders. Preceding the articles are almost two pages explaining how the parties to this convention are 'recalling', 'affirming', 'recognizing', 'considering', 'aiming', 'desiring', 'noting' and further are 'convinced', 'conscious' and 'bearing in mind'[36] different aspects related to preceding international meetings such as the 1972 Stockholm Declaration on Human Environment and the 1992 Rio Declaration on Environment and Development. To imagine that the government representatives present were actively recalling, affirming, desiring and so on is to overstretch it a bit. The first two pages of the Convention text also state the general reasons for the process leading up to the Convention. These two pages are not only a rather stark reminder of the reliance of the Aarhus Convention on prior processes but also in how it is embedded in normative and liberal assumptions of how a better future might be achieved:

> <u>Desiring</u> to promote environmental education to further the understanding of the environment and sustainable development and to encourage widespread public awareness of and participation in, decisions affecting the environment and sustainable development.[37]

As the above implies, the Convention text is 'not an entity of its own but a collective patterning of intention'.[38] This is particularly clear given that the text is full of references to preceding agreements and conventions and that the national delegations have arrived at the lowest common dominator of what they can accept. The countries and delegations negotiating the convention text have tried to arrive at a common understanding of intentions and ambitions. They have also sought to connect this process to others in the sphere of environmental politics.

The Convention text stipulates norms and provisions and is divided into sections of two basic types. First, there are the sections that are meant to stipulate the Convention's validity, its 'entry into force', how arbitration measures are to be carried out and the role of the Convention secretariat. A general feature of these sections (articles 1–3 and 10–22) is their stipulation of the procedures according to which the Convention is meant to function. They also include provisions on how the 'review of compliance' should be developed in the future:

> The Meeting of the Parties shall establish, on a consensus basis, optional arrangements of a non-confrontational, non-judicial and consultative nature for reviewing compliance with the provisions of this Convention. These arrangements shall allow for appropriate public involvement and may include the option of considering communications from members of the public on matters related to this Convention.[39]

Second, there are the sections covering the three pillars of access to information (articles 4–5), access to public participation (articles 6–8) and access to justice (article 9). These articles (4–9) can be understood as the substantive part of the Convention, on which the focus on legal interpretation, claims and counterclaims for the most part rests.

At the heart of any international convention is a text signifying ambitions, intentions, ideologies and politics, ultimately leading to policies and practices related to the convention. This text is the result of negotiations and deliberations by a number of states trying to agree upon a general legally binding framework to regulate a given sphere of international and national behaviour. But it also works as the basis for claims made by environmentalists.

Chisinau, take 2

Returning to the Chisinau meeting, one of the issues facing the meeting was to choose the country to host the next MoP. According to Norwegian government delegates with whom I spoke during one of the lunch breaks, Belarus surprised the delegations by volunteering to host the next MoP. This had happened during the closed sessions. Apparently, objections had been raised due to the boycott of the Lukashenko regime. Norway – as one of the biggest donors per capita – was encouraged to host the next MoP; it was Western Europe's turn, according to some delegates. Norway nevertheless declined. The Convention text says nothing on the order in which countries shall host the MoPs, although passing the baton among different member states is regarded as a sensible procedure. On the final day of the public session, Ukraine offered to host the next MoP. This caused some embarrassment and was greeted by a rather muffled response. The problem – from what I heard from the delegates – was that Ukraine was also considered one of the least successful countries in its implementation of the Aarhus principles and the EU was thus against the proposal. Soon after, the head of the Polish delegation asked for a short adjournment to discuss the matter with the EU member states. On returning, the EU thanked Ukraine for its offer and asked for the decision to be postponed. This motion was granted by the MoP.

On the final day of the meeting, a decision regarding Armenia's implementation was taken. Prior to this, an international NGO had voiced its support for its Armenian colleagues, a sign that the Armenians had done some networking in preparation for the meeting. This invoked an image of a pan-European network of concerned citizens and organizations, although the size or level of cooperation was not mentioned. This does not make the network any less real. As Riles has pointed out, merely invoking a network is to confirm its existence.[40] In the deliberations that ensued, the Armenian government official wanted a passage in the decision to be rephrased. None of the other parties supported the Armenian official, to which he exclaimed in frustration, 'Can't we at least change the Russian version?' Laughter was heard, but the subtext was serious enough. For the government official, it was important to return to Yerevan with a more favourable decision to show to his superiors. No doubt he would be showing them the Russian version, especially if it had been changed. The MoP thereupon decided that Armenia was in breach of the Convention's articles on public participation and access to justice. There is no need to detail everything here, but suffice it to say that Armenian authorities were held to have failed to give the public relevant possibilities and means to participate in decision making and to have put the relevant procedures in place enabling access to justice. These are basically formal or procedural issues and shortcomings. The network of Armenian activists involved tried to approach this in several ways, as we will see in the next chapter.

The MoP also had to consider applications from countries outside the UNECE area to join the community of ratifying parties to the Convention. One such petition came from Mongolia. The MoP expressed its gratitude for Mongolia's interest, but decided to postpone the exact measures until it had considered the threshold criteria such non-UNECE states needed to fulfil. However, it did decide to encourage 'the propagation of the important and unique protections offered by this international environmental rights treaty on a fully global scale'.[41]

In addition to taking part in decision making, delegates were also part of the Aarhus community. For instance, for the Norwegian delegates, who represented a country in which the Aarhus Convention is neither contested nor seen as an important issue – Norway is assumed to be in compliance almost by default – the MoP gave substance to the Convention as a network. For other delegations, such as the Belarusian and Ukrainian, whose offers to host the next MoP were rejected, the Convention was a far more concrete affair given the results they had to report back to their respective governments.

Armenia's focal point

Every party to the Convention is obliged to report regularly on implementation progress. The MoPs, on the other hand, according to article 10 (2), are obliged to 'keep under continuous review the implementation of this Convention on the basis of regular reporting by the Parties'.[42] These reports are usually submitted by a nationally appointed focal point. Although such an appointment is not stipulated in the Convention, it is common practice for the focal point to liaise between the respective governments and UNECE secretariat.

Armenia's focal point to the Aarhus Convention is responsible for submitting Armenia's national implementation reports to the UNECE secretariat. The focal point is also involved in liaising between the Government of Armenia and Convention bodies. Working outside the ministry, Armenia's focal point is not responsible for the implementation of the Convention in Armenia but to oversee and keep the Convention secretariat updated on progress.

Armenia's focal point was a woman named Hasmik whom I had met in 2006 at YSU's Faculty of Law. We were both there to plan a series of lectures to be given by a colleague later the same year. I met her again on the first day of the first of a series of FNI seminars (September 2006), where Hasmik spoke about civil society and the Aarhus Convention in Armenia. Before addressing challenges facing Armenia's implementation of the Aarhus Convention, she introduced briefly the main rights and provisions stipulated in the Convention text, which she linked to the rights of civil society to be involved under the Convention.

Besides being a professor at the law department at YSU, Hasmik was also a founding member of an Armenian NGO. In the course of establishing the Armenia project, this NGO became one of FNI's prospective partners – although the partnership never materialized in practical terms. As an independent analyst and informant, Hasmik offered frank assessments of the Armenia's poor implementation record: Most MPs have connections in the business community, they are corrupt and do their best to torpedo any threatening parliamentary bills. She also described relations (back in 2006) between the government (e.g. the ministries) and NGOs as rather bad. NGOs were not invited to arrangements when they should have been, she said, and those invited tended to be the least critical. I talked with her once about the status of the Aarhus Convention in Armenia.

Me: What can you say about the challenges in Armenia when implementing the Aarhus Convention?

Hasmik: As you know, the convention consists of three basic rights. Access to information, access to participation and access to justice. We have problems with all three aspects. First of all we need to find out what shall be defined as 'environmental information'.

Me: As opposed to business sensitive information for instance?

Hasmik: Yes, exactly. We need to develop a better understanding of this. Then there is the question pertaining who should be invited to participate in decision-making. NGOs from Yerevan or local communities? Whoever claims to have an interest? Thirdly, there is the issue of lacking procedures for securing access to justice, fear of liabilities etc.[43]

At the time, I remember thinking that this was a fairly sensible analysis and a fairly critical one. Hasmik was nevertheless clear that more work and legal deliberations were needed to clarify the issues at hand: what constitutes the 'environmental' in environmental information, who should be included in the participation measures and how can sensible legal remedies be developed? Her assessment points to various challenges and practical measures Armenia has to consider and settle. It is one thing to be formally entitled, another is to get to enjoy one's entitlement in practice: to claim a right is not the same as having it in material terms. Hasmik always encouraged me at the end of our conversations (aka mini-lectures) to ask if there was anything else I wanted to know. Although she was critical of the situation in Armenia with regard to environmental rights, Armenian activists have increasingly questioned the independence of Armenia's focal point. Hasmik probably found herself between a rock and a hard place, defending what modest progress Armenia may have achieved in front of demanding NGOs.

Described by one of my informants as a 'very convenient person for the government', Hasmik as the focal point had multiple roles. Through her work in EPAC, she was credited with – even by her critics – playing a vital role in making the Aarhus Convention known in Armenia. From 2008, she was also leader of the newly formed Environmental Law Resource Centre (ELRC) at YSU. ELRC is located on the premises of YSU and is meant to be an independent centre facilitating the implementation of the Aarhus Convention in Armenia and providing guidance to the Aarhus Centres in legal matters. Until 2011 it was financed by OSCE, but after disagreements over its management, OSCE withdrew its financial support. The centres and the focal point find themselves increasingly isolated from civil society. In November 2010, I arrived at the ELRC for a scheduled meeting with its director, Hasmik. She was not there, but two junior members of staff were. Although one of them was in the middle of a phone conversation, I was invited in and served tea by the other junior official who was later elected to the Compliance Committee of the Aarhus Convention at the 2011 MoP. Several Armenian NGOs were worried in case she only represented the opinions of the focal point and lobbied on behalf of the official Armenian view. The other junior staff member, Gosh, ended his phone conversation. As I understood it from the phone call and what he told me, he was advising the Armenia Copper Programme on how to respond to complaints filed by the NGOs in question in this case.

As the above indicates, both Hasmik and the Armenian member of the Compliance Committee have to defend their independence as focal point and Compliance Committee member, respectively, in a landscape of contested claims by Armenian activists, the Armenian government and Armenian businesses. Even though the focal point is an independent role, it might be useful to consider Hasmik and her role within a framework of bureaucracy. Although bureaucracies and bureaucrats are often treated as 'corrupt and unimaginative', they should perhaps be regarded as 'all-too-human agents', many of whom regard themselves as 'servants of the people'.[44] When serving the people, bureaucrats used to working within specific fields of competence and knowledge may not realize how much power they are exercising.⁴⁵ Armenia's focal point to the Aarhus Convention is an example of such a bureaucrat. However, it should be clear from the way bureaucrats can obstruct as well as foster solutions that their practices and embodied knowledge should be approached with the same eye for detail as anthropologists usually use on their informants. As such, the bureaucratic logic or 'cosmology'⁴⁶ with its embedded practices and knowledge is necessary for the state to function.⁴⁷ In a way, it is the bureaucratic *metis*. For this reason, Herzfeld has called for ethnographic research on the 'interactions between bureaucrats and both their clients and legislative masters'.⁴⁸

Hasmik embodied this interaction insofar as she, in a sense, worked in all these capacities herself: as an expert and professor in environmental law, she advised the government; as the appointed focal point, largely a bureaucratic function, she was responsible for reporting and liaising with the secretariat. The 'intimate knowledge'⁴⁹ of bureaucrats or people in contact with the state can be illustrated by something a Georgian environmentalist told me when I asked about how the right to access information was exercised in Georgia. His reply was revealingly straightforward. If he wanted information from the Georgian Ministry of Ecology, he would never use official channels as he is entitled to by the Aarhus Convention. He would use his contacts instead – informally – to find out what he needed to know. According to people I have spoken with in Armenia, the same applies there too. So, we see how 'formal schemes of order are untenable without some elements of the practical knowledge that they tend to dismiss'.⁵⁰

The bureaucratic *habitus* in Armenia is probably still influenced by its Soviet predecessor and it would not be unreasonable to suspect that power relations, in Herzfeld's words, 'long survive[d] particular ideologies of governance'.⁵¹ But it has also been argued that bureaucratic and anti-bureaucratic impulses 'can be seen as complementary rather than contradictory',⁵² because anti-bureaucratic practices are necessary for a bureaucracy to function. Better then, as indicated in the case above, to utilize whatever contacts and networks you may have. The importance of local knowledge and *metis* should therefore not be underestimated. Many actors have local knowledge and skills in getting round bureaucratic resistance, not only environmentalists.

The same skills are used by the bureaucrats themselves. They replicate the old Soviet tradition of *blat*, 'the use of personal networks and informal contacts to obtain goods and services in short supply and to find a way around formal procedures'.[53] There is reason to believe that *blat* occurs to a certain degree today, although the goods and services that are in short supply vary. However, information, as environmentalists experience again and again, is also a commodity in short supply. This practice of 'unfree flow'[54] indicates that some elite networks may be recycled. As has been suggested elsewhere,[55] the Soviet *telefonnii zakon* (telephone law) is still in effect: bureaucrats tend to work according to orders given by telephone rather than basing decisions on transparent rules and regulations. This form of decision making is rather different to what the Aarhus Convention seeks to foster. In Armenia, former civil servants in the environmental management sector often get to work in NGOs, either full-time or in addition to their regular job at, for instance, the Ministry of Nature Protection. Supporting this observation is Ishkanian's claim that [Soviet] elites in Armenia continue to nurture and exploit their networks.[56] She further argues that civil society actors 'are embedded in webs of social relations and structures which influence their decisions and behaviours'.[57]

Is this really the case when it comes to Hasmik's multiple roles and her undoubtedly numerous connections in the higher echelons of Armenian society? The wording seems to cast a shadow of suspicion onto the civil society actors and somehow invokes ideas of ulterior motives and decisions shrouded in secrecy. Even though we know that Armenia – in common with many other former Soviet republics – is rife with corruption, I think we should be careful when addressing or discussing individual decision makers or advisors close to people in power. Some of my informants are frustrated by the focal point's multiple roles related to the Aarhus Convention and some find her a biased advocate of the government's view. However, the activists' stance on issues related to environmental rights is likely to be based on a more superficial and idealistic understanding of the law than Hasmik's, who is well aware of all the jurisdictional pitfalls, inconsistencies and issues that are open for interpretation in Armenian legislation. This knowledge Hasmik uses to the best of her ability to argue the view of the government.

Returning to the discussion of *blat* and elite networks, I want to end this section by arguing that in settings in which everyone seems to expect corruption and dishonesty all around them, as analysts we should investigate how these claims work rather than simply taking them for granted. The problematic issue revealed by the discussion noted above is how much of the literature on democratization seems to imply – as I have briefly mentioned before – that the 'recipients' are playing a game,[58] to conspire and move tactically in order to acquire international funding.[59]

I find it more instructive to employ the concepts of network and performativity as developed by Riles[60] and Barad,[61] among others. These perspectives allow us to understand, for instance, Hasmik's actions quite well, without implying whether she or other informants are driven by cynicism or worse. Hasmik is skilled at networking within and without her policy field, advising on legislative changes, while also acquiring funds for her NGO and acting as Armenia's focal point to the Aarhus Convention. What she does in these different capacities falls within the ambit of the prescribed rules, procedures and practices, such as performing her duties as the focal point. It may obviously be contested whether her performance as legal expert or focal point actually benefits civil rights, but it is nonetheless within the confines of expected behaviour of a government-appointed official. This issue will be further exemplified by Hasmik's written correspondence in the following chapter when we discuss the deliberations concerning Armenia's alleged non-compliance with the Arhus Convention.

Hasmik's role as focal point is but one expression of the Aarhus Convention's reach in Armenia and how it shapes individual careers and positions. The Convention has also given rise to institutional proliferation in Armenia typified by the Aarhus Centres that are scattered across Armenia.

The Aarhus Centres

The Aarhus Centres are a unique feature of the Aarhus Convention. Although several other countries have similar centres, the actual number in the Armenian regions makes Armenia a special case. Most other countries in the region have one or two centres; Armenia has fourteen. To take Azerbaijan as an example, the only Aarhus Centre there was situated (in 2008) in a building occupied by the Ministry of Ecology and Natural Resources. When we tried to visit it in 2008 (Chapter 4), the building was undergoing renovation and the centre was temporarily closed. There was a joke going around about it – with reference to the Soviet period – that the only thing missing was a sign saying *remont* – 'under repair'. It was the usual Soviet trick, disguising a political decision to close something down by calling it renovation.

The establishment of Aarhus Centres came about under the ENVSEC.[62] The OSCE has been responsible for setting up the Aarhus Centres in cooperation with the Armenian ministries of territorial administration and nature protection. Working with the government of Armenia, the OSCE opened an office in Yerevan following a decision at OSCE's 241st plenary session in 1999. The OSCE office was intended to promote 'OSCE principles … in all OSCE dimensions, including the human, political, economic and environmental aspects of security and stability'.[63] An appointed ambassador heads the office, with several experts seconded from OSCE member states. The head of the OSCE office during most of my involvement was a Russian ambassador. In the field of environmental activities, the programme was headed by various foreigners, with local staff providing personnel stability. These were the people we worked with on the Armenia project. During fieldwork in 2010, eleven Aarhus Centres were up and running across Armenia and several more were planned. Their purpose is to foster Armenia's implementation of the Convention by facilitating dialogue and 'opening up' the environmental management sector to the public. Although the establishment of these centres is clearly no guarantee of actual changes on the ground, they provide environmentalists and concerned citizens with a new opportunity to acquire environmental information.

In ENVSEC's own description of the South Caucasus regional cooperation for the implementation of the Aarhus Convention project (2009–10), we can read,

> Overall objective of the project is to promote regional cooperation for implementation of the Aarhus Convention through networking among the Aarhus Centres and Public Environmental Information Centres within the region by capitalizing on the varying strengths of the countries of the region and responding to their varying challenges in relation to the three pillars of the Convention. In line with the work program for the Aarhus Convention (2009–11) and the Long-term Strategic Plan, the project facilitates the implementation of the Convention at the regional level, particularly in areas that respond to the priorities identified by the ENVSEC regional assessment for South Caucasus.[64]

Once again – although in different words – we note the ambition to make a common framework, while being sensitive to and taking account of regional differences. As the quote shows, it is apparently possible to 'capitalize' on differences as far as interconnected programmes and institutions allow.

In Armenia, the ENVSEC project is de facto run by Anush,[65] a local employee at the OSCE office and one of my informants. Decisions pertaining to the project are taken higher up in the OSCE hierarchy, but for the daily operations, Anush's role is essential down to the smallest details. Although representing an institution funding the Aarhus Centres in Armenia, she very much regards herself as a colleague and companion of the people at the Armenian Aarhus Centres and also with the mayors with whom the OSCE cooperates closest; at one point, Anush referred to them as 'our mayors'. Relations between OSCE and the Armenian government have had their ups and downs. In theory, after the initial project period, the centres should have been financed by the government directly, but after a ministerial employee stopped paying the managers of the centres, OSCE decided to fund them themselves. Whether this was a calculated intervention by the Ministry of Nature Protection or merely expression of a fight to subdue the centre managers is unclear. In the opinion of another of my informants, the ministry had clearly wanted to tame the centres, which makes it tempting to analyse the event as a throwback to Soviet times when everything was controlled by the government; indeed, this was an interpretation invoked by my informants. Some in the higher echelons of government viewed the centres' independence as a threat.

This conflict arose in 2007 and 2008 when a new official within the ministry was given the Aarhus desk. I met him together with Anush in a ministerial building in one of the *mikri*[66] surrounding Yerevan city centre. This was before the conflict and I had been invited since the OSCE and the Armenia project considered the new contact to be a promising choice. It was certainly a reminder of the relative precariousness of professional relations I encountered in this field. Everyone seemed to know everyone else and at some point will have crossed swords, although at other times relations were portrayed as excellent. Networks are precarious and volatile, yet they are described as stable in project documents. The network of the Aarhus Centres in Armenia and the occasional connections outside Armenia are seen as important to the functioning of the Aarhus Centres and related institutions such as the ELRC at YSU. The disagreement and ensuing cancellation of OSCE's financial support of ELRC was due to a breach in personal trust, according to several of my informants.

One may also ponder whether and how the network functions as a connective tissue linking meetings and seminars that occur on an irregular basis. Like Riles, networks exist, I believe, inasmuch as they are claimed to exist by their participants but also inasmuch as they function to legitimize connections between temporally distant events. One such networking effort was a seminar Anush had attended and which she told me about on one of my many visits to her office. It was an international seminar on the role and development of the Aarhus Centres or the more or less similar Public Environmental Information Centres (PEICs), established in several other members of the UNECE. The seminar, held in January 2010, was organized by the Office of the Coordinator of OSCE Economic and Environmental Activities in Istanbul, Turkey. One issue at the seminar was to define and regulate the affiliation and legal status of the centres. Some were hosted by the government; some centres were NGO-based.

The seminar attempted to reconcile the procedures of the various centres and devise a general set of guidelines for them. One of the speakers ended by asking several questions: 'What can be done to make the Guidelines work?' 'How feasible are the guidelines?' 'What aspects might be difficult to implement?' This speaker also touched on 'Making strategic decisions, using the Road Map' and 'Building a Network'.[67]

Clearly process-oriented, these questions indicated not only the constant need to reaffirm and legitimize the network but also the wish and belief in standardized solutions across a very diverse region and differing political landscapes. Claims are thus made regarding the scale of Europeanization and closer alignment with European environmental law via the Aarhus Convention. One of the many mundane manifestations in Armenia – and for that matter elsewhere in the region – was precisely the establishment of the network of Aarhus Centres. In Armenia, centre managers work together quite closely and Anush refers to them as 'my colleagues', indicating close relations and mutual trust. One of these managers is Ashot, based at an Aarhus Centre in central Armenia.

At the Aarhus Centre in Hrazdan – intimidation and lack of information

In conjunction with the Armenia project, I had met Ashot, the manager of the Aarhus Centre in Hrazdan, Kotayk marz (province), on several occasions. We had on these occasions spoken about the centre he led in Hrazdan and in 2010 I decided it was time to accept his invitation to pay him a visit. The drive from Yerevan took me not only through beautiful late-autumn scenery where the mountaintops were covered with snow but also through an industrial wasteland and dilapidated buildings on former collective farms (see Figure 2.1). The Aarhus Centre I visited was in the building of the municipal authority, a typical late Soviet-era structure in dire need of renovation. Ashot met me outside and we climbed the barely lit stairs up to his office. There I was greeted by an American who happened to be volunteering at the office. He had spent time there as a US Peace Corps volunteer in Armenia some years back and now that he had retired, he had returned as a volunteer without organizational affiliations, choosing to work with Ashot at the Hrazdan Aarhus Centre. Ashot was a prolific champion of the Aarhus Convention in Armenia and 'one of our best guys', as Anush at the OSCE office had been telling me. He was one of those people who saw themselves as activists rather than neutral interlocutors between citizens and government. In his opinion, this was especially important and warranted because the town lacked local environmental NGOs. So not only did this office facilitate dialogue, arrange meetings and the like, it also initiated and investigated cases. One such case was the – unsuccessful – attempt to obtain information about plans to permit the mining of iron ore close to the town.

The plan apparently included open-pit strip mining. 'Apparently' is important here. It was hard to be certain about anything; information was in scarce supply. In 2009, Ashot had been apprised of this 'news' by contacts in Yerevan. He learned subsequently that two public meetings had been held in Yerevan, with only three people attending the second. The town's mayor had allegedly been informed in 2008 and a public hearing had followed in February 2009. According to Ashot, scientists at the Yerevan-based American University of Armenia (AUA) had said the project was dangerous, due to its proximity to an irrigation channel. Iron deposits are often intermingled with deposits of chrome, copper, nickel and arsenic. So what did Ashot do about this? He went to the mayor he knew had already been informed of the plans; the mayor

Figure 2.1 Hrazdan, Kotayk province
Source: The author.

told him the plans had not been approved and had been sent back for further work.

Several organizations decided to launch a petition campaign. They collected about two thousand signatures. According to Ashot, many more were opposed to the plans but were afraid to sign. In the end, uncertainty over what was actually going on had reached the president's office. Staff there seemed confused and to know little. Later, however, more was learned about the firm involved, its ownership and the possible involvement of a former Armenian minister of nature protection, Vartan Ayvazyan (later a member of parliament, an office which gave him immunity).[68] Back in 2010, however, information was scant. Ashot told me that ministry sources had indicated that the Republic of Armenia (RA) presidential office had commissioned an environmental impact assessment (EIA) whose purpose was to prove the AUA scientists wrong. The EIA was eventually published, but the publicly available downloadable file was full of empty pages. 'The process is stopped – we don't know if we had an impact.' Lack of transparency, decisions shrouded in secrecy, allegations of corruption and nepotism – no one seemed to trust anyone. Being industrious and full of initiative, Ashot turned his attention to businesses involved in the recycling of plastic waste into plastic bags – the process was allegedly harmful to workers. He wrote a letter to the head of the state inspection agency, urging an inspection of the businesses in question. Plastic was recycled as plastic bags by a process of heating, melting and reconstitution, Ashot told me, but it was done without special equipment, protective gear or other safeguards. Sometime after sending the letter, Ashot received what he felt was a threatening call from a representative of the inspectorate. Ten minutes later, he got another call came from a head of one of the implicated businesses: 'Why are you trying to harm me? I simply earn money for my family.' Either way, although an inspector came from Yerevan, no findings or conclusions were published. In Ashot's opinion, the inspection had been a hoax.

Ashot still retained a sense of optimism: 'There have been big improvements in environmental activism, not only by NGOs, also by Facebook campaigns and more. Our [the Aarhus Centre's] role is to foster dialogue, facilitate and be a catalyst.' A short while after my fieldwork, however, Ashot decided to follow in the footsteps of many of his compatriots and migrated to Russia.

The Aarhus Convention as an assemblage

The Aarhus Convention is but one example of the 'institutional proliferation of particular globalization projects'.[69] What does adherence to the Aarhus principles involve in terms of scale making? Or, put differently, is the Aarhus project one in which Armenian environmentalists can 'imagine globality'?[70] The Aarhus Convention and its platform of Europeanization can be regarded as a project of 'relatively coherent bundles of ideas and practices as realized in particular times and spaces'.[71] If we follow that train of thought and pay attention both to the ideologies of scale as well as projects of scale making,[72] what do we find? Understood as a project of scale, the Aarhus

Convention seeks to mould several European environmental laws and practices into a more or less coherent whole. The ratifying countries have ample discretion to interpret the Aarhus Convention and adjust and/or introduce domestic practices in a given field as long as the practices comply with the spirit of the Convention.

One hallmark of the Aarhus Convention is the access it grants to environmental information. Writing about the consensus of experts in international development cooperation related to poverty reduction, David Mosse found that it marries neo-liberalism with 'new institutionalism'. Because bad governance and corruption are seen to impede development, existing forms of state rule need to be dismantled and replaced with strong, accountable institutions.[73] There is neo-liberal agreement on methods, such as 'harmonization' and 'alignment'. At the same time, the emphasis on participation, partnership, brokerage and consultation means that aid agencies can claim they are merely supporting the conditions necessary for promoting development rather than intervening in domestic politics.[74] The wording of the title of this chapter indicates that the former communist states need to be 'helped', which is the phrase used by UNECE.[75] What these countries need apparently is 'assistance' to help them replace corruption and authoritarianism with strong institutions and international connections.

Transparency and Europe

I have argued that one way of understanding the Aarhus Convention is by analysing it in terms of the networks it gives rise to in Armenia. By Riles's definition of network, we understand institutions and knowledge practices that generate effects in a tautological, self-reflective way.[76] The MoPs are patterned processes of intention of pan-European reach, familiar in their regularity, with each new MoP adding a new layer to the pattern of Aarhus practices. The institutions and practices are not given; rather, they are the result of the continuous work being performed in Armenia, at the multilateral MoPs and elsewhere. The suggestion that the Convention is pan-European is an indication of the ambitious scale that is invoked throughout the Convention area by politicians and environmentalists alike. To use an analogy, the Parties to the Convention make up a tribe, with the EU as the dominant clan and the post-Soviet states as a far less coordinated one. Norway, as one of the main donors to the Convention, is perhaps the tribal wizard. Further, the MoP is a tribal ritual and the Compliance Committee a gathering of tribal elders. In this tribal order, central and peripheral, global and local movements, institutions and practices are forged together[77] through the dreams and claims pertaining to environmental rights.

For Armenia, the Aarhus Convention is part and parcel of the republic's effort to become a truly European democracy, to become 'Europeanized'. It has spurred practices and networks and involved a range of domestic as well as international actors, first and foremost the OSCE and its office in Yerevan. This chapter has attempted to map and understand the Aarhus Convention and its institutional offshoots in Armenia and elsewhere as a process of scale making, specifically with a view to Europeanizing Armenia. Through the reading and analysis of the ethnography of international meetings and law texts, of the Aarhus Centre in Hrazdan and the role of the focal point, I have endeavoured to show the breadth and magnitude and sheer reach of the process of Europeanization. Resistance to and participation in this process by a variety of Armenian networks, institutions and individuals are a sign – I have argued – of the reach of the assemblage and agency required for the Convention to become part of the Armenian environmental discourse. Agency is also a keyword here inasmuch as I have employed post-socialist readings of 'transition' to this ethnography. It has led me to a tentative conclusion: that agency – at least with regard to some elements of the post-socialist literature on civil society and democratization – is inadequately accounted for. People are either portrayed as cynically adapting to donor priorities or as passive recipients. It would give us a better understanding of their practices, I argue, if we reconstituted these NGO activists and others by making use of the literature on networks and performativity from other strands of anthropology.

While this chapter has looked at the Aarhus MoPs as various institutional performances as well as the role of the focal point and Aarhus Centres in Armenia, the next chapter will discuss how Armenian activists make use of the Aarhus Convention and its mechanisms as part of their activism.

3

Save Teghut!

This chapter addresses the Aarhus Convention from a slightly different angle by looking at how Armenian activists perform their environmentalism through the staging of street protests, court cases and international petitions. In the following sections, I present ethnography from various protests and petitions organized under the Save Teghut Civic Initiative (STCI), but most notably from correspondence between the Aarhus Convention's Compliance Committee, coalitions of Armenian non-governmental organizations (NGOs) and representatives of the Armenian government related to the same case.

I argue that although the activists and activism analysed in this chapter rely on numerous strategies, they had meagre success. The protests and court actions discussed in this chapter are indicative not only of the multiple ways in which Armenian activists fight but also of how the environmentalists are able to scale up their demands. The activists are occupied with how laws and rights may enable them to foster change, and yet it turns out to be an existential drama for some of the organizations as their legal standing is disputed. This is an example of how Europe and transparency are enacted in Armenia. The efforts themselves are based on a (moderately optimistic, perhaps) view of the rule of law in Armenia. The activists have their own interpretation of different laws and the rights they perceive to 'trickle down' from them or the degree to which they believe themselves to be entitled. As 'newly transnationalized locals',[1] activists in Armenia challenge the relationship between the global community, the nation state and civil society, usually understood as a vertical topography. These networking efforts and environmentalist activities coincide with court rulings that in some ways threaten some of these organizations' claim to be acting on behalf of the wider population. One characteristic of this activism is the prominence of references to a wider global or regional context, demands for adherence to the law and other general principles, even sometimes at the expense of the case the argument is about, namely the mining prospects at the Teghut deposit.

In one sense, then, this chapter is a combination of ethnography of environmental activism in the streets and environmentalism through allegations of environmental rights violations. I want to show that these different elements can basically be understood as aspects of the same thing, as various ways of establishing, nurturing and maintaining networks as well as assembling environmental rights.

Environmentalism in this chapter is understood as advocacy on behalf of cultural and social change where 'success depends on the extent to which [the advocates] can persuade others that their interpretation of reality is correct and that the changes they advocate are important and necessary'.[2] In what follows, I analyse the actions of the involved environmentalists in response to a plan to allow open-pit mining in Armenia. The question is whether the Armenian government fulfilled its Aarhus-related obligations to consult with 'the public' when it gave the mining company a license. Environmentalists are thus concerned not only to protect the environment from what they perceive as damaging exploitation but also with 'society's habitual way of doing things'.[3]

We saw in Chapter 2 how the provisions and rights provided for under the Aarhus Convention were established in a legal and universal manner, or in other words how the assemblages of environmental rights and Europeanization are established. How these rights are practised and observed in Armenia (and elsewhere) is obviously an ethnographic question and will be dealt with in this chapter with regard to the mining license issued for the Teghut deposit in northern Armenia.

The Teghut case

The environmental issue at the heart of the conflict was a license granted by the government to a mining company to extract copper and molybdenum from deposits in the Lori region of Armenia. Different activities aimed at stopping the proposed exploitation of the Teghut mine were organized by Armenian organizations and activists. In the following section, I examine the different settings in which these activities – from street protests and petitions to senior Armenian power-holders, the courts and the transnational institutional set-up under the Aarhus Convention – took place.

The Teghut mine is located in Lori Marz, close to two villages, Teghut and Shnogh. The territory allocated for mining is almost 1,500 hectares, of which more than 80 per cent is wooded.[4] For the environmentalists, this is important as deforestation is a huge problem in Armenia where only about 14 per cent of the territory is still covered by forest. The exploitation license (number HV-MSH-13/33) was granted to the Armenia Copper Programme (ACP) by government decree in 2004 and was preceded by a license to ACP's predecessor Manes and Vallex CJSC in 2001.

As with the other metal mining companies in Armenia, the state's share is nil, but more importantly with regard to ACP, ownership of about 80 per cent of the shares is undisclosed due to offshore registration rules.[5] In a country where allegations of corruption and suspicions of alliances between politicians (one of the parliamentary privileges in Armenia is immunity) and oligarchs are seldom far away, this has caused a lot of speculation. Environmentalists questioned the decision's ecological merits but also objected to it in light of what they regarded was the public's lack of involvement in the decision making. The issue thus has a substantive component and a procedural component. My ethnography deals with the latter. The conflict related to the license led to various protests, court cases and a case brought before the Compliance Committee of the Aarhus Convention.

In 2007, the STCI was established, consisting of individuals as well as NGOs. Several of the people involved in this network also brought the cases to the Armenian courts and the Compliance Committee under the Aarhus Convention. Some of them are also informants of mine.

The activists fought unsuccessfully, however, and the mine was officially opened in 2014.[6] They did succeed in challenging powerful actors in Armenia and beyond.[7] While the relationship between NGOs and informal groups is an interesting topic,[8] the purpose of my analysis is slightly different. Rather, I want to discuss how this activism was performed through the assemblage of environmental rights, and how the activists subjected themselves to the Aarhus Convention.

Save Teghut – in the streets

On a Saturday evening in the autumn of 2010, I was walking to a park near the Komitas State Conservatory, in the centre of Yerevan, to join some of my informants in a demonstration against plans to allow open-pit mining in Teghut. One of the activists had told me about it via Facebook and emails. Several organizations and networks had organized the demonstration under the slogan 'Save Teghut Civic Initiative'. In the park, they delivered speeches and we listened to a concert aimed at attracting the attention of the public and raising awareness of the issue. I saw several familiar faces from the national and international organizational scene together with clergymen, musicians and a few members of parliament. The area was full of campaigners wearing 'Save Teghut' t-shirts and people handing out leaflets and selling homemade bags to support the campaign. After walking around for a few minutes, taking photographs and receiving leaflets, I saw Hermine, an NGO campaigner and activist, and walked over to join her.

She told me that the organizers had had several problems, because the city authorities had refused permission to stage the protest. Under Armenian legislation, the mayoral office can allow protests to go ahead after due notification. Sometimes, however, organizers have to fulfil additional criteria. In this case, the mayor's office gave what the organizers believed – based on their interpretation of relevant Armenian law – was an insufficient answer. They were urged to *consider* another venue, but without any indications as to where that might be. The authorities did not explain why they were against an event being held close to the Komitas Conservatory. Given the lack of detail, the organizers chose to proceed as planned. The day before the protest, some of the organizers were called by the city police, who advised them in no uncertain terms to refrain from organizing the announced protest.

The organizers had a deal with a nearby café owner to supply electricity for the protest and the following concert. The proprietor was also contacted by the police and decided to cancel the agreement. By this point, as Hermine said, 'we were afraid'. They proceeded as planned, and since they had no power, megaphones were used for the speeches and the now acoustic mini-concert was held.

The police arrived and tried to persuade the organizers to stop the protest, but when a former minister of foreign affairs and now oppositional member of parliament intervened on the protesters' behalf, they were allowed to continue.

Whether Hermine is right in her legal interpretation does not really matter, because it shows us how legal knowledge and an ability to argue along legal lines became assets in the hands of Armenian environmentalists objecting to cases of urban development and risks to the environment. These capacities can probably be attributed to the discourse on environmental rights that emerged in Armenia in 2001, when Armenia ratified the Aarhus Convention. The Aarhus Convention and its provisions and the transparency discourse engage people like Hermine as it allows them to frame objections and problems in Armenia in a more general way and link them to rights that Armenia has formally endorsed. However, we should not forget the possibility of a gap between formal rights and the sociopolitical contexts in which activists like Hermine try to promote them.

This applies to the Teghut demonstration in that while Hermine refers to different laws and provisions, their rights as campaigners are being infringed by late-night calls, threats and what seems like a deliberately exaggerated police presence. Besides showing the Armenian state's ability to exercise power, it is an indication of how the activists claim adherence to a wider context of human and environmental rights, yet stumble upon petty hindrances:

> Even if our bridge aims toward the most lofty universal truths – the insights of science, the freedom of individual rights, the possibility of wealth for all – we find ourselves hemmed in by the specificity of rules and practices, with their petty prejudices, unreasonable hierarchies and cruel exclusions.[9]

Nevertheless, the assemblage of environmental rights has 'fixed' itself onto an Armenian context where a complex Soviet heritage of corruption and petty bureaucracy accentuate the importance of informal connections. The way I understand it, Hermine and her fellow activists still believe that the legal avenue will bring them success. Whether this reflects the lack of other options or an actual belief in their ability to succeed is harder to tell. These campaigners are not likely to have much trust in the legal system or its judges. The petty problems they had to overcome and the intimidation they faced were a reminder of the blunt instruments used by the police and authorities to throttle opposition. The discrepancy between ideals and felt reality suggests that promoting environmental rights in Armenia is in many ways a 'sticky engagement' between local police practices and lofty ideals of transparency and equality before the law. Friction is created when abstract claims to legal rights unfold in specific sociopolitical contexts.

Save Teghut – in Armenian courts

In 2009, several Armenian organizations decided to let the Armenian courts test the legitimacy of the Teghut mining license. These organizations were Ecodar,[10] Transparency International Anticorruption Center and Helsinki Citizens' Assembly Vanadzor. In view of what the plaintiffs considered inadequate public consultation, they asked the court to render invalid the licenses obtained by the ACP along with the environmental impact assessment and declare a government decree on land use 'null and void'. In the event, the Administrative Court refused to hear the case because the appeal 'contains no justification of how or by what the rights of the non-governmental organizations that act as the plaintiff have been violated'.[11] According to the Administrative Court of Armenia, because the plaintiffs lacked 'environmental protection' or some such phrasing in their organizational mission statements, their petition was invalid.

The plaintiffs appealed this decision to the Republic of Armenia (RA) Court of Cassation, which in October 2009 reversed the Administrative Court's decision to deny Ecodar's – which has environmental protection as one of its statutory goals – standing.[12] But it did uphold the Administrative Court's decision not to grant standing to Transparency International Anticorruption Center and the Helsinki Citizens' Assembly, because these organizations did not have environmental protection as one of their statutory goals. Ecodar returned to the Administrative Court alone – the two other organizations having been relegated to the position of informal supporters – but the court once again refused to hear it, this time because 'persons that have such standing are already stipulated by the Administrative Procedure Code … However, non-governmental organizations are not among them'.[13] Taking an earlier decision of the Armenian Constitutional Court – which addressed legal standing – into account,[14] the Armenian Court of Cassation, in its final verdict, rejected the claim of the plaintiffs. They had now, in the words of the Compliance Committee, 'exhausted all domestic remedies'.[15]

These court decisions brought the NGOs to a critical juncture. Is NGO legitimacy in legal terms restricted to what is mentioned in the organizations' statutes? Or more specifically, does an organization have the right to submit before the courts environmental decisions taken by institutions? And if not, is their network viable at all? It all built up to something of an existential drama for the organizations in question. The ruling that two of the organizations had no legal standing regarding environmental matters in effect raised questions concerning the legitimacy of the NGOs. NGOs and civil society at large tend to base their legitimacy on a claim to speak on behalf of a wider public or citizenry. It is called *actio popularis* in legal parlance and is applied in a quite restrictive manner in Armenia, something the focal point of the Aarhus Convention also acknowledged.[16] The implication was that the Transparency International Anticorruption Center and Helsinki Citizens' Assembly Vanadzor – to the dismay of the involved activists – were denied an opportunity to stand before the courts because they lacked mention of 'environmental protection' or similar phrases in their statutes.

One of the avenues environmentalists seized on in Indonesia, Tsing writes, was to use liberalism against itself.[17] In a similar vein, the Armenian activists tried to use the Convention's liberal provisions of access to information and so on to obtain information from the Armenian authorities. Reliance on the legal avenue means that once a verdict is reached and appeal possibilities exhausted, the activists' options are limited. Obviously, in the Armenian case one can question whether this was a process in which a liberal state is resisting a call for action or if Armenia is a semi-authoritarian state merely posing as a liberal democracy.

Although unsuccessful this time round, the entitlement to environmental justice gave environmentalists an opportunity to pursue lawsuits as a means of challenging the state. Dependence on the law may delay other strategies, notes Tsing, by closing the 'political imagination' whereby activists rely solely on technical solutions.[18] But the political imagination of the Armenian activists, I suggest, was not closed by pursuing the case through the court system. By combining this strategy with street protests and other forms of environmental activism, the political imagination, despite relying very heavily on court cases at certain junctures, and testing whether the court system was a viable avenue, did not shut down. The activists continued to pursue different avenues to achieve their ultimate goal: to stop the mining and gain more insight into the process by which the Teghut license was granted to the ACP.

So what was the activists' answer to their failure in the courts? They scaled up their fight and claims even more. It was now time to engage at the international level, for example, with the Compliance Committee of the Aarhus Convention. In my analysis of the documents and use of the Compliance Committee, I show how civil society, by bringing the case before an international arbitration body, circumvented the Armenian state and government, challenging the very topography of state–society relations to which many a government official in Armenia seems to subscribe.

Documents, networks and artefacts in international law

Strategies, written communications, judicial processes and international guidelines on development policies also make up important aspects of the ethnography. Indeed, Lisa L. Gezon, in her study of land rights in Madagascar, says that such documents 'expose tensions among identities, cultural logics and discourses of rights and responsibilities between people and nonhuman environments'.[19] What exactly constitutes these 'nonhuman environments' obviously varies, but in my case they involve documents, policies, law, flow charts and goal hierarchies in project management. Now, these various artefacts should be understood not merely as representative of a given organization or practice but rather as themselves constituting objects.[20]

Central to our understanding of law as practice is how we understand documents. Documents, I believe in line with Riles,[21] do not simply have representative qualities; rather, they are artefacts in and of themselves. In discourse analysis, the representative dimension of documents is conceived as the manner in which documents construct objects (for development purposes or otherwise).[22] If documents are essentially understood as bearers of representative or referential qualities, it will be important to keep this in mind when discussing the role of documents in a programme of transparency such as the Aarhus Convention. Perhaps we should rather focus on the circulation and production of these documents and the kind of power relations they may coincide with? In an ethnography of colonial archives, Stoler stressed the need to acknowledge their nature as 'epistemological experiments'.[23] Analytically, I also consider documents to be constitutive in part of 'rules, ideologies, knowledge, practices, subjectivities, objects, outcomes and even the organizations themselves'.[24] This is the case with the list of documents to be discussed in Chapter 5 insofar as they show how the Aarhus Convention's Compliance Committee attempted to establish what had happened regarding a specific environmental issue and whether it was in compliance with the Convention.

Documents in this sense are therefore taken to have representational, aesthetic qualities, as well as being artefacts of an institutional practice.[25] Practices related to the compliance mechanism are thus understood as 'a set of institutions, knowledge practices and artefacts thereof that internally generate the effects of their own reality by reflecting in themselves'.[26]

We should regard documents, I suggest, as something more than representational artefacts. For instance, I will argue that the introduction of the logical framework (LOG frame) hierarchy in project application forms has an effect on how given projects are conceived and portrayed. It is as if it guides or encourages changes in projects and project descriptions simply because of its formal requirements. The LOG frame lives a life of its own, and once it is implemented in a new sphere, it affects this sphere.

Elaborating on legality as a practice, Brunnée and Toope have argued that

> [l]aw is created, maintained, or destroyed through day-to-day interactions in communities of legal practice. Legal obligation cannot be reduced to the existence of fixed rules; it is made real in the continuing practices of communities that reason with and communicate through norms.[27]

While legal norms differ from social norms in that they are legally mandated,[28] legal norms also require a shared understanding and support: it is in this context that NGOs, states and transnational organizations matter because they, in varying degrees, 'articulate, promote, apply and work to shift international norms'.[29] Even though legal norms can be soft (as in 'soft law'), they are distinct from other social norms, the authors argue, in that their influence derives from the concept of legal obligation.[30]

In contrast to domestic law, international law has a fairly limited range of sanctions at its disposal (in the absence of a central authority). Yet international law, through the creation and monitoring of conventions and social pressure, is a 'global order' in the making.[31] Governments comply with international law largely out of a sense of reciprocity between states and a wish to appear 'civilized'.[32] Under the mechanisms, rights and obligations stemming from international law, the sovereignty of nation states is narrowly circumscribed.[33] During the Cold War, the East and the West seemed to follow two distinct paths in the development of human rights. Whereas the former saw them as social and economic rights, the latter (especially the United States) focused on civil and political rights. Where the Soviet Union guaranteed work, food and health for all, the United States focused on free speech and eventually civil rights.[34]

What makes the human rights system different from other parts of the international legal regime is that it is premised on the rights of individuals, rather than the regulation of relations (trade, etc.) between states.[35] The Aarhus Convention lends itself to this interpretation insofar as it mainly regulates the obligations of the ratifying states to their citizens. Merry argues that the anthropology of international law involves 'studying up',[36] by focusing on how rules and procedures are shaped in the corridors at international meetings, how knowledge production of a transnational character circulates and how both are connected to larger economic and political contexts.[37] In the case I make in this chapter, we will see how Armenia's implementation shortcomings are negotiated, affirmed and contested at such international meetings.

International legal knowledge practices produce truth and define identity[38] and can be understood as global forms, and inasmuch as they are articulated in specific places, they constitute global assemblages.[39]

I have so far discussed theories of post-socialist transformation, development policies and legitimation as well as anthropological conceptions of civil society and law. The material I am about to present shows how the framing and perception of real-world problems are as important as the projects themselves. The strength of the network around such projects (not only the Armenia project, but the Aarhus project as such) relies on its ability to construct 'slices of manageable reality'[40] where the network forges links between means and end.[41] On the other hand, it can also be argued that the motivation to maintain a network is the reason behind the development interventions – that organizations' decisions are driven more by the need to maintain relationships than to observe policies and guidelines.[42]

The practice of documenting environmental rights

The parties to the Aarhus Convention agreed to allow members of the public to raise issues of compliance. When someone in a ratifying state, as a member 'of the public', decides to bring an issue before the Compliance Committee, they first have to submit a request to the Committee. The Compliance Committee, upon receiving the request, decides on its admissibility. Anonymous, unreasonable, irrelevant or incompatible requests are rejected. More importantly, the Committee has to decide whether the communicant (the party submitting the complaint) has exhausted all reasonable domestic remedies before applying to the Committee. If the case is admitted, the secretariat gives the case a reference number and communication will ensue, typically entailing requests for further information, English or Russian translations of relevant domestic laws, minutes of public hearings and questions the Committee wants the implicated party and/or the communicant to answer. The party, communicant and others of relevance to the case may be called upon to provide oral statements at the Committee's meetings. Some of these oral statements are included in the communication.

How can we produce ethnography from a list of formal documents? I describe in the following section the documents and the communications in a way that reveals what I will call the 'social life' of these documents. It does not take much imagination to understand that behind these documents (and indeed within them) lie a long series of deliberations by the Compliance Committee, tactical and ethical considerations on behalf of the communicants, and tactics and lines of defence on behalf of the government.

The number of documents involved in each and every case brought before the Compliance Committee obviously varies. In the three cases related to Armenia, there were 34, 42 and 36 documents respectively. I discuss below the two latter cases, both of which concern the Teghut license. Some of the documents circulate twice. The case numbers assigned by the UNECE Secretariat to the cases were ACCC/C/2009/43 and ACCC/C/2011/62. The years refer to the date of submission. The two cases were eventually decided at two Meetings of Parties (MoPs) in 2011 and 2014, respectively. Following this, Armenia was asked to present progress reports. These reports entailed new document lists.

On the recommendation of the Compliance Committee, three subsequent MoPs[43] assessed Armenia's compliance. Armenia accounts for three of the twenty-seven cases of non-compliance addressed by the different MoPs. The assigned titles of these decisions are not the same as those assigned to the case preceding the MoPs. The first of these decisions (III/6b) was an adjunct to a general decision on compliance by Albania, Armenia, Kazakhstan, Lithuania, Turkmenistan and Ukraine. The two following decisions (IV/9a in 2011 and V/5b in 2014) addressed implementation measures to be taken by Armenia and were more specific.

The case documents, including the entire communication between the Compliance Committee, the communicant – for example, the individual or group that initiated the communication – and the implicated party, are available to everyone. The party here refers to the Armenian government and the government-appointed national focal point, who is responsible for overseeing the implementation of the Aarhus Convention. This was Hasmik, whom we met in the preceding chapter. This person is assumed – in principle – to be independent of the government. The list of relevant documents does not contain minutes of the Compliance Committee meetings unless they were sent to the implicated party and communicant.[44]

Save Teghut – beyond Armenia

The following cases indicate how international law is primarily the hard work of continuous practice insofar as the Compliance Committee is involved in meetings,[45] deliberations and legal interpretations that also take place in the periods between the MoPs. In the two periods covered below, the Committee held thirteen meetings between the MoPs of 2008 and 2011 and twelve between 2011 and 2014. Following the first decision of the Administrative Court, Ecoera and Transparency International Anticorruption Center decided to submit the Teghut case to the Compliance Committee. In September 2009, they sent a letter to this effect to the UNECE Secretariat asking for the case to be evaluated. Ten days later, the Compliance Committee found the case to be admissible, although all domestic remedies had still not been exhausted. This was clear from the communication, as the communicants had stated that after the initial rejection by the Administration Court, they had appealed to the Court of Cassation. That decision was still pending. The case was assigned the number ACCC/C/2009/43 by the UNECE Secretariat. The documents 'involved' in this case are listed in Figure 3.1.

The secretariat asked the communicants to identify who had challenged the decisions of the Administrative Court. The implicated party received further detailed questions to enable the Compliance Committee to establish the facts. The communicants urged the

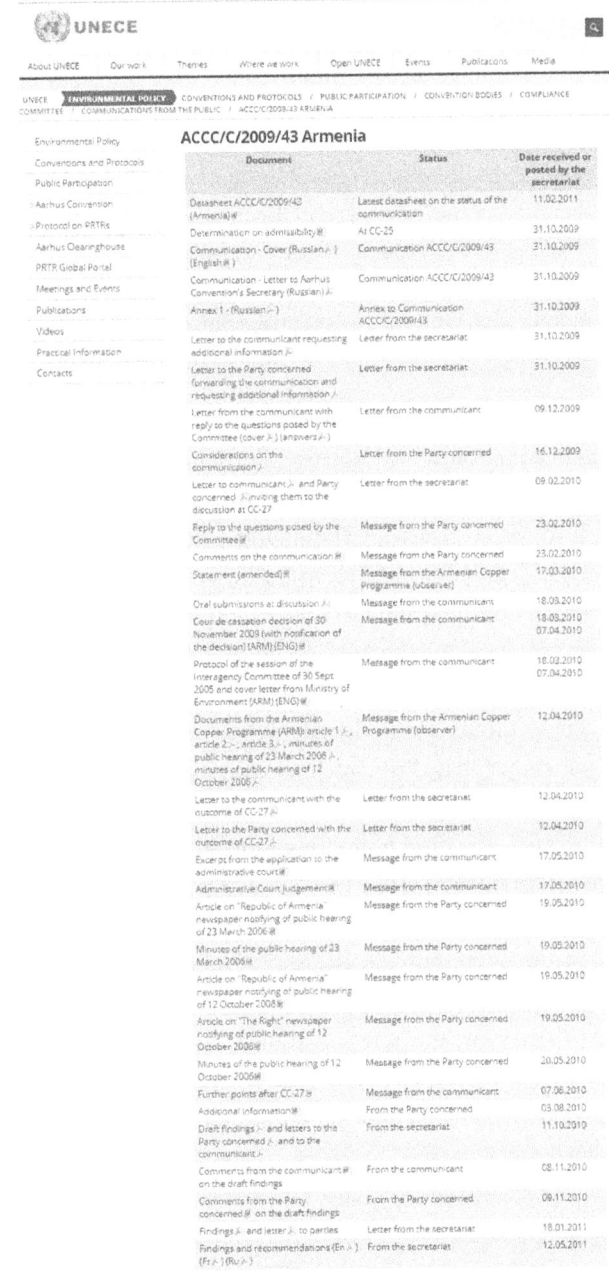

Figure 3.1 Overview of communication ACCC/C/2009/43 Armenia.
Source: Available at www.unece.org/env/pp/compliance/compliancecommittee/43tablearmenia.html (accessed 21 September 2014).

Compliance Committee to look into the case, even though it was still pending in Armenian courts:

> We do not find the decision of Cassation Court as fair in respect with non-recognition of the 'Transparency International Anti-Corruption Centre' NGO as a concerned party. Thus we would like to request the Aarhus Convention Compliance Committee to continue reviewing our communication with particular consideration of violations of our access to justice.[46]

By denying the local branch of Transparency International legal standing before the court, the Cassation Court had acted in accordance with Armenia's 'restrictive approach to actio popularis', as the focal point put it to the secretariat,[47] although the focal point did concede that Armenian legislation needed to be improved. The verdict went to the very heart of the conflict. Who can represent what the Aarhus Convention refers to as members of the public 'having a sufficient interest'?[48] This was now up to the Compliance Committee to decide.

While the communicants claimed to be 'the public concerned', we must remember that the Armenian courts rejected Transparency International Anticorruption Center's and the Vanadzor-based NGO's claim to the same. The focal point found the decision of the Cassation Court to be substantiated, since the Civil Code of RA requires a legal person's civil rights to correspond with the purposes of the activity enshrined in the organization's statutes.[49] The courts therefore had to decide whether environmental protection was indeed included in their statutes. In their view, the activists argued, the Teghut license issue also concerned a question of transparency and anti-corruption, the promotion of both being mentioned in the organizations' mandate and statutory goals.

One of the challenges for the Compliance Committee, as the communication shows, was to determine what had actually happened during the decision process within the Armenian government. In a letter to the secretariat, the communicants included a list showing what they contended constituted the decision-making process. One of the decisions on the list is an undated 'Decision on exploitation of the [Teghut] deposit'.[50] The communicants placed this decision prior to the issuance of the license. In a response, the focal point denies that any such decisions had been taken and since the communicants had no date or document to prove the veracity of what they said, they had no substantive case; moreover, there were no legal requirements in Armenia regulating or stipulating such decisions.[51] As this disagreement indicates, while Hasmik as the focal point argued on a formal level (about what can be proved), the activists alleged that the real decision had been taken before the public was notified. This was obviously difficult for the activists to prove, even though they, like most Armenians, believed that corruption was endemic in government circles and society in general and represented a serious problem.[52]

After this August 2010 communication, the Committee's draft findings were made available online on 10 October of the same year, some two weeks after the 29th session of the Committee. The findings summarize the chronology of the previous communications and preliminary decisions of the Committee at meetings 25–29. The findings stipulate timeframes for future communication and anticipate the Committee's conclusion that Armenia had failed to comply with 'article 3, paragraph 1 ... and article 6, paragraphs 2, 4 and 9, of the Convention'.[53]

The communicants at this stage had succeeded in persuading the Compliance Committee that their right to information and participation in decision making was infringed, at least to some degree. But, notably, the Compliance Committee did not consider the implicated party – Armenia – to be in non-compliance with article 9 regarding the issue of legal standing although it did suggest that in addition to seeing if 'environmental protection' is mentioned in an organization's statutes, its de facto activities should also be given some weight. A restrictive interpretation risks, at the very least – according to the Committee – 'being inconsistent with the Convention'.[54]

Obviously, given their prior statements, the communicants objected to the Committee's response: 'The Compliance Committee did not recognize the failure of the Party to comply with article 9 (2)'.[55]

Responding to this objection on behalf of the Armenian government, the focal point largely accepted the Committee's findings and referred to changes in the pipeline, as evidence of how seriously the government was viewing this issue:

> Party concerned accepts recommendations and conclusions made in the sections (i) and (iv). In this regard there is a need to assign amendments, addendums to RA legislation on EIA and other related legislative acts (Subsoil code of RA, Law 'On environmental expertise' and etc., which are on the schedule of RA Government).[56]

Further details of the focal point's reply on behalf of the government are unnecessary, as no comments regarding legal standing were made there. A month or so later, the Compliance Committee issued the final version of its draft findings. Nothing had changed concerning legal standing and article 9, and it barely noted that Ecodar had been granted standing.[57]

When I attended MoP-4 in Chisinau in 2011, the plenary session was about to consider the preliminary findings of the Compliance Committee in this case. Back in the conference hall, I was, as we recall, sitting with some of the Armenian activists involved in the case. An international NGO voiced its support for the Armenian activists in the discussion following the opening of the case. The findings of the Compliance Committee were adopted unchanged, although there was disagreement as to whether parts of the Russian version could or should be amended.

Following the meagre results of MoP-4, the activists decided once again to bring the Teghut case before the Compliance Committee; it duly reappeared on the agenda of the MoP of the Aarhus Convention at MoP-5 in 2014. How could these activists mount their claim to act as 'concerned citizens' when they were in effect denied legal standing in Armenia, that is, their activity was not recognized in judicial terms? The list of documents involved in this case prior to MoP-5 in 2014 can be seen in Figure 3.2. They are largely the same as the Compliance Committee had studied while reviewing the case from 2009 to 2011. In addition, the communicant was asked to submit English translations of five different court decisions during the period July 2009–April 2011.[58]

Save Teghut!

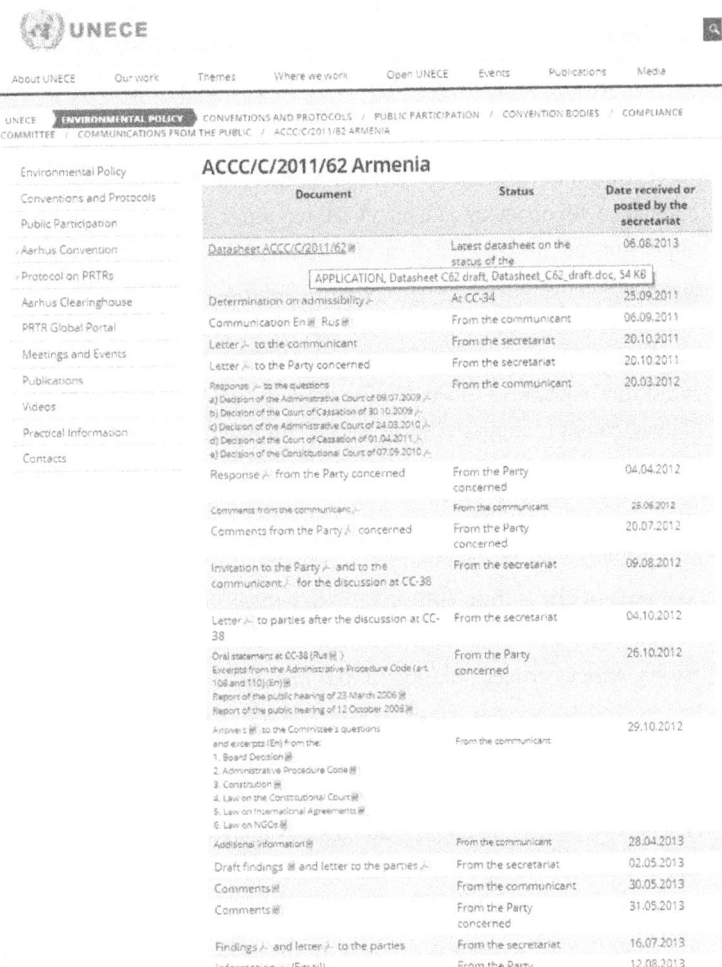

Figure 3.2 Overview of communication, ACCC/C/2011/62 Armenia.
Source: Available at http://www.unece.org/env/pp/compliance/compliance committee/62tablearm.html (accessed 22 September 2014).
Screenshot of UNECE's Aarhus website, showing all the documents involved related to the Teghut case, ACCC/C/2011/62. The final verdict came at MoP-5 in 2014.

In April 2012, Armenia's national focal point answered the Committee's questions in a document without a letterhead, date or signature. This caused the communicant to challenge the focal point's mode of communication:

> [The] informal manner of communication of the Republic of Armenia, with no letterhead, no official requisites and signature raises a question on who should bear the responsibility for the provided information. More specifically, we are confused with the incorrect information provided to the Compliance Committee ... We feel that the requirement for an official form of correspondence with respective authorities' signatures ... would raise the responsibility for the quality of information for both Parties as well as communicants.[59]

This spurred a response from the focal point ensuring that all communication with 'the Secretariat of the Aarhus Convention is being circulated in the Ministry ... and sent to the Secretariat with the consent of the public authority'.[60] The focal point then addressed what she regarded as the communicants' misinterpretation of court decisions, which 'proves once again that the "EcoEra" NGO had in fact had access to justice even if it expresses discontent with the substantive issues of the judgements of Armenia's court system'.[61] Doubtless to the communicant's dismay, this latter correspondence still lacked a letterhead and official insignia, although it was signed on this occasion.

The documents in this newest case also consisted of transcripts of public hearings. At a public hearing in 2006,[62] municipal officials and local residents were evidently positive to the plans, mainly because of the prospect of more jobs. Scepticism was mostly voiced by Yerevan-based NGOs, international organizations and journalists.[63] Although the job prospects were welcomed – an issue that often pitches rural populations against environmentalists from urban centres – there was considerable uncertainty about the consequences for health. The hearings covered topics ranging from reforestation and alleged male impotence and female sterility in the mining town of Karajan, to the prevalence of cancer and shorter life expectancy in nearby Alaverdi.

Alaverdi is home to a Soviet-era copper smelter which ACP wanted to replace with a new one if they were allowed to increase output in their copper extraction. This led the ACP official to say, 'I can assure you definitely that the exploitation of the Teghut deposit will have a positive influence on the environmental situation in Alaverdi.'[64] Pressed on the reforestation issue, the ACP official was vague. The inclusion of these documents in the second round of the Teghut deliberations of the Compliance Committee is indicative of the Committee's efforts to establish what had actually occurred as regards the Teghut case.

In the ensuing correspondence, the communicants described once more what they perceived to be the (continued) breach of their right to have access to justice after the prior case was brought before the Compliance Committee.[65] In this document, it was further argued that Ecoera was also considered devoid of legal standing: 'Article 9 par. 3 was violated by finding that "Ecoera" NGO has no legal standing to claim against administrative acts listed hereafter.'[66] Thereafter the communicants proceeded to list the deficiencies in Armenian legislation concerning the 'Administrative Procedure code, the Law on Non-Governmental Organizations and others' on how the 'public concerned' is defined.[67]

This was followed by a decision of an NGO of legal experts in Armenia 'which is closely cooperating with the RA Constitutional Court.'[68] The communicant listed prominent members of this NGO, including a former minister of justice, the prosecutor general of Armenia and dean of the Faculty of Law at Yerevan State University. Although the NGO essentially supported the decisions of the court, it also urged the national assembly to stipulate 'legal provisions on applying to court for defending others' rights within their jurisdiction ... more unequivocally and specifically through amendments to relevant legislation.'[69] This should be implemented in the Law on Public Organizations – what the communicants refer to as the Law on NGOs, Civil Procedure Code of Armenia and Administrative Procedural Code of the Republic of Armenia.[70] This supports the argument of the plaintiffs to some degree, as it at least acknowledges that interpretations of different legal acts may vary in Armenia.

After receiving all this documentation, the Committee spent six months and three committee meetings elaborating and substantiating its findings. At the MoP in Maastricht in 2014, the parties held that Armenia's alleged non-compliance was not due to systemic errors but was caused by the inherent possibility of misinterpretation of the various laws.[71]

It is time to look at a few defining characteristics of the communications and documents. First, the documentation in both cases is massive and repetitive. Second, they reveal an ongoing process of networking via documents in which claims and counterclaims are made. The communicant's distrust of the focal point is apparent in questioning the focal point's style of communication and lack of official insignia, as noted above. The alleged informality of the communication and lack of letterheads or other insignia frustrated the communicants. Process and documents are in focus rather than the substantive issue of mining at Teghut. The activists had dedicated considerable resources to pursuing their case beyond Armenia. This, I argue, is yet another incident in which the Aarhus Convention and the use of its mechanisms divert attention from the substantive issue (e.g. mining at Teghut) to formal requirements and practices. The activists turn 'liberalism against itself',[72] that is, they use liberal provisions such as the Aarhus Convention against Armenia as a ratifying state, arguing that Armenia is not living up to Convention standards. However, in this process, the same activists and NGOs largely fail in their purpose. After all, if they had not brought the cases before the Armenian courts and had their legal standing denied, no one would even have thought about disallowing the same organizations from protesting the Teghut case.

In *Living in a Post-Traditional Society*, Anthony Giddens suggests that we are all caught up in everyday experiments that reflect the changing and perhaps diminishing role of tradition,[73] where expertise is reappropriated and displaced.[74] Seen as an everyday experiment, the Aarhus Convention arguably redefines expertise, or at least the right to confront expertise and to consider oneself a citizen with legitimate concerns and sufficient competence. The Aarhus Convention perhaps fosters a 'specialized social expertise' based on knowledge of the Aarhus compliance mechanism, its consequences compared to Armenian law and how it can be turned into an asset for the network.

By bringing the case to the attention of the Compliance Committee and ultimately the delegations at the Chisinau and Maastricht MoPs, the Armenian activists were given an opinion on the concept of legal standing in Armenia and the degree to which Armenia complied with the Aarhus Convention. The Compliance Committee urged the Armenian government to consider not only the NGOs' statutory goals but also their de facto activities when considering whether a given organization should be granted legal standing. In essence, this is an argument for a more pragmatic approach than the Armenian authorities and courts have tended to follow. This present case, I argue, is precisely an example of how international law is a continuous practice. In fact, its very legitimacy hinges on the practices of documentation, interpretation, formulation of tentative decisions and findings and so on, in which the Compliance Committee is involved. The Aarhus Convention in Armenia is not merely a *lex superior*; it is a practice in which Armenian activists, the focal point, the Armenian government, the Compliance Committee and the ACP are involved by adding performative substance to the Convention, thereby Europeanizing Armenia. This point can hardly be overstated.

The Aarhus Convention is a 'social process of producing norms, knowledge and compliance'.[75] It is important to investigate how various groups champion, lay claim to, implement and think about those claims to norms, knowledge and compliance.[76] Law is practised in small places, like the villages anthropologists have studied for a long time. And international law, much like law in small communities, is based on deliberations and consensus rather than imposition.[77]

The practice related to the Aarhus Convention – in addition to the everyday work of the secretariat and the MoPs described above – is one of documenting and assessing claims of infringements of environmental rights. The legal obligation of a convention has to rest on a sense of 'reciprocity or mutuality of expectation among participants in a legal system ... collectively built and maintained'.[78] While this covers reciprocity between states participating in a given legal regime, it is more important for my purpose that a certain reciprocity also obtains between the authorities and the public. Conventions can aim for stability and increased regulation, but they can also promote normative change.[79] The Aarhus Convention is rather heavy on the normative side, especially if we take into account the ambition of the 'Environment for Europe' process of urging members of the former socialist club to learn from Western democracies. In this manner, the Aarhus Convention may have had a constitutive effect for some countries, been regulatory for others and merely acted as a confirmation for countries considered to have been in compliance from the start.

If we consider the notion of development as hope, administration and critical reflection,[80] it can arguably be applied to the issue of Armenia's implementation of the Aarhus Convention. Whereas the Aarhus Convention came about as a *hope*, envisaging the standardization and Europeanization of environmental management, the very practices it leads to result in a form of politics and administration that may, in turn, result in a one-way street of procedural issues. It certainly confirms the argument that international law rests on continuous practice, in that, as I have argued above, attempts at forging a link between the specific Armenian context and the environmental rights assemblage do indeed require continuous practice.

Save Teghut – in the conference halls

In 2010, getting the government to withdraw the ACP license permitting the mining of copper from the Teghut mine had become one of the most important projects of the various groups campaigning for environmental rights. In spring 2010, I discussed with Hermine her ideas about sending a letter to international organizations operating in Armenia, such as the United Nations Development Programme (UNDP), OSCE and several others. As I understood it, she was worried that these organizations were not aware of Armenia's alleged violations of several Convention principles. Hermine also expressed the hope that these organizations might be able to force the Armenian authorities to change their attitude and practices. I offered to draft a letter for her, after some initial hesitation.[81] Parts of the draft were used in an invitation to relevant Armenian organizations and international organizations with a presence in Armenia.

I was later invited to attend a Teghut conference in December 2010. I was unable to go, but the conference, which was largely a domestic affair but with the inclusion of some organizations from Georgia, had around ninety participants. As the summary of the conference states, only three of the thirty-three invited state institutions attended: the RA Ministries of Health, Agriculture and Foreign Affairs. Interestingly, neither the Ministry of Energy, which handles mining licenses, nor the Ministry of Nature Protection attended. The conference issued a critical statement concerning the proposed mining at Teghut.

In the statement, which was co-signed by twenty-six Armenian and five Georgian organizations, the patterning of intentions seen in the Aarhus Convention is, interestingly enough, repeated.[82] Much in the fashion of the text of the Aarhus Convention discussed in the previous chapter, the signatories 'acknowledge', 'assert' and are 'concerned' with several aspects of Armenia's record of environmental management before they list rather ambitious demands. The Armenian authorities, they demand, should 'suspend Teghut mining project until reassessment of its environmental impacts' and 'arrange for non-biased and comprehensive environmental impact assessment in accordance with international best practice'.[83] Among the Armenian signatories to the petition were several Aarhus Centres whose activities fall in part under the umbrella of the Armenian government. None of the ministry officials signed the petition, however.

Demanding policy changes is obviously the most substantial part of the petition. Yet I find the form to be of equal interest. The stylistic manner indicates perhaps a 'patterning of intention' in which the signatories form an ad hoc network that forges a link between means (NGO activism) and ends (suspension of the Teghut license).[84] The statement also forges links between the specific issue of Teghut, the Aarhus Convention text and the discourse on environmental rights, by mimicking the phrasing and also invoking a network:[85] with the use of such phrases as 'We, the undersigned' and by distancing themselves (via 'othering') from the authorities in expressing concern about irresponsible government action, the ad hoc network generates a reality that reflects on themselves.[86] The network appears to be as real as anything else. The Save Teghut campaigners used similar tactics when some of them wanted to press for a new and independent environmental impact assessment regarding Teghut. The company that had carried out the first environmental impact assessment (EIA) was allegedly owned by the group of investors that was operating the planned mining license. They addressed their demands to the Armenian president.

Can this case bring us closer to a better understanding of the relationship between assemblages and global forms? Can we presuppose that a global form – as we may take the Aarhus principles to be – is closed to deliberation and change? I will argue that my material indicates the opposite and that although the Aarhus Convention text itself is not changed by the Armenian cases, they have affected the practices and processes of the Compliance Committee and MoPs, adding new layers of meaning and interpretation to the Aarhus Convention.

This view hinges on how one understands 'global form'. As an abstraction, a global form can be a mix of concepts, ideologies and policy frameworks that are conceived to be actor-less and context-less. They are not much to analyse and not that 'real'. On the other hand, if one decides to investigate the articulation of a global form such as, perhaps, 'civil society' or environmental rights in a given field, then we are entering the conceptual landscape of assemblages. So what we study is not really the global forms but their articulation, in Armenia or elsewhere. We need to define what constitutes a global form and what constitutes its immediate effects and articulations. This task is probably more pertinent the closer the empirical investigation is to the global level. The Aarhus Convention case indicates that you cannot study a global form empirically, only how it is bundled, employed and practised in concrete situations and assemblages.

Practising Aarhus

One way of understanding the complex surrounding the Aarhus Convention in Armenia discussed in this and the preceding chapter is by applying Richard Sakwa's notions of 'normative state' and 'administrative regime'.[87] The argument – which I believe has validity also for Armenia – is that Russia is what Sakwa calls a *dual state*, where two competing systems coexist more or less parasitically. The *normative state* is represented by the formal constitutional order, laws and so on, whereas the *administrative regime* is 'a second world of informal relations, factional conflict and para-constitutional political practices'.[88] What the population has to put up with are the workings of the administrative regime, whereas the normative state represents the formal ideal. As others have noted regarding the post-Soviet space, there is a tendency to expect the law to fail in its attempts to ensure justice.[89] Another indication of the same measure of disillusionment is that as Russians in general are in favour of living in a law-abiding society but expect laws to fail and be broken again and again with impunity, they generally accept that certain (if not all) laws and regulations will indeed be broken.[90] Something I experienced on several occasions was the ease with which my informants justified not paying taxes while still regarding themselves as law-abiding citizens. This could be an Armenian example of the same thing.

Likewise, the Aarhus Convention, together with relevant environmental legislation in Armenia, can be seen as representative of the normative state, whereas state practices and actual implementation represent the administrative regime. Although this is a tempting metaphor or dichotomy, it does not allow for the full complexity of the case. As my ethnography shows, the dispute between Aarhus, *actio popularis* and the wider mining issue is not so much about two competing systems within the state system but different interpretations and expectations of environmental rights. In other words, the situation is more complex than a set of two competing systems *within* the state. Rather, a host of people, along with domestic and international organizations and state representatives, expend time and effort to strike the right balance between normative procedures and actual administrative practices.

At the same time, I noticed the participation of these activists in the wider world of international partners and internationally legitimated rights with which they could associate themselves. In a somewhat similar fashion, Tsing has elsewhere argued that we should ask 'how the concept of tribe, with all its simplifications and codifications of metropolitan fantasy, comes to mean something to people caught in particular political dilemmas'.[91] The same, I suggest, goes for the 'global fantasy' of civil society, transparency or environmental rights. The point, as Tsing shows, is that these concepts end up being used by the 'target population' as well. In my case, Armenian activists were and are eager patrons of the environmental rights assemblage. We might replace 'tribe' with civil society or transparency or network, and the metropolitan fantasy is quite apparent also in these cases. Terms such as 'access to environmental information' or 'access to participation' work as mobilizing signposts showing the way for people involved in civil society activities in Armenia and beyond. The point is – to pursue this tribal analogy further – that 'cosmopolitan dreams and fantasies forge the categories and narratives through which central and peripheral social settings are segregated and aligned with each other'.[92] One of the ways these categories are forged is through the various practices performed by my informants and others that take part in the present ethnography.

The attempts of Armenian campaigners to make use of the Convention's compliance mechanism involve sticky engagements between universal rights, local bureaucratic practices and the international community. Relevant concepts here are *environmentality*[93] and *decentralized environmental governance*.[94] Discussing the establishment of forest councils and decentralization strategies in northern India, Agrawal introduced the term *environmentality* in order to analyse how local populations are involved in protecting their surrounding environment.[95] Environmentality denotes 'technologies of self and power [that] are involved in the creation of new subjects concerned about the environment. ... The realization of particular environmental subjectivities that takes place within this gap is as contingent as it is political.'[96] When power is decentred, subjects of governance play an active role in their own self-governance. The (neo-liberal) Aarhus Convention is but one example of this, where some of the activists in Armenia devote considerable attention to the Aarhus Convention and the opportunities it offers them to seek reform. Reframing environmental concerns as an issue over environmental rights might be a way of subjecting themselves to a new form of environmentality.

The claims to internationally sanctioned environmental rights of Armenian activists are thus an example of how international norms are utilized, negotiated and resisted at different levels. Yet the interaction between the 'global' and the 'local' in this sense leaves both levels open for change. How? By involving international bodies of arbitration in Armenian disputes, the 'international level' (the Compliance Committee of the Aarhus Convention) becomes involved. We therefore need a theoretical perspective that allows us to take this into account. It is not merely an issue of local adaption to perceived global norms; through the act of claiming these rights, it is not only the activists that get involved in the field in both confirming and changing the discourse of environmental rights, but Armenian authorities – who need to reply somehow to these claims – as well as international experts and transnational actors.

The cases brought before the Armenian courts by the Armenian activists were rejected on different grounds, and the Compliance Committee lent significant support to the position of the Armenian government regarding access to justice, if only indirectly. That the issue is still open for contestation and remains largely undecided can be seen by the fact that the Compliance Committee accepted two very similar cases for review in 2011 and 2014. Apart from the final verdicts in the Armenian courts, the cases were similar. Yet a new complaint was accepted for review dealing precisely with the issue of access to justice. The particular assemblage of environmental rights in Armenia thus abounds with claims, counterclaims, documents, networks, personal connections, uncertainty, trust and mistrust. This may lead us to ask, following Tania Murray Li, what happens after an apparent failure. What do schemes do?[97] The activists' pursuance of the Teghut case before the Compliance Committee is a performance of a transparency scheme, where the transparency activists failed to make some of their basic claims heard, where the Armenian government at the same time received continued criticism for its failure to fully implement the Aarhus Convention principles, and where international donors and partners promoted behind the scenes their transparency agenda. Do the various claims and counterclaims from the streets, at seminars, in courts and internationally amount to more than the status quo? In material terms, the Convention leaves its mark through the reports, minutes of meetings, complaints, seminars and Aarhus Centres in Armenia and is personified by the appointed focal point.

Although it may look as if the implementation of the Aarhus Convention is a failure in Armenia, practices *have* changed. The activities of Armenian activists such as Hermine, Arthur and Anush take place on many stages and in many forms. But as my ethnography indicates, in the one area where they invested most hope and discursive energy – in the assemblage of environmental rights – they made only modest gains. In fact, denied legal standing, the organizations faced an existential threat. And given the vagueness of the wording of the Aarhus Convention's provisions, the discretion granted to implementing parties in its interpretation and, not least, the pervasiveness of certain bureaucratic practices are likely to make these changes very slow indeed. Without considering whether it was right to try to stop the proposed mining project at Teghut, there seems to be hope in new, less formalized and more ad-hoc based forms of organizing activism.[98]

In Armenia, where the Convention is formally a *lex superior*, the government still seems to lack the capacity or will to observe its principles due to inconsistent legal frameworks, corruption, neglect or for other reasons. On a more general note, then, the Aarhus Convention as a scale-making project has failed to make a substantive difference in Armenia, although the scale is still conjured because, among other reasons, different actors benefit from it and/or see no alternative to it.

As such, the Aarhus Convention reflects a belief in the ability to change practices by modernizing and liberalizing government by means of what are perceived as universal solutions to the exercise of environmental rights. As a ratifying partner, Armenia is obliged to implement these rights in domestic politics. Thus, we see a modernizing scheme that will be implemented, negotiated, interpreted and probably resisted at the local level.

I argue, however, that we should rather perceive both state and non-state actors' governance practices without invoking notions of power topographies, the state's vertical features and civil society as something going on 'down there'.[99] Within the assemblage of environmental rights, practices and claims are played out. As has been argued elsewhere, for instance, with regard to Turkish bureaucracy and state services,[100] inward and outward relationships are characterized by all sorts of mediations, dependencies and legitimacies.

One characteristic of such processes is the sidestepping of usual demarcation lines between local and global levels and of power between transnational mechanisms, state powers and civil society. By introducing a new mechanism and new provisions via the Aarhus Convention, Armenia finds itself in a situation where ratification of the Aarhus Convention has reduced the discretionary powers of the state. Armenian environmentalists can profit from this effect by appealing to international mechanisms of arbitration. At the same time, to do so, the environmentalists need to adopt a new modus operandi. It is not enough to challenge state authority via traditional activism; legal know-how and formal petitions to international forums are also things they have to master.

Performing environmental activism

I have described a varied patchwork of activities involving several actors and degrees of formal organization. It is a fusion of grassroots movements, traditional NGO activity and coalitions willing to go to domestic courts while in between bringing up issues with the Compliance Committee of the Arhus Convention. All this activity has not amounted to much. In fact, it has been a series of setbacks in domestic courtrooms and also with regard to MoPs' decisions in the international arena. The relationships and connections between people, organizations and efforts at the grass-roots level are fluid, sometimes tracing a wider circle including, even, OSCE staff, supporters in parliament and the like, while at others being limited to just a few devoted activists. Environmental activists make use of the 'modernizing scheme' – the Aarhus Convention – as an instrument to promote their own agenda on various environmental issues. The modernizing forces are a host of transnational agencies, donor organizations and NGOs, as well as the Armenian state itself.

It may also be argued that what we are witnessing is a shift from an NGO-organized civil society – where civil society was often conflated with NGOs[101] – to something characterized more by 'spontaneous activism'.[102] NGOs in the post-Soviet area seem to have fallen victim to the general lack of trust in these societies. Several grass-roots activists are currently seeking to distance themselves from NGOs[103] by embracing 'more radical and contentious forms of action'[104] while acknowledging at the same time that NGOs can help insofar as they are potential 'resource centres' for the less experienced and organized activists.[105] The STCI is an example of activists and organizations joining forces in such a surreptitious symbiosis.

Viewed either as different projects of scale or as different articulations of global forms (claims to scale, or efforts to assemble), I hold that environmentalists' practices are instigated as a response to opportunities offered by a multilateral environmental agreement that defines standards and procedures for environmental management across a huge and diverse region (the European Union and most of the post-Soviet states) and practices related to Norwegian efforts to promote democracy and enhanced environmental management in the South Caucasus. These stories share a few premises and are part of a discourse on reforming the former socialist countries and turning them into modern European nation states. This calls for an investigation of the discourses and continued relevance of Cold War dichotomies.[106]

As my ethnography has shown, it is filled with incidents in which what we usually refer to as 'locals' or suchlike make use of the assemblages, establish and exploit networks and in this way change not only the situation on the ground but also higher up the ladder of universality and abstraction.

The local heterogeneity in my ethnography is claimed and networked and performed through multiple references, convention texts, project documents and street protests. This happens in reference to the larger scale or assemblages and perhaps we should also think of them as heterogeneous global phenomena inasmuch as they are acted out in a variety of local settings and situated practices. In essence, a connection to the wider world is forged.

Are these Armenian informants trapped in liberalism? Their mission is to increase transparency in Armenian environmental management, yet, as the court cases and Compliance Committee deliberations indicate, they have had limited success. They may well be perceived as trapped inside this mode of organizing and campaigning. A crucial question, though, is what would have happened if they had not tried to change practices in Armenia. Another aspect pertaining to this is how Armenian environmentalists see themselves as Europeans enjoying rights and entitlements on the international scene. The Armenian activists are protagonists and performers of a rights-based environmentalism.

The performative aspect of this activism is characterized by the employment of NGO-harvested knowledge and resources, social networks and individuals, in conducting street rallies, filing cases with the court system and appealing to international bodies of arbitration. These varied activities and their surreptitious symbiosis indicate that the multifaceted and relentless fight of Armenian activists to change decisions regarding Teghut is creative, based on legal competence, but without much hope of success.

Multiple arenas of activism

In this chapter I have addressed various ways in which Armenian civil society deploys its strategies to change environmental management practices in Armenia by employing the assemblage of environmental rights. These practices range from street protests to court cases and international arbitration. Despite lack of success, these activists remain subjects of liberalism, I have argued, while imagining it as freedom.[107] Bringing the case before the compliance mechanism involves a significant number of documents, which adds up to a correspondence that in itself is a 'collective patterning of intention',[108] although the involved actors may not necessarily share the same intention.

The street and court actions described above are indicative not only of the multiple ways in which Armenian activists fought the Teghut campaign but also how environmentalists are able to scale up their demands. The activists are particularly preoccupied with ways of using laws and rights to foster change. This is an example of enacting the scales of Europe and transparency. The very efforts are based on a (moderately optimistic, perhaps) view of the rule of law in Armenia. As 'newly transnationalized locals', activists in Armenia challenge the relationship between the global,[109] the nation state and civil society, usually understood as a vertical topography. By understanding these environmentalists as deploying, in laying claim to environmental rights in Armenia, a variety of strategies through their networks and skills, we can explore their practices without passing moral judgements on their agendas.

After discussing the Aarhus Convention, its repercussions and mobilization in Armenia, the next part of the book will focus on a small-scale development project carried out in Armenia. I will argue that this too demonstrates how efforts are under way to Europeanize Armenia, but this time by donors and project staff from outside the country, in league with the Armenian project partners.

Part Two

Foreign aid in the post-Soviet Caucasus

4

LOG framing: Donor legitimation and unattainable project goals

Perceptions of a given project's success – or failure, for that matter – are things we can better understand by analysing how these perceptions come about and the technical, institutional and political settings in which they are produced: '[T]he ethnographic question is not whether but how development projects work; not whether a project succeeds, but how success is produced.'[1] Success or failure can in this sense be thought of as judgements that are less contingent on on-the-ground practices, shortcomings and results than we are often inclined to think.

This chapter explores this issue by discussing the ethnography of the Armenia project, by closing in on the administrative practices within the project. I address the repercussions and practices at the project implementation level in Armenia in the next chapter. In the present chapter, I want to look at the processes taking place as part of the management of the project and the dialogue with the Norwegian donor. A central question is how the donor–implementer relationship, reporting cycles and adjustments affect and legitimate changes in the project itself and how these changes and relations constitute new project realities.

My main argument is that the introduction of measures and terms to evaluate and define projects, measures that are based on the logical framework approach, or LOG frame for short, affects how the project was perceived rather than how it was implemented. I argue that the representation and implementation of the project followed increasingly diverging trajectories, resulting in a rupture between the project as a policy idea and the project as an operational system. This could happen because the project as a policy idea was, as we will see, justified by a superficial account of the situation in Armenia, whose sheer complexity could not be easily translated or imported into the project documents. In addition, requests on the part of the donor to develop more ambitious project goals further exacerbated this rupture.

By distinguishing between project as a policy idea and project as an operational system, these aspects of project life can be considered analytically distinct, perhaps to a surprisingly strong extent. The project as a policy idea regards issues related to submission of project proposals, final reports and other requirements to do with guidelines and/or (changing) donor policies. In the Armenian case, they entailed practices within project documents and within the donor–recipient relationship. The project as an operational system – which will be dealt with in the next chapter – entails in this respect implementation practices closer to the ground.

Considering the Armenia project as a policy idea shows, I will argue, that the marketing and modifications of how the project was talked and written about grew in importance at the expense of the situation on the ground that the project was intended to change. Two other features are important: first, that project networks were portrayed as stable when they were in fact precarious and volatile; second, that Norway's attitude to its bilateral relationship with Armenia affected project evaluation even though it was not mentioned in the guidelines. In fact, the project essentially served Norwegian foreign policy priorities, where bilateral relations were micromanaged by proxy.

I will argue that the manner in which the Armenia project was justified had less to do with the willingness of the donor to promote change in Armenia and more to do with the need to legitimize Norwegian policy towards Armenia and the wider post-Soviet region. These claims may seem controversial, and obviously I cannot and will not argue that they apply to all kinds of development assistance funded by Norwegian authorities. However, ideas within the ministry on how the project *should* be implemented interfered with and steered practice in ways that diverted attention away from practical needs and challenges.

In this chapter I analyse five arenas or instances of project life that highlight different ways that aspects of development can be attributed to the notion of development as hope, as political and administrative practices and as critical understanding. These cases are (1) the increased focus on formal requirements and the LOG frame and how it changed parts of the project; (2) the information meetings hosted by the Ministry of Foreign Affairs (MFA); (3) other directions given by the MFA to Fridtjof Nansen Institute (FNI); (4) the effort to expand the project into neighbouring Azerbaijan and Georgia; and (5) the process at FNI on whether to prolong the project or call it a day.

'A seminar is not an outcome'

The following paragraphs present the ethnography of how the project narrative changed after an incident when the donor signalled a desire for an increased focus on the LOG frame. It is thus a revealing story of how development projects can end up as the administration of technicalities. Besides marking a rupture between project as policy idea and project as operational system, it also marked a shift from development as hope to administration.[2]

After submitting the 2008 application, I received several calls from the MFA. They wanted me to rework the LOG-frame approach. Until that point, project goals, objectives, proposals and reports had always obtained a stamp of approval. They were now suddenly rejected: 'A seminar is not an outcome,' we were told. The point was valid enough, but it indicated the contingent nature of the management of the financial development mechanism. No recent shift in policy or political leadership could explain it. Rather, it seemed, officials had got hold of a new project evaluation instrument which they wanted to apply not only to future projects but ongoing ones as well.

The upshot was that policy had to be articulated in a different language, forcing the project into what Mosse has termed 'reactive mode'.³ In order to meet these new criteria, time was spent redrafting the project in compliance with the new policy of 'management by objectives'. This involved discussions over the phone with MFA officials concerning what was to be identified as a reasonable, long-term impact of the project; what needed to be achieved within the twelve-month project cycle (outcomes); what outputs and activities were planned in order to reach the outcomes; and what kinds of input we envisioned it would require. In this process, it was suggested that the long-term impact should be to contribute to change in Armenian legislation. Rather than aiming at transferring know-how and skills (which is a lofty but questionable objective) through seminars and workshops, the long-term impact was reconfigured in terms of '[t]he project [contributing] to changes in Armenian environmental legislation'.⁴

That the change in focus happened without anybody consulting our Armenian partners, and solely at the request of the MFA, is telling of the manner in which such projects and LOG frames can evolve. As such, the project thus acquired a long-term objective which I, as project manager, believed impossible for such a small project to achieve.

I was now obliged to introduce indicators that could say something about the progress of the project and of Armenia's implementation, together with a progress report on the project's long-term impact, all of which was overly ambitious. While I redrafted the project, I wondered what it was that motivated the sudden emphasis on management by objectives at the ministry, not least because I was not informed until several months after the application's submission deadline, and then only by phone. The indicators were there in the original application as well, but seminars that the ministry had earlier approved as a project outcome were now relegated to mere input. Requiring the FNI to define the project in line with LOG-frame criteria, which included defining long-term impacts, risks and so on, was obviously one element of this process.

In LOG-frame terms, it made sense to focus on outcomes, outputs and inputs, yet the interesting thing is that the MFA started to question how the project was presented, not the project itself. The original project proposal was submitted in mid-February 2008, while the ministry's additional requirements were communicated by phone in May. What I then had to do was to make connections between the planned project schedule and the obligatory indicators, benchmarks and the baseline situation in Armenia.

One such incident occurred when I was prompted to resubmit the project proposal as discussed above. I had found a fairly recent posting on the internet from the Aarhus Meeting of Parties (MoP) in Riga, Latvia, dated just days earlier. It contained 'Decision III/6b on compliance by Armenia with its obligations under the Convention', where the Compliance Committee had suggested a schedule for Armenia's future reporting that fitted our project nicely.[5] According to this report, Armenia was invited to 'submit to the Committee periodically, namely in November 2008, November 2009 and November 2010, detailed information on further progress in implementing the recommendations set out above'.[6] This was what I needed. The Armenian government was being urged to submit annual reports addressing issues and obstacles to progress in the implementation of the Aarhus Convention. This would obviously be relevant and useful as an indicator for the new LOG-frame submission. Not only that, I could say the project was working to strengthen Armenia's implementation of the Aarhus Convention by feeding into the Armenian reporting cycle to the United Nations Economic Commission for Europe (UNECE) Secretariat.

This seemed a relevant development of the project – where 'synergies' could be claimed if not achieved – as we would be working with more or less the same people and institutions as had been involved in Armenia's implementation of the Aarhus Convention, that is, the Armenian Ministry of Nature Protection, the Organization for Security and Co-operation in Europe (OSCE) office in Yerevan, the national focal point to the Convention and relevant non-governmental organizations (NGOs). I wrote in the revised project proposal submitted on 19 June, six days after the MoP had finished in Riga, 'It is to be hoped that the project's internal processes will feed into the reporting cycle Armenia has agreed with the Compliance Committee of the Convention.'[7]

Later, while conducting fieldwork, I tried to find the reports Armenia had been urged to submit to the Convention secretariat, but with no success. Apparently, Armenia had not taken up the invitation from the Committee. If Armenian authorities have submitted these reports, they have not been published on the UNECE website as similar reports usually are.

A few weeks after I had submitted the revised project proposal, FNI received confirmation from the Norwegian MFA that the revised project proposal was approved. Although I realized that it would be necessary to ratchet up the deliverables a few notches compared to the initial project proposal, nothing much had changed apart from the way the project was portrayed and anchored within a bigger picture involving international compliance mechanisms. As project implementer, FNI changed the LOG frame without involving the Ministry of Nature Protection in Armenia, its main project partner there. I hold, in line with James Scott,[8] that legibility is one of the main characteristics of modernization projects. Viewed thus, we can see how the LOG frame imposes a perspective on very complex issues in very different places by allowing us to look at these issues and places through the same lenses. It is a way to objectify places and issues, disregarding local variations, except for the variations and challenges that can neatly be accounted for in the LOG frame's rubric for risk factors. The priorities and perceptions of the *baseline situation* in Armenia as set by the Norwegian MFA were largely guided by general observations of the situation of civil society and the state of the management sector in post-Soviet societies. These 'general observations' follow in the line of the liberal triumph after the dissolution of the Soviet Union and the coining of these as societies 'in transition'.[9]

Although the process of resubmitting the application delayed funding approval and the project itself, we still had to comply with the yearly schedule and finish before the end of the same year. This process of redefining impacts and outputs should – one would think – affect project implementation. However, reformulating and reconfiguring this particular project did not substantively change its implementation. Implementation was delayed somewhat, but apart from that it seemed as if the deliberations in connection with the LOG frame were disconnected from the social realities in which the project unfolded in Armenia.

As this process indicates, a lot of the work involved in project proposals and narratives has to do with aligning them with formal requirements where project activities are deconstructed and bracketed in different ways such as input, output and outcome. The increased focus of the MFA on the LOG frame told us that we were expected to make the project fit the formal requirements as well as possible, rather than redirecting or changing the project itself. The LOG frame invoked an appearance of legibility in the messy field of post-Soviet governance. The discussions over the phone with MFA officials made it abundantly clear that the ministry was not interested in changing the project. Rather, it was concerned with the level in the LOG-frame hierarchy at which we plotted the different activities that MFA officials and we as implementers had already agreed were part of the project. What mattered was to fit the project within a larger narrative structure and link it to other processes. These links and networks had to be invented as part of the project management process, although they were made 'real' by accompanying statements and claims indicating links between the Armenia project and the process related to the Aarhus Convention.

Did this increased focus on LOG framing have anything to do with the project? In order to answer the question, it would be useful to distinguish between the representation of the project understood as how it was portrayed and narrated in application forms and reports, on the one side, and how it unfolded as regular project activities, on the other. Although they cannot be separated completely, it makes sense analytically to understand them as two different aspects of the project's implementation that at times followed different trajectories. Projects, Mosse has suggested, have to maintain themselves 'as coherent policy ideas, as systems of representations as well as operational systems'.[10] However, the apparent coherence of the Armenia project rested on the premise that the messiness of the challenges in Armenia had to be kept at arm's length from the neat LOG frame we crafted. In this sense, the project as a policy idea was justified by a superficial account of the situation in Armenia; the sheer complexity of the situation could not be translated into the project-speak of the documents.

The reconfiguring of the project to fit the LOG frame had no immediate or long-term impact on the way the project was executed in Armenia: the project arranged seminars in much the same fashion as before. Rather, it seemed as if the whole process was more important to the internal handling of the application within the MFA. This recalls Mosse's observation that externally generated policy changes sometimes change faster than the lifespan of the programme, forcing project agencies 'into a reactive mode'[11] in order to update and preserve their systems of representation and legitimation. As noted, the MFA officials who had asked us to align the project with the specifications of the LOG frame did not suggest changing the planned project activities. What the MFA was concerned with was how the project was portrayed in terms of the LOG-frame hierarchy. When the 'sensible goal' of seeking to change Armenian legislation was crafted as the long-term impact of the project following the MFA's suggestion, the project had to reinvent its tools and inputs in order to achieve this new and ambitious goal within the LOG frame.

From then on, the project as a policy idea and as an operational system followed increasingly separate trajectories. As long as I remembered to use ambitious phrases when talking with the MFA and to readjust to more modest ambitions when talking to Armenian partners, there were no immediate challenges. At one level, the Armenia project claimed to be able to change Armenian legislation. This sentiment was never communicated to our Armenian partners and was really only used in communication with the MFA. After all, it would not be good for future relations to insist that we (the Norwegians) are here because we think you (the Armenian government) ought to change your legislation.

I would argue that the LOG frame largely worked as an invitation to speak doublespeak, to discuss Armenian environmental governance and legislation, to commence the project in a fashion that somehow forged a link between the project and some new legal framework that most believed was unachievable. The LOG-frame alterations became part of the marketing of the project, whereas project practices were largely unaffected:

> Project documentation is not intended to present an objective account of a social and economic situation ... Such documents support particular positions and courses of action within funding agencies where different sectors compete for limited amounts of cash, stating why and how and what amount of money should be spent by whom to contribute toward which policy objective. Consequently, such documents have more in common with marketing texts than with social and economic analysis.[12]

Now, although projects may not necessarily condense challenges into a 'manageable reality',[13] the introduction of new criteria may have the opposite effect of obscuring the process by introducing new and unrealistic objectives. Nevertheless, the project reports were standardized, as different projects supported by the MFA had to be documented and audited in a uniform way.

In 2009, the information required on the application form was updated and harmonized even more with the principles of 'management by objectives'. For the ensuing application covering a two-year period, FNI replaced the goal of changing Armenian legislation with making a contribution to sustainable development. This was a loftier, yet less binding, goal and the outcome was defined as strengthening the implementation of the Aarhus Convention and building capacity with regard to the multilateral environmental agreements (MEAs) that Armenia has ratified. The new outcomes and outputs are shown in Figure 4.1.

> Impact: sustainable development
>
> Outcomes:
>
> 1. Strengthened implementation of the Aarhus Convention
> 2. Increased competence on multilateral environmental agreements in Armenia
>
> Outputs:
>
> 1.1. Analysis of the implementation process
> 1.2. Increased competence regarding Aarhus, EIAs and mainstreaming in the environmental management sector
> 2.1. Materials translated into Armenian

Figure 4.1 LOG frame, the Armenia project 2009.
Source: Project proposal, Fridtjof Nansen Institute.

FNI was also asked to describe the project in brief, and I tried to discuss whether impacts and outcomes were tangible and measurable within the timeframe:

> A general comment regarding results would be that it takes time to develop indicators related to changes in the legal framework and development of policies and also to measure the impact. At the level of outcomes however, it is our contention that it is possible to see changes evolving within a shorter period of time. At the same time, there are potential obstacles that are beyond the control of FNI. We nevertheless have to trust in the willingness of our Armenian partners to participate and the goodwill of the Armenian government to fulfill its obligations under the Arhus Convention. In this respect, we regard the role of OSCE's Yerevan office and the Aarhus centres as crucial to securing progress in this regard.[14]

Was I reinstating hope after the 2008 cycle had ended in administrative measures? Or was it rather what has been described as 'tactically conspir[ing] to misrepresent'?[15] FNI responded to the guidelines, formulas and practices set in place by the ministry. Since FNI was granted support, the project proposal was obviously considered to have been satisfactorily crafted even though it was a step back from the requirements the MFA had insisted on one year earlier. If this seems as if FNI caved in to donor requirements, we will later take a look at the discussions culminating in FNI's decision not to apply for a further extension of the project beyond 2010. The argument I will put forward here is that project documents live a life of their own, with their claims and internal consistencies and inconsistencies: the LOG frame does not direct practice; rather, it requires action to be represented in a way that is acceptable to the donor. This representation, together with other project documents, creates a totality.

Intriguingly, the new LOG-frame requirements meant that more time and effort had to be spent on technicalities and legitimizing the project at the expense of 'real work'. As is apparent from the above, the project – in order to fit the application criteria – was redone to chime with the call's policy idea rather than as a response to needs on the ground in Armenia. Mosse has made the same observation in a different context:[16] after all, there wasn't much room for flexibility and to adapt the project to local needs.

Another aspect of LOG framing is that it introduces yet another element of 'anti-politics' into project management.[17] When the process of LOG framing was finished, the project had been divided into impacts, outputs, inputs and so on. Armenia's legal framework, corruption and environmental management were translated into techno-bureaucratic terms rather than as political issues,[18] insulating them in consequence from Armenian 'reality'.

An interesting argument related to how development and aid work is that aid practices are largely based on a manner of thinking that categorizes the world into entities such as 'poverty', 'rights' and 'results'.[19] These entities in turn are understood as preformed categories with an essential bearing and content, an example of so-called substantialism.[20] The connective tissues joining them together are the varying 'mechanisms'. Eyben contrasts substantialism with relationalism, where the relationships between various actors making up the world of aid are what matters.[21] At the same time, it is important to acknowledge that aid agencies with substantialist policies seem to allow for relationalist perspectives up to a point, which may actually make working in the world of aid better than it would have been otherwise.[22] The point here is not to state an either/or argument but rather to take this into account: the LOG frame and related administrative aspects as accounted for above are largely an answer to such substantialist categories where change is considered as a relatively straightforward procedure and where a given input will ensure a given output.

An example of substantialism's precedence (institutions, categories of poverty and rights, etc.) over relationalism is the 2005 Paris Declaration on Aid Effectiveness. This declaration – to which both the Republic of Armenia (RA) and Norway attest adherence – sets out five principles for effective aid: (1) ownership, (2) alignment, (3) harmonization, (4) results and (5) mutual accountability.[23] The focus on results, for instance, represents a shift of emphasis from inputs to measurable outputs.[24] In some projects, it may be relatively simple to discover what was needed to achieve a given long-term impact. Let us consider an example. If the long-term impact is to improve the health of a village, the output might be to provide access to clean water. The village will need a new well (input) and that will be the result of specific activities (identification of water sources, drilling, digging, etc.). The project may stumble for a variety of reasons, but in a properly designed LOG frame, potential risks will have been identified as far as possible. So far, this is a pretty straightforward procedure and in many ways it is instrumental. But even here, we have to consider that many projects probably come about not because a problem is identified and there is a wish to alleviate it or produce an impact, but rather as a response to donor policies, opportunities to obtain funds and ideas to fix various problems that in the end will be attributed to the input or output levels of the LOG-frame hierarchy.[25]

In the Armenia project, the impact at one point was defined as 'changing domestic legislation', without specifying how this change was expected to come about (e.g. decisions in parliament, draft legislation), and the output was the transfer of skills and know-how and capacity building. Project management then became shrouded in mystery – or at least with rather obscure connections between means and ends and how change can be 'measured'. Are we at any point capable of measuring changes in the capacity of project participants?

What this tells us is that the project as a representational system has gained the upper hand vis-à-vis the 'reality' it is meant to represent and change. The changes required by the LOG frame – at the request of the MFA – were hard to achieve in a context where participation was fetishized[26] and the implementer had scant belief in the project's ethos.

There were no practical measures within the scope of the Armenia project that could legitimate or contribute to such an ambitious impact as the changing of Armenian law. Project practices therefore continued as if it was business as usual, as it were. Yet there was a 'connective tissue', not unlike 'civil society', that was supposed to be holding state hierarchies and the disenfranchised populace in the former socialist bloc together.[27] The connection was constructed around standardized solutions enabling a more efficient environmental management that would also allow the populace to take a more active part in forming environmental policies and practices.

The question is therefore whether these efforts somehow affected project implementation or just its representation. In other words, we (essentially I) had to portray the project not only as a coherent policy idea, but also as if things were actually happening when they were not. Given the donor cycle, project acquisitions between 2005 and 2008 were made for a year at a time. The application submission time was mid-February, and it took up to five months before a final decision came through. Because we had to spend our grant by the end of the year, the five-month delay reduced the time available to use it. These institutional practices and requirements negated the broader narrative of continuity in project cooperation that we sought to pursue (and were in fact encouraged to do by the MFA). So although nothing much happened project-implementation-wise between October/November and June (although rather more project-acquisition-wise), we had to give an impression of continuity. We did this by invoking various networking efforts. For example, we reported what seminar participants had learnt and were meant to 'take with them' to apply in their daily work and bring to the attention of others, thus contributing to 'competence transfer'.

The representation of the project as manageable slices of reality is not something that has to be 'true'; it is rather an endeavour in juggling internal priorities (acquiring funding) and external priorities (MFA policy, changing the law in Armenia) within a project narrative that is acceptable to both implementer and donor. Implementers' tactical willingness to slightly misrepresent,[28] or at least exaggerate, results at the expense of critical considerations will obviously vary from implementer to implementer. Yet in the end, the rupture in our case was largely the result of the unattainable goals the project ended up with. As we will see later, the balancing act in the end proved impossible to sustain.

Norwegian development policies for the post-Soviet area

In 1994, the Norwegian government published a white paper called 'Target Programme for Eastern Europe'. Norway, the government said, should 'contribute to a basic restructuring of post-Soviet societies by securing a democratic and sustainable development'.[29] This reflected nothing less than an ambition to reorganize government and society by encouraging and advocating reforms able to foster 'good governance', a 'vibrant civil society' and a 'marketization of the economy'. Although the ambitious formulations have since fallen out of use, the logic still applies and has informed the project mechanism, as will be seen in this chapter. One of the targets of the project mechanism financing the Armenia project described in this book was to support 'efforts to fulfil commitments made under the framework of the UN, the OSCE and other international organisations'.[30] The project mechanism is financed by a budgetary chapter for post-Soviet countries and approved as official development assistance (ODA).[31] The name of the mechanism was 'Project cooperation in the South Caucasus, Central Asia, Ukraine, Belarus and Moldova' and was administered by the MFA rather than the Norwegian Agency for Development Cooperation (NORAD), which usually manages the Norwegian ODA portfolio. The 'mechanism' was little more than an amount of money allocated in the national budget. Its formal guidelines and policy priorities were overseen by a special unit at the MFA. Covering all former Soviet republics except the three Baltic republics and Russia, the unit oversaw a multitude of projects in countries displaying significant similarities but also significant differences. From 2008 on, 'management by objectives' or the LOG-frame approach became an even more important criterion in the MFA's evaluation of projects, as reflected in the application forms.

A crucial observation is that the MFA had assembled a single policy model, which, with slight modifications, was supposed to fit Armenia, Azerbaijan, Belarus, Georgia, Kazakhstan, Kyrgyzstan, Moldova, Tajikistan, Turkmenistan, Ukraine and Uzbekistan. Did it render the policy overly ambitious or merely superficial in its attempt to encourage these countries to embrace 'European' values? I will argue that, although the invocation of the scale of Europe seems very general, it affects how projects are carried out. First of all, it presupposes an all-out embrace of European values and institutions, even though there is little agreement about what they amount to. Rather than saying something general about the consequences of Europeanization in the former socialist bloc, we need to investigate how it is expressed and embedded in specific projects in specific places.

Plenary information meetings at the Norwegian MFA

Each year, the MFA invites project owners and prospective applicants to an information meeting on the project mechanism. For the project period 2006–10, and for some years afterward, I attended most of these meetings. The meetings seemed to gather the rank and file of organizations involved in development assistance in the post-Soviet area, including human rights organizations, environmental NGOs, educational institutions, research professionals, various businesses, trade organizations and the like. A feature of these meetings was the summary MFA provided of priority policy goals for the coming project cycle (which usually started two to three months after the meeting). The meetings also included a Q&A session where prospective applicants could raise issues regarding funding priorities or application procedures and the like. Various MFA sections usually attended these meetings and gave brief introductions to the revised and increasingly standardized application forms.

Participants frequently asked whether it might not be more efficient to work with local partners such as NGOs rather than government institutions, which in many places were deemed to be corrupt. The response of the MFA – as reflected in the guidelines – was simply that local authorities, as far as possible, should be the main partner. The emphasis on hooking up with local authorities in the recipient countries was usually referred to as 'anchoring'. MFA frequently stressed their desire for projects in which cooperation with Armenian authorities formed a central part, for example, making the projects attractive to local authorities. Preferably, a government agency or ministry should be one of the main project partners. This found expression in the anchoring efforts to be documented later in Chapter 5.

When it comes to Armenia, a country where Norway has limited interests and bilateral contact, MFA officials told the participants that the projects to be carried out in Armenia by Norwegian organizations and companies represented 'our most important form of bilateral contact with Armenia, indeed, almost our only form of contact'.[32] This statement reveals how the Norwegian MFA considered the projects it supported in Armenia as constituting a main component of Norway's relationship with Armenia. Norway has no diplomatic mission in Armenia, although there is an honorary consul based in Yerevan; Armenia's ambassador to Norway works from his office in the MFA in Yerevan.

Remembering what was said at an information meeting at the MFA in 2011 about the project implementers involved in Armenia being Norway's 'only bilateral contact with Armenian authorities', what could FNI have said to advance these bilateral relations between Armenia and

Norway? Throughout the project, FNI worked closely with the Ministries of Nature Protection and Territorial Administration. Whether this represented bilateral contact of potential importance to Norway is not clear. It did not lead to extensive or even sustained contact after the projects had ended. However, while in motion, the project represented a potential point of reference or speech point if government officials from the two countries were to meet. One such meeting occurred when the RA Minister of Foreign Affairs visited Norway in 2010. As part of his visit, he visited FNI, to commemorate Nansen and his role as League of Nations High Commissioner for Refugees. At Polhøgda, the Foreign Minister, his entourage and Norwegian diplomats also met FNI's director and myself as manager of the Armenia project. At the meeting we discussed the project details and its implementation in Armenia, where it served as an example of the growth in bilateral relations between Armenia and Norway in recent years.[33]

Although the project's official legitimacy resided within the parameters of the LOG frame and how this framework coincided with Norwegian development policies in the region, the MFA's focus on the bilateral relationship suggests that it carried equal importance. If this is the case, it marks a rupture between project as policy idea (through the LOG frame) and project as a means of pursuing Norwegian foreign policy interests, where bilateral relations are micromanaged by proxy. International relations can be studied through practices.[34] In my case, I think it is instructive to look at how the project could be understood as a means of micromanaging bilateral Norwegian-Armenian relations. Even though the project is categorized as development aid, purportedly to serve local needs in Armenia, the empirical data suggests that the maintenance of bilateral relations was perhaps also an important component.

The LOG frame is but one example of the imposition of standardized solutions on development project management. Development can be understood as a 'reification of institutional practice in which human agency has a limited role to play'.[35] Such a critical approach is linked to Escobar[36] and Ferguson.[37] In several accounts of foreign assistance to former socialist countries, the opportunities for human agency, as I have noted before, are often reduced to making tactical or cynical adaptations.[38]

However, as I argued in Chapter 2 regarding the role of the focal point, I find this perspective rather unsatisfactory. My material indicates that when considering the project as a policy idea and as an operational system it is neither reasonable to suggest that human agency is limited nor that what we see is the mere expression of cynicism. The empirical material presented in this chapter is, in my view, better understood in light of various perspectives within development studies on how policy and practices are developed and legitimized,[39] and as a managerial practice where project management involves the construction of projects in a way that turns them into 'slices of manageable reality', where outputs identified within the LOG frame can be reached.[40]

As Maia Green suggests, I find it fruitful to understand project management as an endeavour to apply standardized solutions and thus render the project manageable in its representation of a 'slice' of reality. We are also familiar with Mosse's argument about the internal dynamic between upholding the development project as a policy idea but also as an operational system. Even though I have focused on the policy and representational aspects of the project, we should not forget that a project's legitimacy also depends on its operational practices and effects. However, the degree of this dependency is probably less than what one might expect. While this will be discussed more broadly in Chapter 5, suffice it to say for the present that, as I have argued above, the pressure to align a project idea with policy priorities and shifting ideas is not insignificant.

So to what kind of standards and marketing of policy ideas did the Armenia project's descriptions allude? The two different project descriptions as published online in 2006 and 2009 are indicative. The following is the project description from 2006:

> The aim of this project has been three-fold. The first aim has been to explore the implementation process of Armenia's environmental

commitments. Environmental issues have in recent years increasingly appeared on the international agenda. Two of the international agreements focused upon in this study – the Kyoto Protocol and the Convention on Biological Diversity – have introduced the principle of horizontal sector integration of environmental policy. ... Second, the project seeks to establish scientific and educational exchange between Caucasian and Norwegian universities and research institutions within the social sciences. Strong scientific communities in the social sciences are necessary to ensure the ongoing democratization of the Armenian society and good governance. The project has also aimed to investigate, in close co-operation with Armenian educational and research institutions, the role of civil society in the governmental decision making process.[41]

The project was framed as far as possible as one with academic ambitions: implementation processes in Armenia were to be explored and analysed, the role of civil society investigated together with Armenian researchers. Students from Armenia, Azerbaijan and Georgia were invited to attend the University of Oslo's summer school in Norway. Note how this academic approach was mostly abandoned in the project description of a few years later:

> This project aims at identifying challenges with and thereby enhancing the implementation of multilateral environmental treaties in the Republic of Armenia. Through the project we put special emphasis on the UNECE Convention on Access to Information, Public Participation in Decision making and Access to Justice in Environmental Matters, the so-called Aarhus convention. The project seeks to develop Armenia's capacities to fulfill its obligations by facilitating transfer of competence, experience as well as building of capacity on environmental governance among the national, regional and municipal governance sector and NGOs in Armenia.[42]

It seems apparent that the project focused on MEAs, impediments to implementation in Armenia and outreach to academic institutions in Armenia, initially including students in Armenia, Azerbaijan and Georgia. The descriptions are framed in a normative manner where increased internationalization of environmental regulation is a given and no questions are asked concerning the different capabilities of different countries. The Armenia project adopted the grand narrative of legitimizing Western efforts at changing post-Soviet states, which generally is taken to mean changing them into liberal market democracies. This is not a task for the humble. It involved the use of many of the catchphrases of 'democratization' such as civil society and capacity building. The excerpts of the project descriptions show how the project made use of a rather unquestioning normative tone regarding the need for reform in Armenia.

The increased focus on LOG-frame practicalities had a standardizing effect. The LOG frame at certain points in the project phase became more real than the project practices it was meant to guide and depict. As Green suggests, it made it possible to claim success in the delivery of short-term outputs within the project, but at a critical point in the LOG-framing process, with the imposition of changing domestic legislation in Armenia, it became increasingly challenging to claim any kind of success. It was at this juncture, I have argued, that the rift between the project as a policy idea and as an operational system widened almost to the point of breaking apart, with only a few strands connecting it to practical applicability.

Which university to cooperate with?

In 2006, the project had sufficient funds allowing several students from three universities to study at the Nansen School at Lillehammer, Norway, and the University of Oslo's summer school. The students came from Yerevan State University (YSU) in Armenia, Ivane Javakhishvili Tbilisi State University in Georgia and Baku State University in Azerbaijan. The idea was partly to breathe new life into the more or less moribund peace dialogue between Armenia and Azerbaijan. The students were selected by the universities and during their stay in Norway, FNI had no contact with them at all.

At a meeting with the MFA in early 2007, this part of the project was briefly discussed and all agreed that although the idea was laudable in principle, it had little to do with the main purpose of the project. We thus decided not to include it in the project proposal we were about to draft. At the same meeting, we also discussed cooperation with YSU. The MFA urged us to look for other institutions we could work better with in Yerevan. I suggested the American University of Armenia (AUA) as a possible better alternative. At the time of the meeting, I knew almost nothing about the AUA, despite floating the idea. The meeting concluded that we should contact the AUA and start working with them if possible. At this specific meeting, then, we had been told, instructed or encouraged to (1) stop inviting students to Norway, (2) work with the AUA rather than YSU and (3) cut the number of seminar days.

After the meeting I checked out AUA's web pages and was happy to discover that the institution had a centre devoted to research on biodiversity and environmental management.[43] We forged an alliance with the AUA and inserted it into the proposal, as indeed the MFA had encouraged us to, albeit with a few minor alterations. We worked with the AUA for one year only. In 2008, FNI decided to withdraw from the partnership and, ironically perhaps, return to working with the YSU again. There, a new centre funded by the OSCE had been established, the Environmental Law Resource Centre (ELRC), led by the focal point to the Aarhus Convention. The MFA did not comment on this return to YSU.

What can we make of the incidental nature of these shifting collaborations, the motivations for them and their legitimation? In hindsight, the shifts and turns in the project design came about in response to recommendations and shifting priorities communicated to us at pre-submission meetings and discussions with MFA officials. In addition, the annual meetings hosted by the MFA for anyone with an interest in the support mechanism provided valuable information on the political considerations informing the grant scheme. I was still in the dark, however, as to whether the changes would have a substantive effect on the project. Wasn't it rather that the legitimacy of the project within the MFA rested on changes being made that may 'obscure project effects'?[44]

The project mechanism was designed to fit eleven former Soviet republics, but with some room for different priorities in the different countries. It bears noting that for a long period of time, when I and possibly many other project managers were in contact with the MFA, the ministry only had one person in charge of all project-related questions for the eleven countries, including responsibility for reviewing and evaluating project proposals. At the same time, she was acting country desk officer for the same countries. To require this civil servant to give every little detail of every project proposal and implementation with the same amount of attention is obviously unreasonable. The level of professionalism rests – perhaps – on the MFA's reliance on standard solutions and catchphrases regarding the situation in Armenia as one of many post-Soviet states.

Exporting the project in the South Caucasus

Given the notion of the scalability of democratization and development, there was no reason to stop with Armenia. From a 'planetary' viewpoint,[45] Armenia, Azerbaijan and Georgia may look the same in terms of governance challenges and the many post-Soviet impediments to Europeanization. The MFA perspective is an example of taking the scale of Europeanization for granted. In the following, I describe FNI's endeavour to expand its project portfolio in the South Caucasus – in response to ministry encouragement. At a meeting with MFA officials in late 2007, FNI was asked to look into opportunities for 'exporting' the Armenia project: 'Why can't you try to do something of the same in Azerbaijan and Georgia?' On other occasions, ideas were floated about doing the same in Kazakhstan, although this was never seriously considered. FNI was encouraged, however, to design a pilot project to assess interest and possibilities in the two other South Caucasian republics. The plan was approved, and off we went to Azerbaijan and Georgia. We had sixteen meetings and interviews with key government representatives (at the Azerbaijani Ministry of Ecology and Natural Resources and the Georgian Ministry of Environmental Protection), officials at the OSCE offices in both countries, the World Wide Fund for Nature (WWF) offices and a range of other NGOs as well as local researchers.

In Baku, after some initial hurdles, we were granted access to the international department at Azerbaijan's Ministry of Ecology and Natural Resources. At the meeting, the officials voiced their scepticism of the need for a project promoting environmental democracy in Azerbaijan: 'Why is your government interested in this? Why here? Why does Norway want to meddle in our affairs?' was the response of government officials in Baku. It did not make things better when they asked me to explain what we were doing in Armenia. They did not warm to the idea of being on the receiving end of a project originally envisaged and implemented in the territory of their arch-enemy across the border.

With regard to Georgia, we ourselves were not at all sure whether there was any need for such a project. Georgia is 'overdeveloped' inasmuch as it is the biggest aid recipient per capita of the former Soviet republics. This is exacerbated by the fact that Georgia, at least prior to the 2008 conflict with Russia, was considered to be the most convenient country in the South Caucasus for development agencies to operate in. Georgia is the only country of the three South Caucasian republics where international donors can initiate projects involving Armenians, Azerbaijanis and Georgians, because Armenians will not travel to Azerbaijan and vice versa. At separate meetings with two environmental organizations in Tbilisi, in October 2008, we soon realized that FNI was operating in a crowded field with many other participants and competitors: one of the organizations we spoke to seemed willing to work with us but was clearly more experienced than us and had developed a similar but more thorough framework than we had envisaged. The other organization – a 'Trans-Caucasian' organization with branches in the three South Caucasian republics – made no effort to conceal their disappointment at our failure to employ their expertise in Armenia already: 'Why are you doing this, we can do it better,' they said.

After some initial hesitation, FNI nevertheless chose to submit full project proposals, accompanied by letters of cooperation from the OSCE office in Baku (but not from the OSCE Mission in Georgia, which had been closed in the meantime) and the Georgian Aarhus Centre. The two ministries had respectively agreed to sign on as main domestic partners, despite the prevailing sense of scepticism in Baku. In the report on the pilot project we noted that the two republics' commitments, according to the MEAs in question, were rather modest and their ability to enforce obligations stemming from the MEAs was limited. At least, that was our general impression. We also noted significant differences between Azerbaijan and Georgia, especially in the degree to which different voices, dissenters and democratic practices were tolerated.

I clearly remember the atmosphere at some of our meetings in Baku and Tbilisi as we attempted to explain and justify our intentions and commitments to the 'problem complex' that we had sort of inherited from the Norwegian MFA. During these meetings, I wrote down whatever I thought could be used in our project proposals, probably more preoccupied with how things could be framed in a coherent project framework than with identifying local needs and points of view. This sense of unease was characteristic, perhaps, precisely because we were about to introduce a project of scale in a 'sticky engagement' rather than really being open to local perspectives.

The MFA decided to withhold support for the proposed projects. This was probably a good decision. For, as far as the prospective Azerbaijani partners were concerned, we had apparently failed at 'translating the project into their terms'.[46] Second, it looked like the Georgia project would not be needed. That is not to imply that the environmental management sector or the implementation of the Aarhus Convention was not without many of the problems known from Armenia; rather, it was because the country had already experienced its fair share of the seminars and training programmes included in the project proposal and other organizations were better suited to undertake these programmes than the FNI.

The initial pilot project nevertheless indicates how 'development interventions are driven not by policy but by the exigencies of organizations and the need to maintain relationships'.[47] After all, it came about as a result of the Norwegian MFA prompting the FNI to design a project no one had asked for. In Azerbaijan, government officials were openly critical of the initiative. Why then did the Azerbaijani ministry agree to take part? The reasons are unclear. Most probably it was because it was a fairly non-committal deal for the Azerbaijanis to sign up to and it had no financial cost for them.

As the above indicates, foreign development consultants like myself often arrive in places with a 'conception of the problem' and some funding. What we then need to do is find a domestic partner able to give the project an aura of local legitimacy by affirming the need for the project and by participating in its implementation. Any failure at this point will seriously hamper efforts to secure a wider network of support and acceptance for the project's ethos.[48] As we gathered local support in Baku and Tbilisi – though there were certain reservations – FNI's project proposal was rejected by the Norwegian foreign office, which had in fact instigated the pilot in the first place.

The reason, apparently, lay with the project proposal. I agree with Green, who suggests that projects create spaces with their own logic connected to project documents, project mechanisms and guidelines.[49] The network we create constitutes and confirms its own (virtual) reality by way of self-referentiality.[50] As we tried to forge a link between means (seminars, transfer of know-how) and ends (improved environmental management in Azerbaijan and Georgia), we had to invoke a network.[51] This network consisted of the MFA, FNI and South Caucasian environmental ministries, transnational organizations such as OSCE, local NGOs and social scientists. As Riles reminds us, such networks are made real by constantly reflecting on themselves.[52] The reality of the network is never more apparent than in the funding applications and letters of support, tactically conspiring to misrepresent,[53] involving actors who slightly exaggerate the extent of the network, its importance and its capacities in terms of knowledge and skills. If a project proposal fails to win support, the network ceases to exist. At least, it did in this particular case.

Alternating between real places with real problems and benign challenges (the environment in Azerbaijan and Georgia), places with more or less mundane challenges (project acquisition at FNI) and the MFA, which needs to show some kind of involvement in the region to justify its budget requests, such projects or project ideas are characteristically transmogrified into non-places. As such, the network fails because there is no contact between the network partners after a project proposal has been ditched. But was the network in Armenia, which we successfully established and kept going over the years, more of a network than the failed attempts in Azerbaijan and Georgia? Not really. The network architecture is essentially the same and the networks invoked had the same metaphysical appearance involving a Western consultant (FNI), a domestic government authority, local NGOs and transnational organizations with missions in Azerbaijan and Georgia (WWF and OSCE). So why do some projects (or networks) fail before they even start, while others succeed in securing funding over and over again, despite repeating the same repertoire year after year with minimal change and progress?

There are, of course, substantial differences between the projects FNI implemented in Armenia and those we tried to develop in Azerbaijan and Georgia. But they all share the common denominator of being projects no one in Baku, Tbilisi or Yerevan had asked for. They were essentially devised by FNI as a response to project calls and discrete hints or mandates from the Norwegian MFA. One material difference between the countries, however, is that the Norwegian MFA funded fewer projects in Armenia than in Azerbaijan and Georgia and probably needed someone – as officials said at information meetings the MFA hosted – to 'maintain the bilateral relationship'. If this is one of the reasons, it is an example of how multiple justifications for project funding reside with the donor and how some of them, although stated at information meetings, are not included in the official guidelines and projects. Seen thus, the MFA's motivation for considering bilateral points of contact as an additional, informal, criterion suggests that project implementers may knowingly exploit this disparity.

Success or failure – a matter of perception?

To reiterate the gist of Mosse's propositions discussed in Chapter 3, he suggests that projects work largely to consolidate two different aspects of projects, as coherent policy ideas and as operational systems.[54] Assessments of success and failure are policy judgements, he maintains, rather than the results of specific project achievements and limitations.

We can safely say that the main reasons the project was created were the needs and ambitions of MFA and FNI rather than those of the Armenians. In itself, this should not come as a surprise. After all, one cannot expect government officials in Armenia or elsewhere to be aware of the different support mechanisms in distant Norway. On the other hand, the process of applying, implementing, reporting, reapplying and negotiating reveals how the project design served largely to maintain political support in Norway.

Development may be understood as a process in which 'institutions generate their own form of discourse', which simultaneously constructs 'a particular kind of object of knowledge and creates a structure of knowledge around that object'.[55] Within the 'development' apparatus, Ferguson argues, politics is suspended by way of expanding bureaucratic state power, and thus an 'anti-politics machine' is created.[56] This is in line with Mosse's argument noted above on the relationship between policy and practice.[57] I find the latter to offer a more useful approach for my analytical purposes than Ferguson's grand discourse, yet his argument that development practices are to a considerable extent standardized is certainly the case also in my ethnography.[58] Although not universal, in the various recipes for 'developing' Armenia, civil society and democratization have been imperative: development discourse is by and large produced by outsiders and as such risks ignoring and simplifying local particularities that ought to be considered.

As Mosse suggests, policy primarily mobilizes political support, but is it the policy of the donor or the implementer? Or, as suggested in another of his propositions, do 'coherent policy ideas' pertain – again – to the donor or the implementer? These are crucial questions in my case because the policy judgements and frameworks largely belong to the sphere of the Norwegian MFA; FNI had no policy of its own, perhaps with the exception of always having to consider new funding opportunities (though not at all costs). But I find Mosse's arguments instructive because, as we have seen, FNI largely adopted the ethos of MFA policy judgements in order to acquire the projects in the first place. Local needs and perceptions in Armenia were taken into account, but to a much lesser degree.

Mosse's arguments can help us gain a better understanding of the cases presented on the previous pages. The relationship between the donor and the implementer – here MFA and FNI – forges new project conceptions and LOG-frame adjustments that had limited bearing at the level of project implementation and associated practices in Armenia. Yet they were formulated such that it appeared as if the operational features had guided the 'improvement' of the LOG frame.

An extension of understanding success and failure as a matter of performativity is to understand judgements or ascriptions of success or failure not as a 'certain state of affairs' but as performances that are integral to the construction of that very same state of affairs.[59] In other words, successes and failures are performed. As project manager of the Armenia project, it was obviously important for me to perform – portray, frame – the project narrative such that it could be understood as a modest success at the very least. But more important than reaching a conclusion – on success or failure – was to argue the need for continued financial support from the MFA.

FNI counterbalanced the reasons for incremental success with arguments that more needed to be done: the capacity-building measures needed to continue as the challenges in Armenia were immense. This act of performing the project as neither success nor failure but something in between is characteristic of the project reports and proposals. The nature of managing a project portrayed as 'a work in process', while each year writing up the narratives and reports finalizing the project, made for a creative counterpoint of tentative successes and claims of work still in need of being done, which were then included in the next year's project proposal. Thus FNI deployed self-referential tactics,[60] also evident as what in project proposals was formulated as an ambition and in later documents was turned into achievements.

Diversions in project management

Several ruptures in the implementation of the project occurred over the period. I have called the LOG-frame incident the first rupture. Even though there had been from the start a certain disconnect between the project representations in project documents and actual project practices, it had widened, creating an ever larger gap between project as policy idea and as operational system.[61] By accepting the change in the LOG-frame hierarchy – a precondition for continued funding – the Armenia project became increasingly distant from the Armenian reality it was meant to improve. This rupture was characterized by the ever-widening split between what the project did and what the project claimed to do.

A second rupture occurred when we realized that the MFA were also reviewing projects in light of current foreign policy, in the sense that one of the desired outcomes of projects in Armenia was to maintain a minimum of bilateral contact between Armenia and Norway. The reasoning related to maintaining bilateral relations with Armenia was spelled out at information meetings, yet it is nowhere to be found in the guidelines. This was obviously not something that was accounted for or could be inserted into the increasingly important LOG frame. It served, rather, as a tacit, informal reason to back Norwegian development interventions in Armenia. It was also one of the informal motivations and part of policies that may render a development project legitimate, although they were not included in the LOG frame.

In the guidelines, civil society throughout the region is portrayed as weak and plagued by widespread corruption. Europeanization and institution building are the remedy, paving the way for standardized projects that fit the policy model, rather than projects responding to local needs. The point here is not to analyse these storylines but to note that the result (as in FNI's case) is likely to be project proposals that kowtow to the storylines in the calls for project applications in order to make themselves look acceptable and worthy of support. Requests pertaining to changes in the LOG-frame hierarchy had a greater effect on how FNI portrayed the project than they did on how the project was implemented in Armenia. For instance, there are, as I have argued, formal guidelines on development policies for parts of the post-Soviet area. But there are also tacit, informal rules defining what can be considered legitimate, such as maintaining bilateral relations. The MFA's request to cooperate with local authorities (anchoring) is another example to which I return in the next chapter.

The Armenia project involved donors, NGOs and others in a modernizing scheme. Scott's critique of states has relevance for the international aid system as well.[62] Armenia is a state where NGOs operate as modernizing forces and where 'democracy has become a project'.[63] Armenia is undergoing processes of Europeanization from different sides by different actors constructing project spaces that are manageable slices of reality. At least, this is the case in project documents; whether these slices are manageable in practice is another question.

Jim Igoe says that NGOs that manoeuvre to position themselves as recipients of development aid deploy 'strategies of extraversion',[64] in that one central feature of such NGOs is to consider the outside world of donors rather than local realities, which may ultimately lead the organizations away from their (imagined) constituencies. In the same vein, the Armenia project was more tailored to suit MFA priorities, instrumentally speaking, than to the less tangible 'local needs'. The world of development projects is probably teeming with similar examples. The Armenia project is but one to successfully deploy the scale assumptions and collude with the ethos of the donor call through LOG-framing practices. FNI performed Europe through the LOG-frame alterations that paid scant regard to the project practices to be discussed in the next chapter.

The project spaces resulting from foreign aid and project cooperation support mechanisms are, on the one hand, constructed so as to be manageable, whereas their legitimization relies on striving for goals and impacts that are – in the end – unattainable. The concepts these projects introduce or are surrounded by are not neutral. 'Civil society', 'democratization', 'capacity building', 'international obligations', 'good governance' and 'anti-corruption' should be treated as empirical objects rather than taken for granted. As such, this project can be understood as part of a wider scale-making project,[65] as discussed in Chapter 1. Projects are sites of social and institutional reproduction,[66] in which, I argue, a specific story of international relations and post-Cold War rhetoric exists: the West won, now you are welcome to become like us.

The tailoring of the project to suit the various demands and the need for legitimacy within the Norwegian MFA is revealing of international project cooperation insofar as it is an embedded practice in Norwegian foreign policy. The practices depicted rest on project performances and regularity (seminars, study-trips on an annual basis), competence and background knowledge (terms of reference, applications and experience) and discursive and material factors ('helping the post-Soviet states' and financial means). By perpetuating the aid relationship, the transition is 'suspended' between past and present and may perhaps be prolonged.[67] We are thus left with the question of whether our efforts to 'do good' are actually doing harm.

I have shown how formal requirements in project auditing and documentation lead to the creation of project goals that are unattainable and have little to do with on-the-ground project practices and needs. This hypothesis supports Mosse's argument that success or failure can be produced irrespective of what happens on the ground.[68] The two aspects adhering to project life both nurture each other and – when the rift is too wide and long-lasting – can cause the end of the project.

5

'Never mind, it's not a good idea'

In this chapter I analyse the Armenia project as a developmental encounter in Armenia between researchers at the Fridtjof Nansen Institute (FNI), Armenian civil servants and bureaucrats at different levels, Armenian non-governmental organizations (NGOs), international organizations with 'missions' in Yerevan and Armenian educational institutions. The Norwegian donor will be kept at 'arm's length' in this chapter.

I make use of the term 'project spaces'[1] and the notion of networking[2] to argue in this chapter that the project spaces created by the Armenia project in Armenia and beyond are contested and that various project spaces important for the project had to be muted in the official descriptions of the project. The professional network on which the project relies is important, yet the origin of the network in social encounters is toned down. These project spaces, I shall argue, are materially and physically contested spaces based on historical and national contingencies, rather than merely constituting virtual non-places in the project world.

But I will also argue that documents such as formal letters of cooperation bring social networks to life and that both document-related networks and social networks are constitutive of the project space. Some of the physical spaces discussed in this chapter, nevertheless, are more contested than others. They include the venue of the first seminars hosted by FNI in Armenia, the Miami Hotel on the shores of Lake Sevan. The hotel had been built in 2005 as a holiday resort. With the relative success of efforts to restore Lake Sevan to its original size with its original seabed, the Miami Hotel in fact ended up being flooded.

International projects promoting democratic change and development in the former Soviet republics have frequently been informed by a discourse in which these republics' civil societies are considered incapable of mobilizing the population behind political change. This has led to a broad range of projects where fly-in Western experts offer seminars and lectures, to which the locals pay 'ritual lip-service'.[3] It can also be argued that participation is not only an important effort in networking; it can be said to come about as an effort to assemble experience and strategies to better position oneself in the world of aid:

> While I have never heard of a course or workshop dedicated to exposing informal dynamics and decision making procedures of aid agencies to potential clients, many recipient players attend capacity-building lessons in search of precisely such strategic information.[4]

This range of projects has local effects as well. Arguably, the Armenia project can be said to part and parcel of an approach in which participation is *fetishized*, for example, it is subject to the belief that 'participation in Western-style forums will inculcate in people a sense of democracy and trust'.[5] Fetishization of participation is nothing new to people who have lived under Soviet socialism, but it has since taken on a new form.[6] To what extent, then, can we understand this participation as yet another aspect of a Europe performed in Armenia?

A central feature of the analysis will be the discussion of the project practices and how they can be understood as a project of scale making with global connections, networking efforts and 'sticky engagements'. I have argued that project reports and preceding funding applications concentrated towards the end on a narrative totality that was largely disconnected from the project as an operational system.[7] I will now consider project practices in Armenia, in other words, the project as a localized operational system. This chapter shows how the Armenia project established networks across different dimensions, socially and professionally. These networks, it is argued, were mutually dependent. The different private, semi-professional and professional networks are aspects of the same thing, yet they have to be separated in project documentation. In fact, the social aspects of the network would have disturbed the professional representation of the project: insofar as actors within the networks also employed their own personal networks and knowledge, they became an inescapable part of the project, imperative to its very working. At the same time, it also led the project slightly askew, as we will see below in the discussion about where seminars should be held during the first two years of the project. As I described in Chapter 4, the project came about when FNI became aware of the project mechanism of the Ministry of Foreign Affairs (MFA). But how did the project come about in Armenian terms?

The project was instigated by a phone call in 2005. FNI's director called the Armenian Ministry of Nature Protection (MNP) to ask whether they might be interested in establishing a partnership in order to initiate a development project targeting environmental management in Armenia. After recovering from their initial bewilderment, the Armenian ministry put FNI's director in contact with the civil servant who was most adept in English, Karen. Within minutes, the two realized they already knew each other, having participated at international meetings together in the early 1990s. The conversation ended in an agreement: FNI would apply for funds with the Armenian MNP as its partner.

Working within the Department of Bioresources at the MNP, and prior to that as deputy head of one of Armenia's national parks, it seemed sensible to carry on working with Karen during the preparation of the project. He is well connected with Armenian NGOs through his membership of a small NGO set up by civil servants.

Seminar locations under water

The practical challenges of aligning project visions and practices can be illustrated by the following example. The main activities in practical terms throughout the project period were seminars on environmental management and Armenia's international obligations. The participants, for the most part, were civil servants involved in environmental management at national, regional and municipal levels, mayors and NGOs.

Both the 2006 and 2007 Armenia project seminars were held at the Miami Hotel, in Gegharqunik Marz, on the shores of Lake Sevan, which at 940 square kilometres is Armenia's biggest lake, covering 5 per cent of the country. Lake Sevan constitutes most of the Sevan National Park and, being just an hour's drive from Yerevan, is a popular destination for Yerevanis during the hot summer months. Lake Sevan is located at approximately 1,900 metres above sea level, whereas Yerevan is about 1,000 metres above sea level.

During the first seminar, in 2006, plenary discussions revealed several seemingly inconsistent facts about the location of the hotel and the role of Sevan National Park, making its use as a venue for a seminar on international environmental commitments problematic for the project implementer.

Because the agricultural sector in Armenia has always been desperately in need of water, the Soviet Union initiated large-scale irrigation projects, including a plan to channel water from the lake into the Hrazdan River. This was accomplished by digging a tunnel several metres below water level between the lake and the river. Hydropower plants were also built in the 1930s. Between 1930 and 1980, the lake's water level fell by 18 metres,[8] which nevertheless was far less than the initially calculated 40 metres. To prevent erosion caused by rivers and streams flowing into Lake Sevan, Soviet authorities undertook several reforestation and afforestation projects, the effect of which was to increase Armenia's forest cover from approximately 8 to 11 per cent over a period of forty years.[9]

As the water level diminished, plans to make use of the reclaimed land for agricultural purposes were drafted. They proved unsustainable, and in 1981, work on a 50-kilometre tunnel to divert water from the river Arpa into Lake Sevan got under way. This increased the water level by 1.5 metres. The surface area of the lake was still at least 200 square kilometres less than it was originally: an island with an old fortress and two churches dating back to the eighth century became a peninsula. The impact on the lake's biodiversity was dire, especially the endemic Sevan trout. Over the years, several hotels and resorts were illegally constructed along the new shoreline, the venue of the project's first two seminars being one of them. When asked why this had happened, answers varied from corrupt authorities to the more mundane need of the national park to earn money to make ends meet. A certain level of commercial activity had to be allowed, we were told.

Uneasy about hosting a seminar at a venue of disputable legality, I tried to find another for the 2007 seminar; this proved unsuccessful, however, due to budgetary constraints. The project's local partners had their own preferences with regard to which region the seminar should be organized in. I have no indication that someone was lining their pockets, although the suspicion is never far from anyone's mind in Armenia. The question is an important and difficult one; an informant working as an anti-corruption activist explained that she thought that just by participating and collaborating with Armenian authorities, our project contributed to and necessarily was in tangential contact with corruption. Matter-of-factly, she stated that money from our project was probably diverted to some senior official in the MNP to secure institutional support. I was never able to verify this, but similar and indeed more detailed statements were made by several sources familiar with the workings of the ministry in other internationally funded projects. Nevertheless, in 2007, we were once again back at the same hotel discussing Armenia's implementation and governance challenges and so on. In 2008 the venue did change, on my insistence. In 2009 and 2010 the water level in Lake Sevan continued to rise steadily and several of the shoreline resorts ended up under water; see Figure 5.1.

As of today, Lake Sevan has stabilized at 1,905 metres above sea level. Every now and then, environmentalists express alarm at the outflow volumes allowed by the MNP. A news feed reported that an MNP official had been charged with pocketing money meant for cutting trees now under water. He had allegedly cut a 50/50 deal with the tree-felling

Figure 5.1 Picture taken from the closed gate of the grounds of the Miami Hotel, partly submerged in 2010. Between 2006 and 2008, the shoreline had receded about 150 metres away from where the picture was taken.
Source: Photo by Karen Jenderedjian.

company. In the event, the trees were never felled. Interestingly, the official referred to the *telefonnij zakon* (telephone law) in his defence,[10] claiming that he got orders from above. The charges were later dropped and the official was allowed to come back. The person in question was Artashes, department head at the Armenian MNP and participant at several FNI-organized seminars. The analytically interesting aspect, however, is how the Miami Hotel constituted a contested project space. The Miami Hotel and its dubious history could not be communicated in the official descriptions of the project. Although seminar participants agreed that the resorts along the shore of Lake Sevan were a significant problem, government officials seemed indifferent or unaffected by how such places could exist: 'The national park needed an income'. The Armenia project – unknowingly the first year – had thus affiliated itself with a contested place stemming from decades of failed environmental and economic policies in Armenia.

Seminars and preparatory work in Armenia

The first project seminar was hosted jointly by FNI and the Armenian MNP at the Miami Hotel in September 2006. The invitation to the prospective participants (civil servants, NGO representatives) is reproduced in Figure 5.2.

FRIDTJOF NANSENS INSTITUTT
FRIDTJOF NANSEN INSTITUTE

Dear_____

The Fridtjof Nansen Institute, in co-operation with the Ministry of Nature Protection of the Republic of Armenia and technical support of Professional and Entrepreneurial Orientation Union, has the pleasure of inviting you to a **Seminar on international obligations in environmental management** in Armenia.

The seminar is to be conducted at Hotel Miami, Sevan, Gegharquniq marz, 25-29 September, 2006.

Environmental management and sustainable development are increasingly on the international agenda. Numerous international conventions have came into force, containing provisions and proscriptions for how nations should keep their environment sustainable. If environmental issues earlier were presumably of domestic concern – if at all – the notion that the utilisation of natural resources and the sustainable development of Earth's environment are, and should be, an issue of trans-national concern has got an ever-broader appeal.

Most international environmental conventions do not foresee means of coercion. Governments that fail to implement the commitments required are not subject to sanctions by the international community, though declining prestige may be an undesirable consequence of non-compliance. On the other hand, the fact that those governments are legally required to pursue certain policies make it easier for domestic groups like environmental NGOs or the local population to make pressure on authorities. In this way the inter-linkage between international and regional actors may work as an effective tool to change national environmental policy. The role of the civil society in achieving sustainable development has gained increasing attention and recognition in international forums, and under some of the international conventions, governments are explicitly required to take into account the needs of the local population. The Convention on Access to Information, Public Participation in Decision-Making and Access to Justice in Environmental Matters (the Aarhus Convention) is the most visible example of this recognition.

In the years following the collapse of the Soviet Union, Armenia has signed a number of international environmental treaties, yet the implementation of the commitments taken is still only in its early stage. This seminar will focus on the following issues:

- International environmental politics in general
- Brief introduction to four international treaties which are ratified by Armenia
- management structures
- the role of other actors in implementing environmental commitments: NGOs, and business actors, other stakeholders

Civil servants from national, regional and local levels are invited to participate, alongside with a selected number representatives of NGOs and the scientific sector. Please see the enclosed program for details. The seminar aims to train participants in the basic commitments that derive from Armenia's ratifying of the relevant treaties and to increase awareness among civil servants and NGO representatives towards contemporary issues in international and national environmental management.

P.O. Box 326, NO-1326 Lysaker, Norway. Visiting address: Polhøgda, Fridtjof Nansens vei 17, Lysaker
Tel: +47 6711 1900 Fax: +47 6711 1910 E-mail: post@fni.no
www.fni.no

Figure 5.2 Invitation to seminar participants, 2006.
Source: Fridtjof Nansen Institute (FNI).

The invitation invoked terms such as sustainable development and environmental management and stressed the importance of involving civil society. Considering projects of scale making as bundles of coherent ideas, these notions, I argue, were bundled such as to enable the creation of two ideal types: the environmentally concerned citizen and an environmental management sector capable of and willing to foster change, both pointing in the direction of *environmentality*.[11] On this point – at least around the seminar table – everyone seemed to agree. Scale-making efforts, allegiance to international values and agreements, a 'vibrant civil society' and so on were things all participants said they were involved in.

The seminar, which lasted five days, had four days of lectures and one day for an excursion around Lake Sevan, stopping off at Lchashen Cove and other sites highlighting some of the environmental challenges facing Armenia.

At the seminar, several Armenians presented various multilateral environmental agreements ratified by Armenia and spoke of the challenges they had faced in their implementation. The speakers were mostly civil servants from the ministries, but there were also some research professionals. Many were government-appointed focal points for each of the respective agreements. Among the conventions covered were the Convention on Biological Diversity, Convention to Combat Desertification in Armenia and the Convention on Wetlands (Ramsar Convention, after the city in which it was adopted). There was also a talk on 'Civil society and the Aarhus Convention', given by Hasmik, whom we met in Chapters 2 and 3.

As for the seminars we conducted, there was obviously much talk concerning the environment, but it was largely indirect in tone, for example, in terms of whether management procedures and laws related to the environment worked or not. When concrete issues were raised, such as the Sevan case, municipal tax collection or suchlike, they largely served to illustrate the futility of remaining hopeful – an ultimately exhausting exercise. Except for the occasional excursion, which provided a look at some of the issues discussed at the seminars (waste management, management of wetlands, etc.), little was said about the environment in terms of the immediate natural surroundings. I take this as an indication that the discourses or assemblages that are invoked, rephrased, contested and negotiated are so pervasive that the heart of the matter is somehow lost from view.

These assertions add substance to the assemblage of environmental rights by making claims to a linkage between international conventions and domestic Armenian politics. On the other hand, however, whatever environmental challenges there may be at the local level or elsewhere were not really up for debate. In this regard, seminars resemble repetitive acts invoking the Cold War hierarchy of First, Second and Third World countries and citizens. In a post-Cold War ethnography,[12] we should acknowledge the participation of those perceived to be at the receiving end of development projects but also analyse development professionals and local participants within a common framework.[13] One way to understand this better is to investigate the different social and professional aspects of project life insofar as they constitute project spaces and networks. This will be done below in presenting several social settings in the project and how they formed an integral part of project life.

In spring 2007, I was back in Yerevan to plan a follow-up seminar together with our Armenian partners in the ministries and NGOs. The topic had changed slightly since the previous year, but the main goals were the same. My visit started on a personal rather than a professional note. Just hours after arriving, I was one of a procession of people visiting Tsitsernakaberd, the national memorial for the Ottoman genocide. I was with Karen, who told the history of his family. His was one of the many Western Armenian families forced to flee into the deserts, where possibly millions perished. Karen's grandfather died and his father was born there. After we had laid flowers at the memorial we walked back to town with tens of thousands of others. The day continued at Karen's home with toasts to friendship and plenty of food. It was not until the day after that we got to work on planning the next seminar. I felt a certain uneasiness during these initial planning meetings as I had to explain the principles of the project, formulated as they were in response to the Norwegian MFA's call for projects.

The project's modus operandi appeared set. I was there on a planning trip, interviewing people and organizing meetings. After agreeing to a tentative schedule, I flew home, discussed the outcome with colleagues and continued preparations at FNI. During the following months, drafts and ideas were sent back and forth, while invitations were sent to prospective participants. A week before the seminar I went back and settled the final details.

The project cycle was punctuated by several bursts of activity throughout the year. Although most of them concerned the administrative practices accounted for in the previous chapter, they also affected how the project evolved in Armenia. The schedule generally went like this: January to mid-February was spent on drafting project proposals, acquiring support letters and identifying possible new project partners. During the spring, when some of the planned activities were about to start, I usually had to prompt the MFA for a response to our application. It usually took a couple of months, confirmation arriving sometime in the period May–July. It happened in some project years that I travelled to Armenia before we had secured financial support, confident that we would get it anyway. Although the amounts we received were often lower than the budget we had applied for, we always managed to get a grant from the MFA.[14] Prior to the Norwegian summer holidays in July (taking into account that Norwegians tend to go on summer holidays earlier than Armenians, who end their holidays in early September), I needed to plan for the upcoming activities while keeping in contact with our Armenian partners. Then came the actual seminars and lectures in Armenia, usually in September or October, with the time immediately afterwards spent on accounts and reports and closing the books with partners in Armenia.

The project year was thus interspersed with hectic activity and disjunctures. This can be attributed to various factors. For example, the project funding mechanism had a reporting and application cycle that undeniably left a mark on project implementation. Other contributing factors were, of course, the distance between Armenia and Norway and how we communicated with our project partners. However, as noted in the previous chapter, we needed to smooth over these disjunctures in our reports to the Norwegian MFA, in project proposals and elsewhere.

The project spurred different kinds of joint networking efforts by Armenians and the FNI. In 2007, Anush, who worked at the Organization for Security and Co-operation in Europe (OSCE) office in Yerevan, visited FNI for a week in connection with a programme funded by the OSCE, with a view to learning more about environmental management. FNI had little to offer since her visit coincided with our summer holidays – but we were happy to welcome her. Her visit did give me an opportunity to add to the new project submission that it had prompted the creation of various networks that had been paid for, moreover, by other parties. It was a reflection of the project's sustainability and relevance. Once again, the development project invoked self-referentiality in order to account for and legitimize changes and practices.[15] As OSCE and Anush were primarily preoccupied with the Aarhus Convention, it also marked an increased focus on the Convention, to the detriment of other conventions and issues in Armenia.

State reserve barbeque

In mid-November 2008, I was in Yerevan, a few days ahead of a project seminar. The day after my arrival, I received an early call from Karen. He had been invited to attend a social gathering together with a colleague, Astine, who also worked in the ministry, by the deputy director of Khosrov Forest State Reserve in Ararat Marz. Karen wondered if I'd like to come along, which I said I would. He picked me up at the hotel and we drove down to the marketplace where all kinds of household appliances and materials are sold. Karen picked up some appliances he needed for his apartment and then we collected Armine, who lives in a small house on a hillside surrounding Yerevan.[16] We then drove back to Karen's apartment block to pick up his wife and son. On our way to the valley, we stopped by a fish farm. Karen wanted to buy fish (Lena sturgeon, as it turned out) to serve at the seminar's opening reception. Karen is always proud to be involved in negotiations that can make things cheaper, either for the project management team or his personal finances.

The fish farm consists of a few dozen outdoor basins (artificial ponds) containing sturgeon, rainbow trout and carp. One of the managers, an acquaintance of Karen's, gave us a guided tour. After ordering the sturgeon, we moved to the office building, where we were offered tea and soorch (Armenian coffee) and chatted with the owner, an Armenian living in Russia most of the time. With the trunk filled with sturgeon, including a few fish to be eaten later that day, we continued down the Ararat valley. Although it was mid-November, the temperature was in the mid-20s.

Nearing the reserve, we met the deputy director, Martiros, and a nephew of his. Karen and I joined them in their Lada Niva,[17] and Karen's son drove the family's car along the road leading to the reserve. On the way up, I was asked the usual questions about what I was doing there and why Norwegian authorities would want to fund projects in Armenia. Nansen's role in Armenian history was also discussed. We stopped at a village. Martiros had already bought fowls to be barbequed, but we needed one more. A huge poster by the roadside told us that we were now entering the Khosrov State Reserve. We met a herder on the road, from whom the entourage bought fresh ox tongue to add to the barbeque.

The cars pulled over at an old and rusty rest stop by a small river. There, Astine and I walked off to collect firewood while the others prepared the khorovats barbeque (a mixture of ox tongue, poultry and fish). Finally, when we had found our places, the meat was cut into small pieces and spread onto pieces of *lavash* (a soft Armenian bread) and handed around. It was then time to open the first bottle of wine. We sat chatting and eating together, interrupted by the occasional toast. Suddenly, Martiros started singing an Armenian folk song. I responded to this – in the spirit of cultural exchange – with a Norwegian Halling (folk song), 'Rotneims-Knut'. After a couple of hours, we headed back to Yerevan. Astine invited us in for more soorch, served with fruits. Finally, the sturgeons in the trunk were carried in to be stored in Karen's refrigerator.

As it happened, neither Astine nor Karen knew Martiros very well, although they had met professionally. Martiros had invited them to the barbeque precisely to develop relations between the three of them. And this is how they really got to know each other, since closeness in professional relationships is reached through sharing a meal and making toasts. Either way, such gatherings are really appreciated, and years later Karen and Martiros still maintain contact on a personal note rather than a professional level.

In mapping the social life of projects, I find it important to discuss and analyse not only how the project was implemented but also how personal networks and social contacts were established in informal ways, which otherwise cannot be accounted for in the 'slices of reality' created by the system of management by objectives.[18] The stories recounted above show how personal and professional relations are intertwined and function as a basis for future cooperation.

In *The Network Inside Out*, Annelise Riles discerns two types of network: social networks and document-related networks.[19] I take the latter to imply the professional aspects of project life. The project created a platform through which network participants could organize certain activities. Why all this sociality? Working through a network is a better way of making sure everything works out, according to Karen. Although I was enjoying myself, I wondered from time to time whether the Norwegian MFA would be happy about supporting this type of activity. When on a different occasion I told Karen of my doubts, he simply refused to scale back on social activities. Social activities were necessary for the project to succeed. I told him the MFA had asked us to not spend entire days on field trips during the seminars. Karen agreed. 'Never mind whether it's a good idea or not,' he said, 'we have to do it as your ministry says.' In Karen's opinion, however, a day spent on a field trip benefited the seminar anyway; it is, after all, what most participants expect. After some deliberation, the invitations to the four-day (i.e. the number of days that the MFA requested) seminar were sent out, with one day still set aside for field trips. Karen's 'never mind' could be interpreted as 'Never mind the MFA, we have to do whatever works best.'

The MFA had not objected to the changes in the reports we submitted to the ministry. There were differences of opinion on other occasions as well, not least because of the different perceptions in Armenia and Norway on the need for social activities. The coexistence and co-dependency of sociality and professionalism contrast with the exclusion of the former in the official project representations.

We can understand this process better, I argue, by using the notion of project spaces. Based on the notion of non-places,[20] Green thought it a good idea to look at projects in much the same manner.[21] Like Augé's conception of airports as non-places, project spaces are characterized by a certain kind of deterritorialization:

> [T]hose coming together for a project only do so through the project itself and represent not themselves but a professional position for an agency which is explicitly operating not only outside its place of origin but to agenda determined in the national and multilateral policy spaces where the content of international development is negotiated.[22]

The multilateral policy space is what we visited in the previous chapter, with logical frameworks (LOG frames), project proposals, guidelines and the like. At this juncture, however, I believe we need to appreciate that projects also consist of contested social spaces. Since this happens in a creative mix where one of the project's main partners acts as both government official and NGO representative, the negotiations within the artificially created project space become even more complex.

At the same time, as I have argued above, participation is somewhat fetishized. Green's non-places argument is valid up to a point but too inflexible, in my opinion. Although project participants meet in the 'project space', or perhaps project non-space in my interpretation, people represent more than their professional roles, as Green apparently seems to argue.²³ Rather, they (or we) get together and combine professional necessities in project implementation with social activities such as dinners with relatives and friends, celebrations and the like. The private and social aspects of project implementation are thus important prerequisites for the project to move forward. They get the project going and perhaps they are an aspect of what induces people to participate.

Green's project space is constructed by an agenda set by international donors, but she risks overlooking its local and social consequences. In terms of local practices, I would argue, project spaces should definitely not be understood as non-places, and although the notion of project space as a non-place is captivating, it should not be taken as an invitation to assume that relations within project spaces are as non-committal as they are in Augé's non-places such as airports and the like.

Project life – both in its professional and social connotations – arguably entails a dual form of participation. On the one hand, there are the professional aspects that may be relayed to a manageable slice of reality attributed to a virtual non-place, that is, the factors portrayed in project documents. On the other, we find the social aspects of project life, which in many ways are equally important. This duality finds its parallel in Riles's coining of networks and personal relations as 'versions of one another seen twice'.²⁴ If we see participation in projects as a duality, we have to acknowledge, at least based on my observations from the Armenia project, that some only participate in the professional sphere. They include, for instance, the minister who signed the Letter of Intent and others who were not at the seminars but in various ways lent it legitimacy. Most participants, however, appear both in a professional as well as a social capacity in the project. In this respect, we should not see the network and the social (or personal) relations as always consisting of exactly the same people and connections. Although we should use the phrase 'versions of one another seen twice' with some caution, social and professional life take on various performative aspects, aspects that are more than merely representational,²⁵ which seems to inform the idea that development professionals do not represent themselves, only their institutional affiliation.[26]

I would now like to return to the proposition that we ought to find ways to understand development professionals and development recipients within a common framework.[27] The discussion so far indicates that sociality and professionalism are highly interconnected, not least because development professionals and local participants largely participate in the same professional and social arenas and it would be contrived to separate these two main categories in the analysis. Obviously, the relationship can be understood in terms of asymmetrical power relations, the ramifications of which should not be brushed aside. However, perceived in terms of participation, from both aisles of the 'development encounter', we are, I find, generally in the same boat.

This fact of co-dependency relies on the need of development aid mechanisms to identify an 'object' to develop while the 'object' itself needs funding and other kinds of support. This form of coexistence within a common framework comprising development policies, projects, post-socialist transition and so on is given substance through performance.[28] The concept of performativity implies a rejection of persons, things and words as simply representatives of positions, relations or policies and the like.[29] As participants in a given project we perform within a common framework, even though our performances have different motivations and reasons. For instance, FNI as project implementer and the MFA as donor and project partner in Armenia invoked the same scale of Europeanization as part of the performative articulation of the project's relevance.

Anchoring the project among Armenian authorities

Tying the projects in Armenia and elsewhere in the region to local government bodies and encouraging them to get actively involved were both an indisputable formal requirement of the MFA's approval and funding. In Chapter 4, I described how MFA officials attached importance to these elements at the information meetings, even at the expense of what was best for the project. The argument was somehow that this was the best way to secure local cooperation and ensure that governments in the recipient countries were not against it. However, it may also be the result of a kind of micromanagement of bilateral relations: as we remember from the description of an MFA information meeting, officials stressed the role of Norwegian projects as the only bilateral points of contact between the two governments. In this sense, the MFA appeared to see the FNI and others as a vehicle of the government's foreign policy.

Artifacts indicative of such cooperation were the formal agreements (letters of cooperation, etc.) with local authorities in Armenia. Throughout the project's lifetime we concluded several agreements with various government institutions in Armenia. One of the many letters of support from the Armenian MNP to FNI is reproduced in Figure 5.3.

In the process of submitting a new project proposal to the MFA, I had told Karen – the project's head contact person in Armenia – how important these letters of cooperation were; we needed to attach them to our new project proposal for the next two-year period. Karen told me later what one of his superiors had said: 'Tell him that he can write whatever he wants and the Ministry is happy to sign it.'

The person Karen had spoken to, Artashes, was the head of the department and would eventually be signing the letter. He had, over the years, been involved in the project from afar, dispensing legitimacy by virtue of position in the ministry but without being involved in any practical sense. One of the first times I met Artashes was in 2007, a few days ahead of the seminar we were organizing together with his section. I had been invited to his office to explain the purpose of my visit. After Karen had said a few words about our common project, he left me alone with Artashes. From then on we barely spoke about the project; he invited me to join him in a separate room in his office suite, with several sofas. We sat down and I was offered grapes and Ararat to drink.[30]

ՀԱՅԱՍՏԱՆԻ ՀԱՆՐԱՊԵՏՈՒԹՅԱՆ
ԲՆԱՊԱՀՊԱՆՈՒԹՅԱՆ
ՆԱԽԱՐԱՐՈՒԹՅՈՒՆ
ԿԵՆՍԱՌԵՍՈՒՐՍՆԵՐԻ ԿԱՌԱՎԱՐՄԱՆ
ԳՈՐԾԱԿԱԼՈՒԹՅՈՒՆ

ՊԵՏ   HEAD

REPUBLIC OF ARMENIA
MINISTRY OF
NATURE PROTECTION
BIORESOURCES MANAGEMENT
AGENCY

0010, ք. Երևան, Փ. Բյուզանդի փ. 1/3
Հեռ.՝ +374 10 527952
Ֆաքս՝ +374 10 527952

1/3, P.Buzand St., Yerevan 0010, Armenia
Tel.: +374 10 527952
Fax: +374 10 527952

"23" 01 2009թ.

N° 022/17

To: Mr. Peter Johan Schei, Director
Fridtjof Nansen Institute
Fax: +47 67 111910
P.O. Box 326, N-1326 Lysaker, Norway

Dear Mr Schei,

Since its inception in 2006, the co-operation between the Fridtjof Nansen Institute and the Ministry of Nature Protection of the Republic of Armenia has promoted good governance and stakeholder involvement to ensure an efficient implementation of multilateral environmental treaties in Armenia.

It is now time to assess the progress this far in the co-operation. When assessing such progress we keep in mind that several of the achievements come rather as a result of concerted efforts than of as the result of a single process. The long-term effect of the co-operation is too early to assess, but we are confident that such co-operation contributes in several ways in a positive manner. To sum it up, the co-operation between the Institute and the Ministry has contributed in three major areas:

  (i)   awareness-raising,
  (ii) confidence-building through dialogue, and
  (iii) implementation into law.

The project co-operation with our Norwegian partner has led to increased awareness and knowledge of Armenia's international obligations, as laid down in the various conventions, such as the Convention of Biodiversity (CBD), the Ramsar and the Aarhus. Outside the environmental management sector, knowledge of the obligations and how to implement these are limited. Various socio-economic challenges as well as underdeveloped sector-integration contribute to this. Through the project, representatives of several ministries as well as municipalities, non-governmental organizations and businesses have taken part in seminars. The knowledge acquired has led to increased awareness of environmental policies in the various sectors.

The seminars have facilitated an important dialogue between various governance sectors and levels as well as with civil society. The Aarhus convention seeks to guarantee the right to access to environmental information and public participation, and we thus welcome every effort to promote and secure the rights guaranteed by the convention.

This co-operation is of particular importance in this respect as it in practice shows us how this dialogue can be developed and maintained over time. Armenia still faces some challenges in its implementation of the Aarhus convention, and through the co-operation we can take advantage of the way our Norwegian colleagues has implemented the Aarhus convention.

Figure 5.3 (*Continued*)

'Never mind, it's not a good idea' 169

During three years of co-operation, the Fridtjof Nansen Institute has provided us with information, experiences from the Norwegian implementation of its obligations into national regulations and legislation. Among the issues discussed have been the Norwegian regulations concerning environmental impact assessments; as we here in Armenia still need to do a lot in this area of environmental regulation. Another issue discussed has been the unique Norwegian Environmental Information Act, which has secured the rights and obligations under the Aarhus convention. Under the CBD, the Cartagena Protocol on Biosafety has been a challenge to implement into law in the Republic of Armenia. The draft now sent to the National Parliament, is largely based on the Norwegian way of implementing it into law. It is our hope that this process can be succeeded by other legislative changes after advice from our Norwegian partners.

For these and several other reasons, we are pleased that the Fridjof Nansen Institute whish to continue their project in Armenia. The project will further seek to strengthen the three areas described above. In particular, the Institute's proposed focus on the implementation process of the Aarhus convention in policies and legislation, as well as awareness-raising among the environmental management sector in the regions are seen as very welcome. We look forward to continue our cooperation with our Norwegian partner on these and other issues in 2009 and into the future.

Sincerely,

Artashes Ziroyan

Figure 5.3 Facsimile of the letter sent to FNI by the Armenian Ministry of Nature Protection stating the ministry's continued support for the project.
Source: Fridtjof Nansen Institute (FNI).

Considering that the ministry had probably needed help to write the letter, I submitted a few paragraphs containing strategically important aspects in support of our project. Since it would accompany our project proposal, it was indeed crucial. Yet, as I stressed in the email to the ministry, they were free to edit, delete and add whatever they wanted. The support letter was signed and faxed to FNI in January 2009, approximately three weeks before the submission deadline. I cannot say that I was particularly surprised when the letter of support turned out to be more or less as I had drafted it. Again, it was an example of how 'we tactically conspire to misrepresent'.[31] At least it seems reasonable to interpret this as a performative aspect of project collaboration. Both sides – FNI and the MNP – together with the Norwegian MFA, are probably aware that many letters of cooperation come about in a similar fashion. Yet such letters are instrumental in getting project proposals approved.

At first glance, the Ministry obviously wanted to improve our chances of obtaining project grants by showing that we had credible and interested local partners to work with. Nevertheless, the manner in which these letters came about tells us a lot about the inner logic and workings of the project world. Whatever the motivation, letters of support have a few defining characteristics: they establish links between the implementation of the project and improved environmental management in Armenia. They express gratitude to FNI (and thus to the Norwegian MFA) for the project. They affirm that participation is broad and representative (which in many ways it was). And they underscore the temporal continuity of the project. In other words, they are instances of networking by use of documents,[32] in which the project world 'constructs' a unity that can hardly be said to reflect the situation on the ground. The manageable reality that projects construct in this way can be understood as the performative aspect of projects.

The process of acquiring and producing support letters is testimony to the view that success or failure depends on the wider network of support one is able to drum up.[33] As a project-within-a-project, the process of obtaining the support letter was successful to the extent that it enabled us to apply for funding once more in accordance with the official guidelines. In essence, the support letter invoked a network – although it probably overstated the network's importance and level of integration and cooperation. On the other hand, one may wonder whether the process of acquiring this support letter and thus establishing and reconfirming the Armenia project's wider support network was not in itself an act of reciprocity with the entire process proving perhaps that officials at the ministry trusted FNI and knew that by being flexible on this point, the ministry could still claim to be part of an international project.

However, relations with local authorities can lead to disturbing affiliations, as this following incident indicates. A week or so before the 2008 seminar, an Armenian journalist was beaten up on the streets. Edik Bhagdasaryan was hospitalized the day after he published an article about alleged acts of nepotism by the previous RA Minister of Nature Protection, Ayvazyan. The attack sparked protests outside the prosecutor's office in Yerevan – on the first day of the seminar. Several seminar participants skipped the last part and the following dinner to show their solidarity with the hospitalized journalist. As it turned out, the anchoring of the Armenia project went all the way up to former minister Ayvazyan. FNI's first letter to the RA MNP, sent in 2006, suggesting the development project had been addressed to Ayvazyan and received a positive reply. These letters of support also demonstrate the self-referential order such projects can end up being.[34]

Standard solutions such as LOG frames are examples of turning complexity into manageable chunks and share in many ways a common denominator in their susceptibility to scalable claims. These scalable claims find their expression – among other ways – in anchoring. The efforts to anchor the project, and the resulting letters of cooperation, are ritual reminders of the different scalable claims of Europeanization and democratization as well as standardized managerial practices. These letters of cooperation therefore become a concrete embodiment of the scalable claims and as such can be seen as having performative qualities.

The way ahead – time for critical understanding

Our seminars in Armenia in 2006–10 often had a final section hosted by FNI's director named 'The Way Ahead', where participants were given a chance to discuss how they intended to use their recently acquired knowledge in their daily work. They could also discuss their ideas on the future direction of Armenian environmental management (obstacles and achievements) and the project itself (shortcomings and successes). After the final seminar in Tzaghadzor in September 2010 and the following financial closure of the project while I was still on fieldwork in Yerevan, it was time to think about whether FNI should try to prolong the project and submit a new proposal to the MFA. In other words, it was time to consider whether the 'way ahead' for myself and FNI also included the extension of the 'Armenia project'.

Over the years, an inbuilt tension in the Armenia project became apparent as year after year FNI had little else to offer than a repetition of last year's activities, with some minor alterations and improvements. We had to justify our approach by balancing our claims of modest progress with explaining why it was still necessary to proceed more or less as before:

> As the seminar systematically focused on Armenia's international commitments it was the first of its kind in Armenia as it also focused on the need to achieve a mutual understanding across management sectors. ... That such a seminar was conducted was highly appreciated by the participants who at the same time maintained there was a need to continue. ... A future challenge would be to reach out to an even broader section of the Armenian management sector, in order to foster a broader understanding for the need for sector integration and mainstreaming. ... Like many other post-Soviet states, Armenia's bureaucratic structure is distinctly vertical with only limited contact between corresponding management levels across sectors within the government structure. This illustrates the need for a continued emphasis on horizontal sector integration, a field in which Norway is a pioneer and can thus contribute its experiences.[35]

To call this 2006 seminar the first of its kind in Armenia obviously depends on how other environment-related seminars are characterized and bracketed. What we were told was that the Armenians were happy to take part in a seminar in Armenia focusing solely on Armenia, rather than being lumped together with Azerbaijani and Georgian officials somewhere in Georgia (the only place to meet, given Armenia and Azerbaijan's conflict over Nagorny Karabakh). At FNI, we incorporated in our project a catchphrase I had often heard at MFA meetings: 'in areas where Norway has comparative advantages'. The paragraph above is but one example of a text in which we endeavoured to bring the project closer to what we believed were the prevalent perceptions and signposts at the MFA, thus increasing the likelihood of a favourable response, instead of considering the Armenian situation per se.

Until 2010, FNI's annual Armenia applications in the years 2005–8 and a two-year project in 2009 had all been approved. For this reason, during the last months of my stay in Yerevan, in the autumn of 2010, I visited possible partner organizations to explore the avenues such a project might take. But more important was my discomfort with the Armenia project in the first place. When I arrived in Armenia in September 2006, I knew little about the project I had agreed to manage. During the first few days in Yerevan, I met Karen at his home and at the ministry and drove around with him in his car. At that moment in time it was all about practicalities and preparations for the seminar commencing a few days later. After just a few days in the unfamiliar country of Hayk (the legendary patriarch and founder of the Armenian nation), I felt ill prepared to resolve these practicalities.

When I first managed to turn my attention to the project design, it felt strangely familiar. It was 'democracy export' and 'capacity building' all over again. I was expected to be one of the agents, albeit a rather unwilling one. At a seminar FNI hosted in Armenia, we sat outside one evening drinking beers and chatting around a fire. Together with an FNI colleague, we joked a bit about the early days and the upcoming field excursion. We soon realized that we shared a perception of the project design and its validity or soundness. We simply did not believe Armenia could learn much from listening to what had been done in Norway. Yet here we were, having a good time and enjoying getting acquainted with a new country, feeding our academic interests in environmental management and post-Soviet challenges of various sorts.

But the challenges facing Armenia required far more than we could offer. Of course, no one expected the Armenia project to revolutionize Armenia's environmental management sector. But expectations were running high all the same and the project did generate some positive feedback. The OSCE was also eager to stress the importance of the project and, as a project partner, had issued several press releases to that effect, as well as lauding the network it facilitated; see Figure 5.4. Still, the project had been conceived because the Norwegian MFA was looking for projects in the South Caucasus. One of the reasons FNI

Organization for Security and Co-operation in Europe
Office in Yerevan

Environmental governance issues discussed on municipal level with OSCE office support

TSAKHKADZOR, Armenia, 5 Noveber 2009 –Municipal challenges for environmental governance were in the focus of a two-day seminar, "Securing environmental rights at the municipal level - implementing the Aarhus Convention in Armenia" that ended today in Tsakhkadzor, Armenia.

Representatives of municipal authorities, public environmental information Aarhus centres, regional environmental organizations and NGOs discussed ways to address environmental issues at full capacity at an event organized by the Fridtjof Nansen Institute with the support of the OSCE Office in Yerevan in co-operation with, the Ministries of Nature Protection and Territorial Administration.

"Effective environmental protection includes transparent and accountable management of environmental issues at local level. I believe joint efforts with the local authorities and public participation will help secure environmental rights both at local and national levels," said Christoph Opfermann, Economic and Environemntal Officer at the OSCE Office.

"Effective municipal governance is essential to the country's environmental protection policy. This seminar was helpful to outline effective environmental governance approaches and practical co-operation with the civil society representatives to address environmental problems in the regions of Armenia," said Ashot Giloyan, Head of Sef-governmental Bodies, Ministry of Territorial Administration

The international experts from Fritjof Nansen Institute delivered lectures on the international practice of environmental governance and transparency and accountability tools. "We hope that the knowledge of international governance tools will contribute to the ongoing policy reform of self-government bodies," said Peter Johan Schei, the Director of Fritjof Nansen Institute.

The OSCE supports the implementation of the Aarhus Convention on access to information, public participation in decision-making and access to justice in environmental matters and values them as positive contributions to democratic, effective and good governance.

For more information, you can contact Gayane Ter-Stepanyan, Senior Press and Public Information Assistant, at (+374 10) 22 96 10/ 11/12/13/14 ext. 5407, mobile (091) 012603.

Figure 5.4 OSCE press release.
Source: OSCE Yerevan Office.

chose Armenia was that we could use Nansen's heritage as a bridge to forge contacts with the authorities. So the project idea and inception came about as a result of Norwegian-based motivations, rather than Armenian needs. This is probably fairly normal in the world of international development projects. Although we did not modify the project concept very much, apart from sprucing it up to satisfy the changing requirements of the Norwegian MFA, and we identified new partners in a more or less haphazard way, whatever we were doing was not responding to local needs.

I therefore decided not to press the matter further vis-à-vis the MFA. My stance was clearly accepted and understood by my peers and superiors at FNI. What remained was to write the final report and submit it to the MFA together with the financial accounts. In 2012 FNI was told by the MFA that, on the basis of the submitted reports, accounts and achievements, the project was officially 'closed'.

According to Mosse, projects are unsuccessful not because they fail to turn 'designs into reality' but because there is a 'disarticulation between practices, their rationalizing models and overarching policy frameworks'.[36] This 'disarticulation' is probably akin to the ruptures I discussed above between the project as policy idea and as operational system. My decision to advise against applying for yet another year of funding was partly rooted in my perception of the widening disconnect between what the project claimed to be doing as formulated in the LOG frame and what it was doing on the ground. In the end, the gap was impossible to sustain. Yet this disarticulation – to use Mosse's phrase – in the case of the Armenia project was also *necessary* for the project to be implemented. It was both a prerequisite of implementation and, in the end, an obstacle to its continuation. We saw above how the foreign office instigated a reformulation of the impact the project was expected to achieve. The small-scale project had to promote an idea of helping Armenia institute legislative reforms. It very soon became clear that this intention could not be communicated to Armenian authorities and legal experts. The stated long-term impact belonged in the LOG-frame hierarchy and nowhere else. Had I sought to align the project as a policy idea and as an operational system, we would have run into problems and even insulted some of our Armenian partners – as well as making ourselves look like naive agents of change with an exaggerated view of FNI's capacity to promote and instigate change. While the notion of the project as both representation and operational system may explain our ability to juggle different policy perceptions and actual implementation practices, disarticulations such as these in projects may, for whatever reasons, have had rather different consequences in the shorter and longer terms.

Armenia in Aidland

The contradictory Sevan case and allegations of corruption indicate a complex situation that is likely to render the entire Armenia project either futile or at least unworkable. Armenia may be one of those places where it is impossible for 'good policy' to thrive.[37] In project terms, we had to constitute and reassemble this knowledge into manageable slices of reality. The complexity is indicative of the critical political challenges facing various sectors of the Armenian environmental management system and the practice of nepotism. The task of the project was rather to convert these critical political issues into technicalities so as to make the entire situation acceptable and manageable in project terms. The obvious way of reassembling them under the LOG frame was to posit the issue of corruption and nepotism as risks. In one of the project proposals submitted to the MFA, we wrote about the risk of corruption and how some of our partners seemed to occupy (many) different roles with shifting alliances. FNI tackled the risk of indirect involvement with possibly corrupt government officials by discussing allegations of corruption in Armenia and seeking to alleviate the risk by vetting who FNI worked with:

> Corruption is a serious problem in Armenia, especially in the Ministry of Nature Protection (FNI's partner) according to some, where officials are said to demand 'fees' to approve projects. This is obviously not well documented. FNI tackled the problem by maintaining close contact with Transparency International Armenia, while our relations with OSCE meant that we have a reliable international partner. In practical terms, all transfers of money were preceded by documentation in terms of receipts.[38]

The important point for the purpose of my analysis is, however, how FNI invoked the network as something that could free us of the risk of involvement in corrupt practices. By incorporating these steps into the LOG frame as indicators of risk, I was able to convert the political question into a matter of technicality.[39] The contradictions related to the Sevan case were smoothed over simply by changing the venue of the seminars, whereas invoking the network within the project and specifically the capacities of the Transparency International Anticorruption Center in Armenia was, in a sense, to acknowledge and authorize their knowledge as beneficial to the project.[40] In terms of project as policy idea, discussed in Chapter 4, the project managed to account for, acknowledge and minimize some of the risks in a way similar to how we had performed the logistics of the LOG frame. This reassembling of project as operational system in order to bring it closer to project as policy idea was, at this juncture, critical to maintaining the connection between the project as a coherent policy idea and as an operational system.[41]

In one sense, it could have worked as an invitation to revisit the anthropological literature on the social life of projects and development professionals,[42] with its captivating descriptions of development professionals.[43] But by focusing on 'Aidland' and the social life of development projects, are we at risk of reifying the aid and development world with our ethnographies of development professionals diverting attention from the power relations imbued in development aid and the wider political and material effects of development?[44] 'Aidland', Elizabeth Harrison writes, 'although often portrayed as a bubble, is in fact not one at all.'[45] But while Aidland might look like somewhere else (imaginary, virtual), it is very real.[46] Harrison's critique is not of the 'Aidland genre' itself, but it concerns the over-preoccupation of certain elements within it: 'development professionals', their hopes, fears, ambitions, relationships and so on.[47] We should look at partnerships and brokerage, she proposes.

A post-socialist contribution here is that of Janine Wedel, who emphasizes the need for 'studying through' when accumulating what she calls 'Aidnographies'.[48] This is rather different from the Aidland genre insofar as Wedel is less concerned with the professionals themselves and more with the social networks they make up. By studying through, as she advises, you can explore a given development project from the viewpoint of the donor and recipient, by moving back and forth between the two.[49] In order to understand aid professionals and target populations using a common framework, assemblage theory has plenty to offer: 'To assemble this heterogeneous set of interests requires … forging alignments, rendering technical, authorizing knowledge, managing failures and contradictions, reposing political questions and reassembling as the ground shifts.'[50] The alignments forged in my ethnographic material are between the Norwegian MFA and FNI as donor and implementer, respectively, and the local project partners (the ministries and OSCE office). In short, the project is *networked* and rendered technical through project documents, [51] work plans and seminar programmes, as something perfectly 'doable'. Knowledge is authorized and legitimized discursively through the relative recurrence and network efforts within policy documents, project proposals, reports and narratives.

The Armenia project: Formalities and informalities

In this and the previous chapter we have undertaken a tour around the inside of a Norwegian development project in Armenia, highlighting how the Norwegian-funded project operated in a particular Armenian context of social practices, networks and contentious issues. Yet one of the main defining characteristics of the project was the ethos of policy making and its legitimation at the Norwegian MFA. Hence, we should ask not only how development projects are managed but also how they are often driven by policies, principles and practices that are external to the 'problem' the project is meant to solve, and how they fail to take the local situation, local perceptions and local needs into account.

There are structural, hierarchical and managerial issues that are of more interest than the mere role of the project manager. The world of assemblages that I found myself in was one where the most convenient and, in fact, only acceptable mode of operation was to adhere to storylines of an underdeveloped civil society in a post-Soviet state, of bad governance and so on. This conception was then transferred to a fairly reasonable LOG-frame hierarchy in which the project assumed responsibility for changing and improving environmental governance in Armenia. That these changes might require far more than any one project could achieve matters less than that the project through the identification of long-term impacts, outputs and inputs assumes this responsibility. In a sense, then, it was the project as a response to the LOG-frame requirements that assumed this responsibility and created this possibility, even though the project management team and the Armenian partners largely considered it to be unfeasible. That does not matter so much as long as the formal structure allowed the project to be portrayed as a manageable project space. It looks good to claim that one is able to 'improve the environmental situation' in Armenia. The agenda was set in Norway rather than in Armenia. FNI, alongside OSCE, the Norwegian MFA and others, was just one of the multitude of organizations carrying out projects to improve and modernize Armenia. FNI, in Li's words, acted as an alternative schemer to the state.[52]

My main point of criticism has obviously been on how reliance on managerial principles in development projects encourages a perspective from which processes of social change are viewed more or less as universals which are scaled up when circumstances necessitate.[53] While contextual specifics are not entirely disregarded, they are certainly not considered to the fullest extent. Development agencies and ministries are well aware of differences in time and place and the need to include them when implementing projects (or when formulating policy documents or calls for proposals, for that matter). Yet the managerial perspective so in fashion today – its main tool being the LOG frame – does not allow project designers to use this knowledge. The point I wish to stress here is that the process of legitimation depends not only on project practices but also to a large degree on the scalability of the project. But this very scalability moved the project even further away from the challenges it was devised to overcome. The project can be seen as entailing performative actions, either pertaining to the management and LOG frame, or to their actual implementation. Performativity gives no preferentiality to words over things, or vice versa.[54] Both aspects are real and come to life through the project networks of documents and in project spaces.

Through the project proposals, FNI deployed 'strategies of extraversion' in order to accommodate the project to policy guidelines and more or less direct orders from MFA officials at various meetings.[55] Did FNI exercise expertise or cunning? Or was it perhaps just the art of adjusting to changing policies? This was how the Armenia project was initiated – or could at least be portrayed – as developmental hope, even though it ended up as politics. The attempt in the preceding chapters was to offer some critical reflections on this.

The Armenia project involved donors, NGOs and others in a modernizing scheme, making Scott's critique of states relevant to the international aid system as well.[56] International organizations such as the OSCE and the World Wide Fund for Nature (WWF), I suggest, have gained the upper hand by offering access to financial mechanisms to the comparatively weak Armenian MNP. Armenia is a state where NGOs operate as modernizing forces and where 'democracy has become a project'.[57] The country is the target of Europeanization projects from different sides and actors characterized by the construction of project spaces that are manageable slices of reality. At least, that is the picture presented in the project documents. Whether these slices are manageable in practice is another question.

Development policy acts to 'legitimize rather than to orientate practice', and developments are mostly driven by organizations' need to maintain relationships.[58] The FNI–MFA relationship is also a practice in which certain policy ideas and systems of representation are maintained.[59] Seen merely as a collection of inconsequential, haphazard and ill-managed micro-practices, the project could be understood as an atypical failure, an underscoring of the need to put prospective project partners and project proposals through a stricter vetting process. This will ultimately lead – at least if the Norwegian MFA continues on the same track – to an even greater focus on the LOG frame. Yet, perhaps the opposite should happen. We need perhaps to rethink the development cooperation industry and set the practitioners free, rather than using projects as justifications for donor policies. The chapters on the project details can doubtless be read as the triumph of politics/administration over hope, where critical understanding played no significant role.

Project spaces and networks

In total, the different Armenia projects funded by the MFA and undertaken by FNI resulted in five seminars, the enrolment of a group of South Caucasian students to a Norwegian summer school, five cycles of lectures at Armenian universities, loads of preparatory meetings and perhaps a better understanding in Armenia of the challenges facing the country in the environmental management sector.

While this chapter has been devoted to practices at project level, in Chapter 4 we saw how requirements to accommodate policy guidelines and reporting cycles led the project somewhat off course. It mirrors the view of post-Soviet realities in which politics rather than practicalities govern the implementation and conception of success or failure in foreign aid reform programmes.[60] To return to the vocabulary of Tsing, the project was one of global connection, with lots of sticky engagements.[61] As development agencies and ministries set out to unroll and provide support for development projects, they tend to force practitioners and participants, I have argued, into a management framework that ignores the local context.

This chapter has addressed project implementation practices close to the ground and interpreted them as constituting contested professional and social project spaces. Focus has also been on how strictly formal and professional project activities are accompanied by a life of sociality. This is but one way in which networks are made and maintained in development projects. It was necessary to downplay this social aspect of project life in the project proposals, yet it had a significance of its own in the actual implementation of the project. It is perhaps the flipside of the professional network. I have argued that the concept of performativity helps us analyse project participants (donors, implementers and recipients) under a common framework.[62] Whatever reasons and motivations people may have as participants, scales are conjured and proposed, assemblages applied and alliances forged from both sides of the development encounter.

Conclusion

The preceding discussion has sought to analyse where Armenia finds itself, between international environmental politics, foreign aid projects and Europeanization. Throughout this book I have discussed two tightly interwoven threads of ethnographic data. The first concerns the environmental activism in Armenia, which seeks to tie itself to European processes related to the Aarhus Convention. The second concerns the Norwegian-funded Armenia project targeting Armenian authorities and organizations involved in environmental management. As I suggested early on, this field consists of engagements situated in various places including Armenia as a signatory and party to the Aarhus Convention; Armenia as an 'object' of and participant in bilateral development projects together with Norway; and fields and sites in Armenia where 'environmental rights' are contested. Yet this field is interconnected ethnographically and socially through many of the same people. Anush, Hasmik, Hermine and Ashot were all active participants in the Aarhus-related issues and the Armenia project. The Convention and the development project were further interrelated thematically.

This can be understood as a distributed network and something with which anthropologists can engage. We can conceive of a network, I have argued, in a way that encapsulates the multiple connections within it, its fluidity and its flexibility. Together with a conceptual framework developed to sidestep binary oppositions such as insider/outsider and donor/recipient, this has enabled me to better understand the field in question and the relationship between me as analyst and what I have observed and taken part in.[1] I have, for instance, attempted to show how environmental rights in Armenia are conjured, performed, created, negotiated and acted out in practice. As I said before, different actors make claims to the same universals for competing purposes and what has interested me is how these claims are put to use in practice and embedded in practices that crisscross local, regional and global arenas.

The practices related to the Arhus Convention in Armenia consist first of the legitimization of the Arhus Convention and its institutional proliferation in Armenia and second of the streetwise and document-wise practices of concerned citizens and coalitions of Armenian non-governmental organizations (NGOs) in making use of the Convention's provisions and mechanisms to launch protests and campaigns against mining projects and other issues. The implementation of the Armenia project, funded by Norwegian authorities, entailed reporting practices and dialogues between donor and implementer in Norway, as well as specific project spaces and practices in Armenia.

One of the things that puzzled me from the very beginning was how 'the locals', who ostensibly are at the receiving end in Armenia, took such an active part in forming, interpreting and making use of new entitlements by establishing networks and connecting themselves to wider narratives and imaginaries of the global, the environment, development and Europe. Here, we can see the active participation of the 'objects' of change. I also noted the disconnect between the Armenia project and the Armenian situation it was meant to alleviate. It was as if the Armenians were mere bit players in an international project.

The various topics I have analysed were conceptualized as anthropological problems. Anthropological problems, we remember, constitute a historical place that is contingent on a more general situation comprising scientific knowledge and political actors. Armenia's environmental politics and practices have been the object and site of this thinking and these practices, as indeed has the development project I have discussed. I myself am part of the project, a member of the network and a contributor to the thinking behind it and its legitimation. These networks of persons, things, documents and laws we should not take for granted; nor should we refrain from questioning their premises. In fact, the things that usually are taken for granted are very often the real anthropological problems. None of the objects, sites, networks and thinking I have attempted to analyse has any primacy over the others. Much as project descriptions, according to Green, represent slices of reality,[2] I have opted to analyse slices within different fields, or perhaps more to the point, as fragments. In doing so I have been able to portray specific encounters that take place within documents, on the streets, in project logical frameworks (LOG frames) and in project spaces. Together, they form social and professional spaces and networks that at times reside more in documents and seminars than in social life. Let me distil the findings as I addressed four research questions and topics corresponding to the four empirical chapters.

The Aarhus Convention as a project of scale in Armenia

The question underpinning the discussion related to the Aarhus Convention conceived as a modernization project, how we can understand it as a social and political process of scale making and how it played out in Armenia.

The Aarhus Convention was analysed in terms of the networks it gives rise to in Armenia. We understand institutions and knowledge practices (or backgrounds and competence practices) that generate effects in a tautological, self-reflective way.[3] The Meetings of Parties (MoPs) are patterned processes of intention of pan-European reach, familiar in their regularity, with each new MoP adding a new layer to the pattern of Aarhus practices. The institutions and practices are not given; rather, they are the result of the continuous work being performed in Armenia, at the MoPs and elsewhere. The Convention is claimed to be pan-European, an indication of the ambitious scale that is invoked throughout the Convention by politicians and environmentalists alike. For Armenia, the Aarhus Convention is part and parcel of the republic's effort at becoming a truly European democracy, at being 'Europeanized'. This has spurred practices and networks and involved a range of domestic as well as international actors, such as the OSCE in Armenia. The Aarhus Convention, with its institutional offshoots in Armenia and elsewhere, is a process of scale making, specifically claiming to Europeanize Armenia. Through the analysis of the ethnography of international meetings and law texts, the Aarhus Centre in Hrazdan and the role of the focal point, I have tried to show the breadth, magnitude and sheer reach of the process of Europeanization.

The Aarhus Convention redefines expertise and reappropriates it in new forms, forms that Armenian environmentalists were eager to seize upon. This is evident in the claims, performativity, agency and participation of actors such as Ashot at one of the Aarhus Centres and Anush in OSCE, but also of Hasmik (the focal point and NGO entrepreneur). It feeds into the argument of how a convention based on neo-liberal assumptions of democracy is filled with hope and leads to discursive and institutional proliferation in Armenia. Resistance to and participation in this process by numerous Armenian networks, institutions and individuals are a sign – I have argued – of the reach of the assemblage and agency required for the Convention to become part of the Armenian environmental discourse. In Armenia, central powers and peripheral activists, movements, institutions and practices are forged together through the dreams and claims pertaining to environmental rights. Agency was also a keyword here inasmuch as I have employed post-socialist readings of 'transition' in this ethnography. Agency is at times inadequately accounted for in some of the post-socialist literature on democratization; there is a tendency either to portray people as cynically adapting to donor priorities or to perceive them as passive recipients. Better then to interpret these NGO activists and others by making use of the literature on networks and performativity in other strands of anthropology. Realizing this led me to understand the proficient practices of the network participants as adaptive claims to the environmental rights assemblage without passing moral judgement.

The Aarhus Convention appears in Armenia in a contingent form that comes to matter not only through institutional proliferation but especially due to the claims and participation of involved actors such as Hasmik, Anush and Ashot.

Multiple arenas and activism

The next question I explored concerned the ways in which Armenian civil society uses domestic and international mechanisms in order to make its networks real and where this takes place. I found that Armenian activists deploy their strategies to change environmental management practices in Armenia through the assemblage of environmental rights. This happens through a variety of activities involving several actors and varying degrees of formal organization. The coalitions of grassroots movements and NGOs that are also willing to take complaints to the domestic courts and the Compliance Committee of the Arhus Convention are revealing of the dynamic network of Armenian civil society.

These practices range from street protests, such as the Save Teghut protest in the centre of Yerevan, to court cases and international arbitration. Not being particularly successful in achieving the desired results, these activists, I have argued, are partly subjects of liberalism while imagining it as freedom. Bringing the case before the compliance mechanism involves a significant number of documents, creating a correspondence that in itself is a 'collective patterning of intention',[4] although the involved actors may not necessarily share the same intentions. Their efforts never amounted to much; they suffered numerous setbacks in domestic courtrooms and in regard to MoP decisions in the international arena. The relationships and connections between people and organizations and grass roots are fluid and filled with incidents in which what we usually refer to as 'locals' or suchlike make use of the scales, establish and exploit networks, and in this way change not only the situation in Armenia but also instigate practices at the Compliance Committee. It all turns out to be a matter of process, writing to the Compliance Committee, awaiting its response and then in the next round the response of the Armenian government to the Committee's findings.

Environmental rights are claimed, networked, performed and made to matter through court cases, references to the Convention text and street protests. It happens with reference to a large scale, and we should also think of the Aarhus Convention as a heterogeneous phenomenon inasmuch as it is acted out in local settings rather than being conceived of as a universal.

The street and court actions in which the activists were involved are indicative not only of the multiple ways in which Armenian activists fought for a reversal in the Teghut case but also of how the environmentalists are able to scale up their demands. The activists know they may use laws and rights to foster change. As activists in Armenia, while campaigning on a transnational arena, they challenge the relationship between the global, the nation state and civil society.

A key finding is that the Aarhus Convention, which was a project of hope ('pan-European legal space'), in effect was transformed into a project of technicalities, administration and politics and setbacks with meagre results.

Project practices legitimating development policies

At this point, the book homed in on the Armenia project to determine the extent to which project reporting cycles and adjustments affected, legitimated and altered project implementation. As I argued there, the project can be seen as consisting of two things in one: as a policy idea and as an operational system. These aspects of project life can be considered as analytically distinct, perhaps to a surprising extent. Even though there had been a certain disconnect from the start between the project's representation in documents and actual project practices, this gap between idea and operational system continued to expand. By accepting the change in the LOG-frame hierarchy – a precondition of continued funding – the project grew increasingly distant from the Armenian reality it was meant to improve.

Another of the desired outcomes – as regards the funding ministry in Norway – of projects in Armenia was to maintain a minimum of bilateral contact between Armenia and Norway. This was not accounted for or itemized in the LOG frame. It served rather as a tacit, informal reason to back Norwegian development interventions in Armenia. It was also one of the informal motivations and policies giving the development project legitimacy. The reasons for maintaining bilateral relations with Armenia were spelled out at information meetings, yet they are nowhere to be found in the guidelines. What does this tell us? Policies work if they are legitimated by projects such as this and projects are more likely to be considered successful if they adhere to the same storylines as the donor. Requests arising from the changes to the LOG-frame hierarchy had a greater effect on how the project was portrayed than on how it was implemented in Armenia. As an exercise in Europeanization, the focus of Norway's support for the project, as administered by the Ministry of Foreign Affairs (MFA), was on how Armenia could become a liberal European state.

The Armenia project was tailored to suit MFA priorities, instrumentally speaking, more than it was to suit the less tangible 'local needs'. The Armenia project is but one to successfully deploy the scale assumptions and collude with the ethos of the donor's call through a performance in LOG framing and collaboration. Europe was performed through the LOG-frame alterations that barely had an impact on project practices. In a way, the project became a technicality.

Formal requirements in project auditing and documentation led to the creation of project goals that were unattainable and had little to do with actual project practices and needs. The two aspects of project life nurtured each other and – when the rift became too wide and long-lasting – caused the end of the project.

Social and professional project spaces – made and maintained

Finally, I sought to investigate how networks and project spaces are made and maintained through development projects. The project funded by the MFA resulted in five seminars, the attendance of a group of South Caucasian students at a Norwegian summer school, five cycles of lectures at Armenian universities, loads of preparatory meetings and perhaps a better understanding in Armenia of the challenges facing the country in the environmental management sector.

The practices depicted rest on project performances and regularity (seminars, annual study trips), competence, background knowledge (terms of reference, applications and experience) and discursive and material factors ('helping the post-Soviet states' and financial means). I explored how strictly formal and professional project activities are accompanied by a life of sociality. The Armenia project constituted contested professional and social project spaces in which networks are made and maintained. It was necessary to downplay the social aspects in the project proposals, yet they had an impact of their own on the implementation of the project. This sociality is perhaps the flipside of the professional network. Whatever the reasons and motivations people may have as participants, project scales are conjured and proposed, assemblages applied and alliances forged through participation from both sides of the development encounter.

By perpetuating the aid relationship, the transition between past and present is 'suspended' and may even be prolonged.[5] We are thus left with the question of whether our efforts to 'do good' are actually doing harm. By perpetuating the aid relationship, Armenia is suspended between past and present.

Armenia is a state where 'democracy has become a project'.[6] Armenia is undergoing processes of Europeanization operated by different sides and different actors constructing project spaces that are manageable slices of reality. The project spaces resulting from foreign aid and the project cooperation support mechanisms are constructed so as to be manageable, while their legitimization, as we remember, relies on striving for goals and impacts that are – in the end – unattainable. The concepts these projects introduce, or are surrounded by, are not neutral: 'civil society', 'democratization', 'capacity building', 'international obligations', 'good governance' and 'anti-corruption' should be treated as empirical objects rather than merely taken as given. As such, this project can be understood as part of a wider scale-making project. Projects are sites of social and institutional reproduction in which,[7] I argued, a specific story of international relations and post-Cold War rhetoric is told: the West won, now you are welcome to become like us.

Environmental and developmental crossroads

From the use of the Aarhus compliance mechanism to the particulars of the small-scale Armenia project, I have described various projects of scale that ultimately 'perceive' Armenia as moving ever closer towards Europe – coaxing Armenia into the European fold. This is a process involving several actors. With regard to the Aarhus Convention, they are the United Nations Economic Commission for Europe and the Compliance Committee, along with Armenian environmentalists. With regard to the Armenia project, project participants, project managers and the donor play active roles. It is this participation, external and internal, that I have been at pains to shed light on.

In the chapters on the Aarhus Convention I mainly discussed agency and participation in hope, where hope mutates into politics, procedural issues and performances of environmentalism. On the same note, the development project morphed into standardized items and technicalities through LOG framing and finally through a network of people, project spaces and documents. These issues are expressions of how modernization schemes are assembled into contingent forms. I sought to develop a framework that allowed me to analyse the influence of both outsiders and insiders in the field in question. It is a field where my informants, I and others take part not merely as professionals but also in a professional guise when we participate in various networks: people meet and interact via email, celebrate each other's capacities in letters of cooperation, and so on.

Obviously, this analysis could have been done differently. I could, for instance, have focused more narrowly on the role of activists, their social life, activities, relations and aspirations. What I believe is a quite novel feature of my analysis was inspired by Stephen Collier and what he said about immersing oneself in the fieldwork and how it may reveal 'critical nodes', highlighting central powers and connections whose intelligibility is to be found beyond the initial point.[8] Ethnography, despite certain fixtures, leads in many directions within the distributed network. What from the start looked like an Armenian 'problem' located within Armenia proved instead to be a plethora of networks, affiliations and projects created elsewhere and related to certain aspects of neo-liberalism and the Europeanization of Armenia.

The analysis has shown how Europe as an idea in Armenia, the legal dead ends encountered by environmentalists, LOG-frame gymnastics and project spaces add up to assemblages to which insiders and outsiders, politicians and activists, and NGOs and project managers attach themselves and claim adherence. In this sense, Armenia finds itself at what I call a Eurovironmental crossroads. I have sought to show how Armenian activists claim adherence to the idea of Europe and how the Norwegian government is involved in Armenia through development projects, a country with which Norway has limited bilateral relations. Both in the description of the Armenia project and with regard to the Aarhus Convention, the analyses have shown how 'we', in various ways, adapt to mechanisms designed in locations far from Armenia (the project mechanism in the Norwegian MFA and the Aarhus Convention). Besides being linked thematically, the Aarhus-related processes and the Armenia project involved many of the same people, organizations and institutions. The way in which the Armenia project attached itself to reporting procedures stemming from Armenia's non-compliance with the Aarhus Convention, by claiming these scheduled reports as indicators of the Armenia project's achievements, indicates the interconnectedness and fluidity of these networks and processes.

Through various and certainly asymmetrically empowered agencies, we act in order to attain certain goals. European politicians and institutions want to advance the regional mainstreaming of environmental management, whereas environmental activists want to stop the mining at Teghut through the use of the Aarhus Convention. Concerning the development project, the Norwegian MFA seeks legitimation of Norwegian development policies in the post-Soviet area, and the Fridtjof Nansen Institute (FNI) is involved in project acquisition.

The conceptual framework was based on the notions of scales and assemblages. What I have discussed shows that what we cannot accept is the notion of global structures as somehow existing outside practices; what makes practices observable are rather claims to scale and universals. I have attempted to show how claims work practically, for instance, how Armenian activists used the assemblage of environmental rights and specific regional measures to articulate their claims in a manner and language that would have been unthinkable before the ratification of the Aarhus Convention in 2001. This is the level, with its various sites, projects, seminars, organizations, and policies and documents, at which these claims are put forward and assemblages negotiated, that I have focused on in my analysis.

The Aarhus Convention and its compliance mechanism are used by Armenian environmentalists to foster change at home, and although the Convention text is finite, interpretations of it are not. And as the example of the development project indicated, the relationship between donors' needs, implementers' capacity, willingness to change and local practices is a complicated one that in many cases confuses the order of the legitimation process. The point here is that, as a discursive formation, 'civil society', 'transparency' and 'environmental rights' are systematized and conceived in such a way that problems and notions are transferred and thought about in a similar fashion.[9]

The various claims and counterclaims with regard to environmental rights can also be seen as a kind of performance. The performativity takes place in very different settings and places. From the level of grassroots mobilization on the streets, via petitions and court cases, to the international level of the Compliance Committee and MoPs of the Aarhus Convention, there is a common feature whereby the Convention and environmental rights are invoked in reference to claims that rights have been abused. The same analytical toolkit was employed on the Norwegian-funded project and how it can be understood as a project of scale, with its focus on the LOG-frame approach and 'Europeanization' of Armenia. This has largely been considered as a practice in which the MFA and FNI construct, contribute to and collude with networks in Armenia and beyond.

I have shown how such schemes work and involve the participation of both sides of the development encounter. Europe and other assemblages are claimed and proposed and thus come into being not as objective truths and universals but as phenomena in relation to which politicians, activists, ministries and project managers act. I have construed the events as existential dramas (such as when Armenian activists were denied a standing before the courts) and policy adaptations on autopilot in development projects. These performative aspects adhere to international politics, development policies, environmental activism and project implementation and have different characteristics. I have addressed them under a common framework, as insiders and outsiders that are part of the same networks.

Environmental rights as an assemblage end up as an epistemological experiment in shifting attention away from the situation at hand to legal processes. For instance, when an international NGO showed support for its Armenian partners at MoP-4 in Chisinau, it was support with reference to the alleged infringement of the activists' rights as Armenian citizens, not to the issue of the prospective mining. By relying on and invoking the assemblage of environmental rights, the activists are immersed ever deeper in power relations as prey to liberalism's seductive language, which to them is imagined as freedom.

This is how, at least, the activists, my material suggests, relied on the Aarhus Compliance Committee and the court cases in Armenia in their fight against the Teghut license.

Post-Cold War anthropology

I found inspiration in the proposal that we should engage with and develop a post-Cold War ethnography, one that accumulated and generated comparative insights from the post-colonial and post-socialist areas and intellectual traditions.[10] As mentioned before, an ongoing effect of 'Cold War representations' is the division of intellectual labour between post-colonial studies concerned with parts of the world that were previously European colonies and post-socialist studies concerned with countries that inhabited the space to the east of the Iron Curtain.[11] According to Chari and Verdery, this spatial partition should be replaced with a single analytical field: the post-Cold War field.

In order for this to happen, a few reflections on the Cold War world order are called for. As has been convincingly argued, the capitalist and socialist empires both rested on utopian ideas of modernity.[12] Where capitalist societies were proponents of mass consumption, mass production was the norm in the socialist East. Both were essentially oriented towards the future, as modernist projects. Viewed thus, the Second World is a space of transition, the Third World a space of development. The First World represents the global centre; the Second and Third Worlds are backward and peripheral,[13] albeit in different ways.

So what does my material on a post-Soviet Armenian experience of 'transition' gain from being analysed from the perspectives of a literature that stems primarily from ethnographies from the Global South and development projects? The case of Armenia – as a major development aid recipient per capita – can contribute to the scholarly discourse on studies of post-socialism, development studies and especially the linkages between them and the continuing effects of the Cold War rhetoric.[14] In the analysis of my ethnographic data, I have used insights from post-socialist studies on 'transition' and post-colonial literature on development comparatively, hoping thereby to contribute to the dialogue between area studies (post-socialist Europe and the post-colonial area) but also refusing to accept the intellectual division of labour in the social sciences inherited from the Cold War. Juxtaposing the dominant modernization theory or even 'transitology' with the development critique of post-colonial scholarship,[15] I was better able to understand the Aarhus Convention and how development projects, policies and practices coexist and legitimize each other in perhaps counter-intuitive ways.

My contribution has been to show how 'global', abstract principles and the idea of Europe can attach themselves to specific local settings. We need to acknowledge that such universals do not exist outside or independently of practice; they are articulated and given substance in many different ways and different arenas. This facilitates a fuller understanding of participation, opening up the analytical field. Rather than regarding them as passive recipients where agency and ulterior motives sometimes gain primacy as analytical objects, I have been able to juxtapose the internal workings of the project world with the policies it legitimizes as well as the project spaces it creates.

Hope in development, hope in anthropology, hope in networks

Being in Armenia as an agent of development change was something I found problematic. This book represents an attempt to resolve some of these conundrums. I have understood my own participation in terms of hope alternating with administrative tasks, eventually emerging as critical understanding. The Aarhus Convention and Norwegian development policies are imbued with positivism and modernism while deploying 'concepts of universal prescription (e.g. social capital, civil society, governance) which focus on the institutional deficiencies of underdeveloped places'.[16] But this notion of simply getting 'their' institutions and practices right is a deceptive one. Devising development programmes often requires us in effect to disregard the pervasiveness of inequality and institutional differences.[17]

There is an inherent incompatibility between different modes of knowledge entertained, for instance, by the people who do work for development and the anthropologists who employ critical perspectives.[18] This divide can seem impossible to bridge:

> Academic critics of development are mistaken if they believe that in development good administration and politics is possible, if only meticulous use was made of their research insights.[19]

How can we reinstate hope after critical reflection? The universal is promoted in development projects through a discourse on rights and aspirations in which local experts or mediators speak for assumed beneficiaries.[20] The problem – if we agree that better communication between the development industry and anthropology would be for the better – is that even though we accept that 'development is a matter of knowledge', to quote Green, 'anthropology always knows better and is always critical'.[21] And, perhaps more critical, is the assertion that policy or research 'may fail to make a difference either by failing to reach its own standards, or, even more tellingly, by disregarding those of its competition'.[22] The epistemic conduct and form of anthropology do not work within development,[23] as I myself understood when writing project proposals with unattainable project goals such as changing legislation in Armenia.

Where does all this lead? An anthropological analysis of any given project could possibly proceed within another discourse than that of the implementing agencies.[24] It would invoke the notion of schism between anthropologists and those concerned with development policy and implementation. This is not because development professionals are ignorant but because anthropology tends to answer questions the development industry has not thought to ask in the first place. Where anthropology and other academic disciplines accumulate credibility on the basis of past publications, citations and peer reviews, the credibility of development-related knowledge relies on unpublished knowledge, on what is considered relevant insofar as it can be applied to ongoing projects and activities.[25]

The encounters to which claims to environmental rights and transparency lead in the real world are in some cases so sticky that the language of hope is a betraying one. What so far has been described may contain only a glimmer of hope, one that ironically resides in the subversion of traditional ways of organizing civil society. Hope is to be found in the challenge to authoritative state power and how a 'surreptitious symbiosis' is reached within civil society between NGOs and social movements.[26] On the same note, aid practices that rely on dividing the world into essentialist categories of poverty, rights and the like[27] may work better if they allow relations to thrive and be supported,[28] for example, by allowing projects to be social and based on trust. Perhaps the tension between social and professional project spaces should be overcome?

I have worked with activists that seem to be part of a fluid network. A path for future research could be to look at how this surreptitious symbiosis through networks of NGOs,[29] activists and ad hoc social movements might evolve in post-Soviet countries where trust in NGOs is waning and authorities are tightening regulations and laws. Future research could address this issue also in a comparative, post-colonial context.

People and documents are assembled in networks. In what way are future Armenian activists likely to organize themselves, what alliances will they forge, will they manage to escape from neo-liberal institutions with their confined and restrictive liberties? Finding themselves between a rock and a hard place, they need innovative activism and projects to move ahead.

Armenia is at a Eurovironmental crossroads, where processes and practices of development, environmental governance and Europeanization converge. This is a disturbing 'place' to be. The various claims, counterclaims and interventions by faraway foreign ministries and transnational organizations are messy and, indeed, sticky. After all, the intervention of the MFA, carried out in large part by a not too enthusiastic anthropologist, was seemingly more sensitive to different policy priorities in Norway and the need to establish something that could amount to a bilateral relationship with Armenia. This was done, if not at the expense of Armenian needs and perspectives, at least with scant regard for them. This was something the Armenian partners themselves acknowledged, most vividly expressed in Karen's comment, 'Never mind, it's not a good idea.' Karen knew that what mattered was what the donor wanted, not what would work.

The practices both in project management and with regard to activism are just a few of many possible. They highlighted the interconnectedness of places, policies, ideas, flow charts, laws and people as our anthropological problems. I have argued that we should resist the temptation or inclination to understand this interconnectedness as an issue over hierarchy, global determinism and fixed relationships. Both strains of ethnography are, to my mind, considerably self-referential, with the anthropologist being but one of the many nodes in the distributed network.

Appendix 1

Excerpt from the Aarhus Convention text

Available from www.unece.org/fileadmin/DAM/env/pp/documents/cep43e.pdf.

The Parties to this Convention,

Recalling principle 1 of the Stockholm Declaration on the Human Environment,

Recalling also principle 10 of the Rio Declaration on Environment and Development,

Recalling further General Assembly resolutions 37/7 of 28 October 1982 on the World Charter for Nature and 45/94 of 14 December 1990 on the need to ensure a healthy environment for the well-being of individuals,

Recalling the European Charter on Environment and Health adopted at the First European Conference on Environment and Health of the World Health Organization in Frankfurt-am-Main, Germany, on 8 December 1989,

Affirming the need to protect, preserve and improve the state of the environment and to ensure sustainable and environmentally sound development,

Recognizing that adequate protection of the environment is essential to human well-being and the enjoyment of basic human rights, including the right to life itself,

Recognizing also that every person has the right to live in an environment adequate to his or her health and well-being, and the duty, both individually and in association with others, to protect and improve the environment for the benefit of present and future generations,

Considering that, to be able to assert this right and observe this duty, citizens must have access to information, be entitled to participate in decision-making and have access to justice in environmental matters, and acknowledging in this regard that citizens may need assistance in order to exercise their rights,

Recognizing that, in the field of the environment, improved access to information and public participation in decision-making enhance the quality and the implementation of decisions, contribute to public awareness of environmental issues, give the public the opportunity to express its concerns and enable public authorities to take due account of such concerns,

Aiming thereby to further the accountability of and transparency in decision-making and to strengthen public support for decisions on the environment,

Recognizing the desirability of transparency in all branches of government and inviting legislative bodies to implement the principles of this Convention in their proceedings,

Recognizing also that the public needs to be aware of the procedures for participation in environmental decision-making, have free access to them and know how to use them,

Recognizing further the importance of the respective roles that individual citizens, non-governmental organizations and the private sector can play in environmental protection,

Desiring to promote environmental education to further the understanding of the environment and sustainable development and to encourage widespread public awareness of, and participation in, decisions affecting the environment and sustainable development,

Noting, in this context, the importance of making use of the media and of electronic or other, future forms of communication,

Recognizing the importance of fully integrating environmental considerations in governmental decision-making and the consequent need for public authorities to be in possession of accurate, comprehensive and up-to-date environmental information,

Acknowledging that public authorities hold environmental information in the public interest,

Concerned that effective judicial mechanisms should be accessible to the public, including organizations, so that its legitimate interests are protected and the law is enforced,

Noting the importance of adequate product information being provided to consumers to enable them to make informed environmental choices,

Recognizing the concern of the public about the deliberate release of genetically modified organisms into the environment and the need for increased transparency and greater public participation in decision-making in this field,

Convinced that the implementation of this Convention will contribute to strengthening democracy in the region of the United Nations Economic Commission for Europe (ECE),

Conscious of the role played in this respect by ECE and recalling, *inter alia*, the ECE Guidelines on Access to Environmental Information and Public Participation in Environmental Decision-making endorsed in the Ministerial Declaration adopted at the Third Ministerial Conference "Environment for Europe" in Sofia, Bulgaria, on 25 October 1995,

Bearing in mind the relevant provisions in the Convention on Environmental Impact Assessment in a Transboundary Context, done at Espoo, Finland, on 25 February 1991, and the Convention on the Transboundary Effects of Industrial Accidents and the Convention on the Protection and Use of Transboundary Watercourses and International Lakes, both done at Helsinki on 17 March 1992, and other regional conventions,

Conscious that the adoption of this Convention will have contributed to the further strengthening of the "Environment for Europe" process and to the results of the Fourth Ministerial Conference in Aarhus, Denmark, in June 1998,

Have agreed as follows:

Article 1

OBJECTIVE

In order to contribute to the protection of the right of every person of present and future generations to live in an environment adequate to his or her health and well-being, each Party shall guarantee the rights of access to information, public participation in decision-making, and access to justice in environmental matters in accordance with the provisions of this Convention.

Appendix 2

Statement from Teghut Conference

Available from www.lragir.am/index/eng/0/society/view/20534.

ՓՐԿԵՆՔ

ԹԵՂՈՒՏԸ

STATEMENT OF NON GOVERNMENTAL ORGANIZATIONS

following the International Conference on the Environmental Safety of Teghut Copper-Molybdenum Mining Project held on December 14, 2010 in Yerevan, Armenia

25 January, 2011

In November 2007, the Government of Armenia approved a project on copper-molybdenum mining in the north-eastern region of Armenia, in the watershed of Debed River, in the region with complex landscape prone to earthquakes and landslides. Allocated area for mining is 1,491 hectares, 82% of which is covered with mountainous forests. Exploitation of the mine will produce about 500 million tones of tailings of hazardous substances and 600 million tones of various other wastes. Dumping tails will be disposed in the gorge of Duqanadzor River, flowing to Shnogh - tributary of transboundary Debed.

Acknowledging that
the mining project may result in the loss of several hundreds of hectares of mountain forests, drainage of water resources, soil erosion and destruction of entire ecosystems, including habitats of endangered plants and animals;
in case of natural disasters or industrial accidents the dumping tails containing silver, rhenium, lead, arsenic, copper, molybdenum, zinc, sulfurous compounds and other chemicals will contaminate the nearby pristine valleys of Shnogh River and its tributaries, affecting food safety and human health;

asserting that
environmental impact assessment report prepared by the mining company covered only the first 8 years of the project - without consideration of consequences within 50 years of project lifetime and beyond, account of emergency situations and risks in a transboundary context; positive environmental expertise conclusion issued by the Ministry of Nature Protection of Armenia failed to consider miscalculations of the environmental impacts and underestimation of ecosystem loss;
decision-making processes related to Teghut mining fell short to ensure effective and timely public notification and participation in accordance with Armenia's obligations under UNECE Aarhus Convention on Access to Information, Public Participation in Decision-Making and Access to Justice in Environmental Matters;
Government of Armenia did not take any step to identify tranboundary risks and enter in consultations with the Georgian authorities and the public in regard with its commitments under UNECE Espoo Convention on Environmental Impact Assessment in a Transboundary Context;
Georgian Government did not recognize the transboundary risks and failed not only to ratify

the UNECE Espoo Convention, but also to demonstrate responsible behaviour and make inquiries as a follow-up of alarms of the public concerned.

and concerned with that
such irresponsible performance by the authorities of two countries may result in the regional environmental catastrophe, whereas the Republic of Armenia as a country of origin of will be obliged not only to remove damages within the boundaries of own territory, but also to compensate for the damage caused to the neighbouring countries;

We, the undersigned non-governmental organizations and individuals from Armenia and Georgia urge that

the Armenian authorities
- suspend Teghut mining project until reassessment of its environmental impacts;
- arrange for non-biased and comprehensive environmental impact assessment in accordance with international best practice;
- commence consultations with Georgian authorities and the public on the potential transboundary impacts of Teghut mining project.

the Georgian authorities
- ratify the Espoo Convention;
- engage in consultations with the Armenian authorities to identify likely environmental impacts in the transboundary context.

Notes

Preface

1 Pål Wilter Skedsmo, 'Europeanizing Armenia: Assemblages of Environmental Rights and Development in Post-Soviet Armenia' (University of Oslo, 2017).

Introduction

1 Its full name is the UNECE Convention on Access to Information, Public Participation in Decision-making and Access to Justice in Environmental Matters, popularly known as the Aarhus Convention, being adopted in Aarhus, Denmark, in 1998.
2 Anna Lowenhaupt Tsing, *Friction: An Ethnography of Global Connection* (Princeton, NJ: Princeton University Press, 2005).
3 Ibid., p. 267.
4 James Ferguson, 'Power topographies', in D. Nugent and J. Vincent (eds), *A Companion to the Anthropology of Politics* (Malden, MA: Blackwell, 2007), p. 397.
5 Marta Bruno, 'Playing the co-operation game: Strategies around international aid in post-socialist Russia', in S. Bridger and F. Pine (eds), *Surviving Postsocialism: Local Strategies and Regional Responses in Eastern Europe and the Former Soviet Union* (London: Routledge, 1998).
6 Sharad Chari and Katherine Verdery, 'Thinking between the posts: Postcolonialism, postsocialism, and ethnography after the Cold War', *Comparative Studies in Society and History* 51/1 (2009), p. 30.
7 Philip Quarles van Ufford and Ananta Kumar Giri (eds), *A Moral Critique of Development: In Search of Global Responsibilities* (London: Routledge, 2003).
8 Chari and Verdery, 'Thinking between the posts'.
9 Paul Baran, 'Some Remarks on Digital Distributed Communications Networks' (Santa Monica, CA: RAND, 1967).

10 Dominic Boyer, *The Life Informatic: Newsmaking in the Digital Era* (Ithaca, NY: Cornell University Press, 2013), pp. 150–2.
11 Paul Rabinow, 'Midst anthropology's problems', in A. Ong and S. J. Collier (eds), *Global Assemblages: Technology, Politics, and Ethics as Anthropological Problems* (Malden, MA: Blackwell, 2005), pp. 40–53.
12 Janice Harper, *Endangered Species: Health, Illness and Death among Madagascar's People of the Forest* (Durham: Carolina Academic Press, 2002).
13 Ferguson, 'Power topographies'.
14 Rabinow, 'Midst anthropology's problems', p. 43.
15 Ibid., p. 51.
16 Ibid.
17 Ibid., p. 41.
18 Ibid., p. 44.
19 Ibid.
20 Ibid., p. 45.
21 Annelise Riles, *The Network Inside Out* (Ann Arbor: University of Michigan Press, 2001), p. 174.
22 Stephen J. Collier, *Post-Soviet Social* (Princeton, NJ: Princeton University Press, 2011), p. 29.
23 Ibid.
24 Akhil Gupta and James Ferguson, 'Beyond "culture": Space, identity, and the politics of difference', *Cultural Anthropology* 7/1 (1992), p. 7.
25 Collier, *Post-Soviet Social*, p. 29.
26 Gupta and Ferguson, 'Beyond "culture"', p. 8.
27 Ibid., p. 14.
28 Ibid.
29 Tsing, *Friction*, p. 271.
30 Knut G. Nustad, *Creating Africas: Struggles over Nature, Conservation and Land* (London: Hurst, 2015), p. 157.
31 James C. Scott, *Seeing Like a State: How Certain Schemes to Improve the Human Condition Have Failed* (New Haven, CT: Yale University Press, 1998).
32 Tania Murray Li, 'Beyond "the state" and failed schemes', *American Anthropologist* 107/3 (2005), pp. 383–94.
33 Anna Tsing, 'The global situation', *Cultural Anthropology* 15/3 (2000), pp. 327–60, 347.

34 Tsing, *Friction*.
35 NORAD – the Norwegian Agency for Development Cooperation – publishes statistics on Norwegian aid on its website, www.norad.no/en/front/toolspublications/norwegian-aid-statistics/.
36 See www.regjeringen.no/en/dokumenter/susprojects/id507666/. The project mechanism has later changed its name to Project cooperation in ODA-approved OSCE countries in Eurasia; see www.regjeringen.no/en/dep/ud/grants/proposals_calls/rules_osce/id747557/.
37 The project lasted from 2005 to 2010. Apart from a 2005 pilot project aimed at identifying possible partners and needs in Armenia (similar pilots were run in Azerbaijan and Georgia in 2008), the main project ran from 2006 to the end of 2010. The application process had to be repeated every year from 2006 to 2008, but the Norwegian MFA provided support for the project for a two-year period, 2009–10. The Armenia project was thus several projects, each requiring separate funding applications and final reports. Every year from 2006 to 2008 – as well as the year of the pilot project, 2005 – the project was named 'Environmental Management and Civil Society in Armenia'. The final project, running from 2009 to 2010, was named 'Transparency in Armenian Environmental Governance', indicating a slight shift in focus. Due to its connectedness, it makes sense to consider it as a single project for the purposes of this analysis. They were in effect bundled together not only because the donor, implementer, and topic remained the same throughout but also because the Armenian partners or 'beneficiaries' did so as well, to a large extent. In other words, the network the project created during its lifetime was characterized by continuity even though it consisted formally of separate projects requiring annual or biannual funding applications and reporting cycles. The main aim of the project was to analyse and provide guidance on how the Republic of Armenia could honour its obligations under the sixteen multilateral environmental agreements Armenia had ratified in a more 'effective way'. It aimed to accomplish this by means of know-how transfers, identification of best practices (included lessons learned in Norway) in dialogue with relevant authorities in Armenia, civil society representatives, and international organizations such as the OSCE. Over the years, the focus of the project changed from several MEAs to the Aarhus Convention.

38 David Mosse, 'Is good policy unimplementable? Reflections on the ethnography of aid policy and practice', *Development and Change* 35/4 (2004), pp. 639–71, 663.
39 Tsing, *Friction*.
40 Riles, *The Network Inside Out*, p. 3.
41 David Mosse, *Cultivating Development: An Ethnography of Aid Policy and Practice* (London: Pluto Press, 2005).
42 My informants – who comprise public officials, people who work in Armenian NGOs or international organizations – have had no objections to being identified by their full names. I have nevertheless decided to anonymize them, except for one who requested not to be anonymized.
43 Riles, *The Network Inside Out*, p. 19.
44 Ibid., p. 20.
45 Ibid., p. 6.
46 As project manager, I discussed the practicalities of the project with many of my Armenian informants, and I obtained informed consent from all of them. Informed consent I hold is something that is based on trust, and following the American Anthropological Association's Code of ethics, it is the quality of the consent, not its format, that matters. I firmly believe and hope I have not failed to honour the trust my Armenian informants put in me. Over time, however, as the nature of this research project changed, I realized that the practices of the Armenia project ought to constitute an important part of my ethnography. This realization occurred in 2012, e.g. two years after the finalization of the project. Several parts of my data stem from meetings that came about while on that mission to run the Armenia project. As will be clear from the ethnographic discussion, the part that involves the MFA is essentially a description and analysis of various management practices displayed in the application and reporting procedures, at public meetings and so on. To a certain extent, I refer to meetings with MFA officials with whom I was in contact over the years, but I have anonymized them. Although the MFA was notified at a meeting of my research work on the Aarhus Convention and environmental rights in Armenia, the later decision to include project-specific experiences was not something the MFA was informed about. These experiences, however, are largely based on data from project documents such as project proposals and reports and an

account of my own experiences and reflections regarding the project. The main emphasis here is on the realization that the Armenia project's design and development might lead to interesting analytical insights on how a project responds to changing donor policies and demands, rather than trying to explain or interpret the very same donor policies and demands. Had I had that ambition, the ministry obviously would have been informed and interviewed.

47 Maia Green, 'Doing development and writing culture', *Anthropological Theory* 9/4 (2009), pp. 395–417, 399.
48 Ibid., p. 411.
49 Mosse, 'Is good policy unimplementable?', p. 666.
50 Quarles van Ufford and Giri, *Moral Critique of Development*.
51 Philip Quarles van Ufford and Ananta Kumar Giri, 'Preface', in P. Quarles van Ufford and A. K. Giri (eds), *A Moral Critique of Development: In Search of Global Responsibilities* (Abingdon: Routledge, 2003), p. xi.
52 Ibid.
53 Philip Quarles van Ufford, Ananta Kumar Giri and David Mosse, 'Interventions in development: Towards a new moral understanding of our experiences and an agenda for the future', in P. Quarles van Ufford and A. K. Giri (eds), *A Moral Critique of Development: In Search of Global Responsibilities* (Abingdon: Routledge, 2003), p. 17.
54 Mosse, *Cultivating Development*.
55 Ibid., pp. 240–1.
56 Quarles van Ufford, Giri and Mosse, 'Interventions in development', p. 18.
57 Maia Green, 'Globalizing development in Tanzania: Policy franchising through participatory project management', *Critique of Anthropology* 23/2 (2003).
58 See Quarles van Ufford, Giri and Mosse, 'Interventions in development', p. 24.
59 Julie Hemment, 'The riddle of the third sector: Civil society, international aid, and NGOs in Russia', *Anthropological Quarterly* 77/2 (2004); Sarah L. Henderson, 'Selling civil society: Western aid and the nongovernmental organization sector in Russia', *Comparative Political Studies* 35/2 (2002).
60 Chari and Verdery, 'Thinking between the posts'.

1 Development and 'transition' in Armenia: Contexts and concepts

1. According to 2017 census. The World Bank, 'Armenia' (The World Bank Group, 2018). Available at http://data.worldbank.org/country/armenia (accessed 12 February 2018).
2. Charles King, *The Ghost of Freedom: A History of the Caucasus* (Oxford: Oxford University Press, 2008), p. 6.
3. Samira Ahmedbeyli and Armeni Karapetyan, 'Concerns Grow over Nagorny Karabakh' (2016). Available at https://iwpr.net/global-voices/concerns-grow-over-nagorny-karabakh (accessed 26 April 2016); Thomas de Waal, *Black Garden: Armenia and Azerbaijan Through Peace and War* (New York: New York University Press, 2004), p. 285.
4. Hostilities continue, however. Shots are often fired across the border by drunken soldiers, occasionally wounding or killing farmers tending their livestock in the border zone. Verbal aggression is the norm, especially after incidents like the murder of an Armenian by an Azerbaijani at a NATO language course in Budapest in 2004 (see de Waal, *Black Garden*). One of the most serious incidents happened in spring 2016, resulting in the death of dozens (see Ahmedbeyli and Karapetyan, 'Concerns Grow over Nagorny Karabakh').
5. Charles King, 'The benefits of ethnic war: Understanding Eurasia's unrecognized states', *World Politics* 53/4 (2001).
6. Ibid., p. 525.
7. Pål Kolstø, 'The sustainability and future of unrecognized quasi-states', *Journal of Peace Research* 43/6 (2006); Pål Kolstø and Helge Blakkisrud, 'Living with non-recognition: State- and nation-building in South Caucasian quasi-states', *Europe-Asia Studies* 60/3 (2008).
8. Armine Martirosyan, 'End in Sight for Last Armenia Quake Refugees?'(Institute for War and Peace Reporting, 2015). Available at https://iwpr.net/global-voices/end-sight-last-armenia-quake-refugees (accessed 3 December 2015).
9. Hovik Y. Sayadyan and Rafael Moreno-Sanchez, 'Forest policies, management and conservation in Soviet (1920–1991) and post-Soviet (1991–2005) Armenia', *Environmental Conservation* 33/1 (2006), p. 66.

10 Sara L. Henderson, 'Selling civil society: Western aid and the nongovernmental organization sector in Russia', *Comparative Political Studies* 35/2 (2002), pp. 139–67.
11 See Chris Hann, 'Introduction: Political society and civil anthropology', in C. Hann and E. Dunn (eds), *Civil Society: Challenging Western Models* (London: Routledge, 1996); Chris M. Hann (ed.), *Post socialism: Ideals, Ideologies and Practices in Eurasia* (London: Routledge, 2002); Henderson, 'Selling civil society'; Sarah L. Henderson, *Building Democracy in Contemporary Russia: Western Support for Grassroots Organizations* (London: Cornell University Press, 2003); Armine Ishkanian, *Democracy Building and Civil Society in Post-Soviet Armenia* (London: Routledge, 2008); Steven Sampson, 'The social life of projects', in C. Hann and E. Dunn (eds), *Civil Society: Challenging Western Models* (New York: Routledge, 1996); Steven Sampson, 'Beyond transition: Rethinking elite configurations in the Balkans', in C. Hann (ed.), *Postsocialism: Ideals, Ideologies and Practices* (London: Routledge, 2002); Janine R. Wedel, *Collision and Collusion: The Strange Case of Western Aid to Eastern Europe* (New York: Palgrave, 2001).
12 Armine Ishkanian, 'From inclusion to exclusion: Armenian NGOs participation in the PRSP', *Journal of International Development* 18 (2006), p. 730.
13 Ishkanian, *Democracy Building and Civil Society*, p. 156.
14 Armine Ishkanian et al., *Civil Society, Development and Environmental Activism in Armenia* (London: London School of Economics, 2013).
15 William F. Fisher, 'DOING GOOD? The politics and antipolitics of NGO practices', *Annual Review of Anthropology* 26 (1997).
16 Janine R. Wedel, 'US aid to Central and Eastern Europe, 1990–1994: An analysis of aid models and responses', in *East-Central European Economies in Transition: Study Papers Submitted to Joint Economic Committee* (Washington, DC: Congress of the United States, 1994).
17 Julie Hemment, 'The riddle of the third sector: Civil society, international aid, and NGOs in Russia', *Anthropological Quarterly* 77/2 (2004); Henderson, 'Selling civil society'; Henderson, *Building Democracy in Contemporary Russia*.
18 European External Action Service, 'EU Relations with Armenia' (European External Action Service, 2016). Available at http://eeas.europa.eu/armenia/index_en.htm (accessed 29 February 2016).

19 Allah Mirzoyan, *Armenia, the Regional Powers, and the West: Between History and Geopolitics* (New York: Palgrave Macmillan, 2010), p. 162.
20 Ibid.
21 Ibid.
22 UNECE, 'Environment for Europe – Home' (2014). Available at http://www.unece.org/env/efe/welcome.html (accessed 8 November 2014).
23 Michael Mason, 'So far but no further? Transparency and disclosure in the Aarhus Convention', in A. Gupta and M. Mason (eds), *Transparency in Global Environmental Governance: Critical Perspectives* (Cambridge: MIT Press, 2014), p. 86.
24 Ibid.
25 Ibid., p. 87.
26 Ibid., p. 86.
27 Ibid., p. 96.
28 UNECE, 'Third Ministerial Conference "Environment for Europe"' (UNECE.org, 2014). Available at http://www.unece.org/env/efe/historyofefe/history.en2011_3.html#/ (accessed 8 February 2014).
29 UNECE, 'Environment for Europe – Home'.
30 Michael Mason and Aarti Gupta, 'Transparency revisited', in A. Gupta and M. Mason (eds), *Transparency in Global Environmental Governance: Critical Perspectives* (Cambridge: MIT Press, 2014), p. 333.
31 Ibid.
32 UNECE, 'Environment' (2012). Available at http://www.unece.org/leginstr/env.html (accessed 7 November 2014).
33 Wedel, *Collision and Collusion*.
34 Katherine Verdery, *What Was Socialism and What Comes Next?* (Princeton, NJ: Princeton University Press, 1996), pp. 15–16.
35 UNECE, 'Environment'.
36 F. Joseph Dresen, 'The Aarhus Convention Test: Environmentalists and Freedom of Information in Post-Soviet States' (Woodrow Wilson International Center for Scholars, 2011). Available at https://www.wilsoncenter.org/publication/the-aarhus-convention-test-environmentalists-and-freedom-information-post-soviet-states (accessed 15 October 2014).
37 The terms 'Meeting of Parties (MoP)' and 'Conference of Parties (CoP)' are employed in various conventions but mean basically the same. They

are meetings convened at more or less regular intervals, to which all countries that have ratified the conventions in question are invited. They are in many ways the 'general assemblies' of these conventions.

38 UNECE, Addendum: Riga Declaration. Adopted at the third meeting of the Parties held from 11 to 13 June 2008 in Riga UNECE (2008). Available at http://www.unece.org/env/pp/mop3/web/Riga%20declaration_v_2008_07_21.pdf (accessed 15 February 2018).
39 Ishkanian, *Democracy Building and Civil Society*, p. 2.
40 Wedel, 'US aid to Central and Eastern Europe'; Wedel, *Collision and Collusion*.
41 Hann, 'Political society and civil anthropology'.
42 Hemment, 'Riddle of the third sector'; Henderson, 'Selling civil society'; Henderson, *Building Democracy in Contemporary Russia*.
43 Armine Ishkanian, 'Is the personal political? The development of Armenia's NGO sector during the post-Soviet period', in *Berkeley Program in Soviet and Post-Soviet Studies Working Paper Series* (Berkeley: University of California, 2003); Ishkanian, 'From inclusion to exclusion'; Ishkanian, *Democracy Building and Civil Society*; Armine Ishkanian, 'Challenging the gospel of neoliberalism? Civil society opposition to mining in Armenia', *Research in Social Movements, Conflicts and Change* 39/107–36 (2016).
44 Verdery, *What Was Socialism?*
45 Cf. Stephen J. Collier, *Post-Soviet Social* (Princeton, NJ: Princeton University Press, 2011); Alena Ledeneva, 'Telephone justice in Russia', *Post-Soviet Affairs* 24/4 (2008); Alena V. Ledeneva, *Russia's Economy of Favours: Blat, Networking and Informal Exchange* (Cambridge: Cambridge University Press, 1998); Katherine Verdery and Caroline Humphrey (eds), *Property in Question: Value Transformation In the Global Economy* (Oxford: Berg, 2004).
46 Wedel, *Collision and Collusion*.
47 Marta Bruno, 'Playing the co-operation game', in S. Bridger and F. Pine (eds), *Surviving Postsocialism: Local Strategies and Regional Responses in Eastern Europe and the Former Soviet Union* (London: Routledge, 1998).
48 Hemment, 'Riddle of the third sector'; Henderson, 'Selling civil society'.
49 Tatiana R. Zaharchenko and Gretta Goldenmann, 'Accountability in governance: The challenge of implementing the Aarhus Convention

in Eastern Europe and Central Asia', *International Environmental Agreements: Politics, Law and Economics* 4 (2004), p. 232.
50 Hann, 'Political society and civil anthropology'; Jim Igoe, 'Scaling up civil society: Donor money, NGOs and the pastoralist land rights movement in Tanzania', *Development and Change* 34/5 (2003).
51 The Convention on Wetlands of International Importance, adopted in Ramsar, Iran, in 1971, popularly called the Ramsar Convention.
52 The United Nations Convention to combat desertification, UNCCD, adopted in Paris in 1994.
53 OECD, 'Compare Your Country: Aid Statistics by Donor, Recipient and Sector' (OECD, 2018). Available at http://www.compareyourcountry.org/aid-statistics?cr=302&cr1=oecd&lg=en&page=1 (accessed 17 February 2018).
54 Ibid.
55 Chari and Verdery, 'Thinking between the posts'.
56 Ibid.
57 Verdery, *What Was Socialism?*; Katherine Verdery, 'The "new" Eastern Europe in an anthropology of Europe', *American Anthropologist* 99/4 (1997).
58 Wedel, *Collision and Collusion*.
59 Hann, *Postsocialism*.
60 Chris Hann and Elisabeth Dunn (eds), *Civil Society: Challenging Western Models* (London: Routledge, 1996).
61 Verdery and Humphrey, *Property in Question*.
62 Catherine Alexander, Victor Buchli and Caroline Humphrey (eds), *Urban Life in Post-Soviet Asia* (New York: Routledge, 2007).
63 Michael Burawoy and Katherine Verdery (eds), *Uncertain Transition: Ethnographies of Change in the Postsocialist World* (Lanham, MD: Rowman & Littlefield, 1999).
64 Michael Burawoy and Katherine Verdery, 'Introduction', in M. Burawoy and K. Verdery (eds), *Uncertain Transition: Ethnographies of Change in the Postsocialist World* (Lanham, MD: Rowman & Littlefield, 1999), p. 7.
65 Ibid., p. 1.
66 Ibid., p. 4.
67 Ibid., pp. 6–7.
68 Ibid., p. 14.

69 Susanne Brandtstädter, 'Transitional spaces: Postsocialism as a cultural process: Introduction', *Critique of Anthropology* 27/2 (2007), p. 134.
70 Chari and Verdery, 'Thinking between the Posts'.
71 Tatjana Thelen, 'Shortage, fuzzy property and other dead ends in the anthropological analysis of (post)socialism', *Critique of Anthropology* 31/1 (2011), p. 48.
72 Ibid. pp. 43–4.
73 See ibid. However, the allegation in the same scholarly article that studies of shortages and property rights (so-called fuzzy property) are dead ends, I find unsubstantiated and unsustainable. As the ensuing debate indicates, their disagreements were not that wide after all (see Tatjana Thelen, 'Economic concepts, common grounds and "new" diversity in the anthropology of post-socialism: Reply to Dunn and Verdery', *Critique of Anthropology* 32/1 [2012]); Elisabeth Cullen Dunn and Katherine Verdery, 'Dead ends in the critique of (post)socialist anthropology: Reply to Thelen', *Critique of Anthropology* 31/3 (2011). But as the debate also makes clear, parts of post-socialist anthropology are theoretically grounded in economic theory inspired by the dissident Hungarian economist Janos Kornai and his concept of 'shortage economy' (János Kornai, *Economics of Shortage*, Contributions to economic analysis [Amsterdam: North-Holland, 1980]). The irony, perhaps, is that Kornai's neo-institutionalist approach based on 'economic man' as rational actor is thus adopted by the very same anthropologists who criticize advocates and analysts of neo-liberal reforms for their assumption of a relative easy transformation to a market economy (see Sabina Stan, 'Looking for a place to stand: Theory, field and holism in contemporary anthropology', in J. G. Carrier [ed.], *After the Crisis: Anthropological Thought, Neoliberalism and the Aftermath* [London: Routledge, 2016], p. 124). This criticism is somewhat misguided, I believe. Although Verdery and Dunn, for instance, make use of the concept of 'shortage economy', to suggest that they are therefore somehow disqualified to criticize the headlong neo-liberal reforms that characterized the 1990s goes a bit too far for me. When anthropologists of post-socialism have criticized various reforms and projects (cf. Verdery, *What Was Socialism?*; Wedel, *Collision and Collusion*), their perspective has largely been from the 'ethnographic gaze' point of view (see Elizabeth Harrison, 'Beyond the looking glass?

"Aidland" reconsidered', *Critique of Anthropology* 33/3 [2013], p. 275), from where they argue that the large-scale reforms failed to take local specificities, needs, and lifeworlds into account. This is standard fare in anthropology, irrespective of the analytical toolkit the anthropologists in question make use of. In my view, it makes sense to criticize neo-liberal economic reform also from the viewpoint of individual actors as rational economic actors. The point as Verdery states it is that one does not need to take transformation to a market economy as a given in the former socialist countries: 'In my opinion, to assume that we are witnessing a transition from socialism to capitalism, democracy, or market economies is mistaken. I hold with Stark, Burawoy, Bunce, and others who see the decade of the 1990s as a time of transformation in the countries that have emerged from socialism; these transformations will produce a variety of forms, some of them perhaps approximating Western capitalist market economies and many of them not ... When I use the word "transition," then, I put it in quotes so as to mock the naiveté of so much fashionable transitology' (see Verdery, *What Was Socialism?*, pp. 15–16).
74 Cf. Verdery, *What Was Socialism?*; Wedel, *Collision and Collusion*.
75 Ledeneva, *Russia's Economy of Favours*.
76 Verdery, *What Was Socialism?*
77 Christian Giordano and Dobrinka Kostova, 'The social production of mistrust', in C. Hann (ed.), *Postsocialism: Ideal, Ideologies and Practices in Eurasia* (London: Routledge, 2002).
78 Nancy Ries, *Russian Talk: Culture and Conversation during Perestroika* (Ithaca, NY: Cornell University Press, 1997).
79 Cf. Catherine Alexander, 'Privatization: Jokes, scandal, and absurdity in a time of rapid change', in K. Sykes (ed.), *Ethnographies of Moral Reasoning: Living Paradoxes of a Global Age* (New York: Palgrave Macmillan, 2009); Caroline Humphrey, *The Unmaking of Soviet Life: Everyday Economies after Socialism* (New York: Cornell University Press, 2002); Caroline Humphrey, 'New subjects and situated interdependence: After privatisation in Ulan-Ude', in C. Alexander, V. Buchli and C. Humphrey (eds), *Urban Life in Post-Soviet Asia* (New York: Routledge, 2007); Verdery and Humphrey, *Property in Question*.

80 Wedel, *Collision and Collusion*, p. 7.
81 James Ferguson, 'Global disconnect: Abjection and the aftermath of modernism', in J. X. Inda and R. Rosaldo (eds), *The Anthropology of Globalization: A Reader* (Oxford: Blackwell, 2002), p. 137.
82 Hann, 'Political society and civil anthropology'.
83 Hemment, 'Riddle of the third sector'.
84 Bruno, 'Playing the co-operation game'.
85 Sampson, 'Social life of projects'; Steven Sampson, 'Weak states, uncivil societies and thousands of NGOs' (2002). Available at http://www.anthrobase.com/Txt/S/Sampson_S_01.htm (accessed 19 January 2005).
86 Marlies Glasius and Armine Ishkanian, 'Surreptitious symbiosis: Engagement between activists and NGOs', *Voluntas: International Journal of Voluntary and Nonprofit Organizations* 26/6 (2014), pp. 2620–44; Ishkanian, 'Is the personal political?'; Ishkanian, 'From inclusion to exclusion'; Ishkanian, *Democracy Building and Civil Society*; Ishkanian, 'Challenging the gospel of neoliberalism?'; Ishkanian et al., 'Civil society, development'.
87 Ishkanian, *Democracy Building and Civil Society*, p. 156.
88 Glasius and Ishkanian, 'Surreptitious symbiosis'.
89 Ishkanian, 'Challenging the gospel of neoliberalism?', p. 119.
90 Ibid.
91 Eric Breit, Lars Rowe and Pål Wilter Skedsmo, 'Evaluering av støtteordningen BarentsKult ("Evaluation of the Funding Mechanism BarentsKult")', in *FNI Report 11/2014* (Lysaker: Fridtjof Nansen Institute, 2014); Pål Skedsmo, *'Doing Good' in Murmansk?: Civil Society, Ideology and Everyday Practices in a Russian Environmental NGO*, FNI Report14/2005 (Lysaker: Fridtjof Nansen Institute, 2005); Pål Skedsmo, 'Demokratisering og miljøkamp på Kolahalvøya ("Democratisation and environmentalism on the Kola Peninsula")', *Norsk Antropologisk Tidsskrift* 18/3–4 (2007); Pål Wilter Skedsmo, *Russisk sivilsamfunn og norske hjelpere (Russian Civil Society and its Norwegian Benefactors)* (Trondheim: Tapir Akademisk Forlag, 2010); Pål Wilter Skedsmo, 'Evaluering av samarbeidet mellom LO og FNPR 2001–2010 ("Evaluation of co-operation between LO and FNPR 2001–2010")', in *FNI Report 05/2011* (Lysaker: Fridtjof Nansen Institute, 2011).

92 Pål Wilter Skedsmo, 'Evaluering av Demokratimidlene (Evaluation of the democracy funds)', in *FNI Report 8/2008* (Lysaker: Fridtjof Nansen Institute, 2008).
93 Glasius and Ishkanian, 'Surreptitious symbiosis'.
94 Cf. David M. Abramson, 'A critical look at NGOs and civil society as means to an end in Uzbekistan', *Human Organization* 58/3 (1999); David G. Anderson, 'Bringing civil society to an uncivilised place: Citizenship regimes in Russia's Arctic frontier', in C. Hann and E. Dunn (eds), *Civil Society: Challenging Western Models* (London: Routledge, 1996); Bruno, 'Playing the co-operation game'; Gerald W. Creed and Janine R. Wedel, 'Second thoughts from the Second World: Interpreting aid in post-communist Eastern Europe', *Human Organization* 3/56 (1997); Alfred B. Evans, Jr., Laura A. Henry and Lisa McIntosh Sundstrom (eds), *Russian Civil Society: A Critical Assessment* (Armonk, NY: M. E. Sharpe, 2006); Hann and Dunn, *Challenging Western Models*; Chris Hann, Caroline Humphrey and Katherine Verdery, 'Introduction: Postsocialism as a topic of anthropological investigation', in C. Hann (ed.), *Postsocialism: Ideals, Ideologies and Practices in Eurasia* (London: Routledge, 2002); Hemment, 'Riddle of the third sector'; Henderson, 'Selling civil society'; Ishkanian, *Democracy Building and Civil Society*; Ries, *Russian Talk*; Wedel, *Collision and Collusion*.
95 Chari and Verdery, 'Thinking between the posts', p. 24.
96 Mosse, *Cultivating Development*.
97 Arturo Escobar, *Encountering Development: The Making and Unmaking of the Third World* (Princeton, NJ: Princeton University Press, 1995); James Ferguson, *The Anti-Politics Machine: 'Development', Depoliticization, and Bureaucratic Power in Lesotho* (Minneapolis: University of Minnesota Press, 1994); Igoe, 'Scaling up civil society'.
98 Escobar, *Encountering Development*, p. 4.
99 Knut G. Nustad, *Gavens makt: norsk utviklingshjelp som formynderskap*, Makt- og globaliseringsutredningen (Oslo: Pax, 2003), pp. 21–2.
100 Ibid. pp. 104–5.
101 Bruno, 'Playing the co-operation game', p. 173; Verdery, *What Was Socialism?*
102 Mosse, 'Is good policy unimplementable?'; Mosse, *Cultivating Development*.

103 Maia Green, 'Globalizing development in Tanzania: Policy franchising through participatory project management', *Critique of Anthropology* 23/2 (2003); Sampson, 'Social life of projects'.
104 Henderson, 'Selling civil society'; Igoe, 'Scaling up civil society'; Ishkanian, *Democracy Building and Civil Society*.
105 Mosse, *Cultivating Development*.
106 Ibid., pp. 14–20.
107 Tania Murray Li, 'Beyond "the state" and failed schemes', *American Anthropologist* 107/3 (2005), p. 279.
108 David Mosse, 'The making and marketing of participatory development', in P. Quarles van Ufford and A. K. Giri (eds), *A Moral Critique of Development: In Search of Global Responsibilities* (Abingdon: Routledge, 2003), p. 45.
109 Jeremy Gould, 'Timing, scale and style: Capacity as governmentality in Tanzania', in D. Mosse and D. Lewis (eds), *The Aid Effect: Giving and Governing in International Development* (London: Pluto Press, 2005), p. 63.
110 Ibid., p. 69.
111 Ibid.
112 Ibid., p. 79.
113 Ibid., p. 71.
114 Raymond Apthorpe, 'Writing development policy and policy analysis plain or clear: On language, genre and power', in C. Shore and S. Wright (eds), *Anthropology of Policy: Critical Perspectives on Governance and Power* (Abingdon: Routledge, 1997), p. 53.
115 Ibid.
116 Stephen J. Collier, 'Global assemblages', *Theory, Culture and Society* 23/2–3 (2006), p. 400.
117 Anthony Giddens, 'Living in a post-traditional society', in U. Beck, A. Giddens and S. Lash (eds), *Reflexive Modernization: Politics, Tradition and Aesthetics in the Modern Social Order* (Cambridge: Blackwell, 1994), p. 85.
118 Context is not a given entity within which one can merely situate one's field of study. Rather, context needs to be investigated as a focus of analysis (see Roy Dilley, 'Introduction: The problem of context', in R. Dilley [ed.], *The Problem of Context* [New York: Berghahn,

1999], p. 37), because 'context is itself problematic, indeed the result of prior interpretation' (see ibid., p. 2). This will take me to places other than Armenia (most notably Norwegian development policies and international institutions and projects related to the Aarhus Convention). But the main locus of my analysis is nevertheless within Armenia. If context is both 'a focal phenomenon and an environment within which it is embedded' (see Ladislav Holy, 'Contextualsation and paradigm shifts', in R. Dilley [ed.], *The Problem of Context* [New York: Berghahn, 1999], p. 49), it should have consequences for how we as anthropologists should proceed. Holy suggests – inspired by Goffman (see Erving Goffman, *The Presentation of Self in Everyday Life* [Harmondsworth: Penguin Books, 1971]) – that 'context as frame' is really the best we have to go by. 'Meaning', he adds, 'is as much context-dependent as context is meaning-dependent' (see Holy, 'Contextualsation and paradigm shifts', pp. 49–50). In other words, context and meaning are seen as being in a dialectical relationship. But if context is just a frame, then one overlooks that 'the "part"/the contexted and the "whole"/the context are not made up of the same "material" – they belong to different ontological domains' (see Chi W. Huen, 'What is context? An ethnophilosophical account', *Anthropological Theory* 9/2 [2009], p. 152). As I see it, the implication of this is that we have to regard context and the process of contextualization as processes in which we consider what we do, not as constructing a single definitive context but rather one of many possible: an instance of a rhizomatic assemblage in the terminology of Gilles Deleuze and Félix Guattari, *A Thousand Plateaus: Capitalism and Schizophrenia* (Minneapolis: University of Minnesota Press, 1987).
119 Stephen J. Collier and Aihwa Ong, 'Global assemblages, anthropological problems', A. Ong and S. J. Collier (eds), *Global Assemblages: Technology, Politics and Ethics as Anthropological Problems* (Malden, MA: Blackwell, 2005), p. 4.
120 Ibid., p. 11.
121 Ibid.
122 Ibid.
123 Ibid., p. 12.
124 Ibid.

125 Ibid., p. 11.
126 Mosse, *Cultivating Development*, p. 17.
127 Chari and Verdery, 'Thinking between the posts'.
128 Cf. David Mosse, 'Global governance and the ethnography of international aid', in D. Mosse and D. Lewis (eds), *The Aid Effect: Giving and Governing in International Development* (London: Pluto Press, 2005); Riles, *The Network Inside Out*.

2 Transparent environment: 'Helping' countries into a 'pan-European' legal space

1 Cf. Michal Buchowski, 'The shifting meanings of civil and civic society in Poland', C. Hann and E. Dunn (eds), *Civil Society: Challenging Western Models* (London: Routledge, 1996); Michael Burawoy and Katherine Verdery (eds), *Uncertain Transition: Ethnographies of Change in the Postsocialist World* (Lanham, MD: Rowman & Littlefield, 1999); Jordan Gans-Morse, 'Searching for transitologists: Contemporary theories of post-communist transitions and the myth of a dominant paradigm', *Post-Soviet Affairs* 20/4 (2004); Katherine Verdery, *What Was Socialism and What Comes Next?* (Princeton, NJ: Princeton University Press, 1996).
2 Anna Lowenhaupt Tsing, *Friction: An Ethnography of Global Connection* (Princeton, NJ: Princeton University Press, 2005), p. 6.
3 Ibid.
4 Armenia's implementation and alleged non-compliance were addressed at MoPs 3, 4 and 5.
5 Sally Engle Merry, 'Anthropology and international law', *Annual Review of Anthropology* 35 (2006), p. 106.
6 Annelise Riles, 'Models and documents: Artifacts of international legal knowledge', *International and Comparative Law Quarterly* 48 (1999).
7 Annelise Riles, *The Network Inside Out* (Ann Arbor: University of Michigan Press, 2001), p. 85.
8 Armenian Aarhus Centers, 'Memorandum of Understanding' (2007). Available at http://aarhus.am/?page_id=662&lang=en (accessed 15 December 2015).

9 UNECE, 'Report by the compliance committee. Addendum: DECISION III/6b Compliance by Armenia with its obligations under the convention' (2008). Available at http://www.unece.org/fileadmin/DAM/env/pp/mop3/ODS/ece_mp_pp_2008_2_add_10_e_Armenia.pdf (accessed 19 August 2014).

10 UNECE, *Convention on Access to Information, Public Participation in Decision-Making and Access to Justice in Environmental Matters* (United Nations Economic Commission for Europe, 1998), Article 4-1.

11 Ibid., Articles 4-1, 4-2, 4-3.

12 Ibid., Article 4-4.

13 Ibid., Article 5-1 (a).

14 Ibid., Article 5-4.

15 Ibid., Article 6.

16 Ibid.

17 Ibid., Article 7.

18 Ibid., Article 8.

19 Ibid., Articles 6-2 (a), (d), 6-4, 6-5.

20 Ibid., Article 6-7.

21 Ibid., Article 9-1.

22 Ibid.

23 Ibid., Article 2-5.

24 Jonas Ebbesson, 'Public participation', in D. Bodansky, J. Brunnée and E. Hey (eds), *The Oxford Handbook of International Environmental Law* (Oxford: Oxford University Press, 2008), p. 703. Jonas Ebbeson, a professor of environmental law at the University of Stockholm, has been chair of the Compliance Committee since 2011.

25 UNECE, *Convention on Access to Information*.

26 The Environmental Information Act was passed to secure the right to access to environmental information. Its definition of what counts as such information is rather wide. More importantly, however, the act goes a step further than the Aarhus Convention in requiring private businesses – not only public authorities as under the Aarhus Convention – to provide environmental information if requested by the public. Should the private sector fail in its duty to inform the public, the public cannot use the compliance mechanism of the Convention since it is not covered under the Convention. For this purpose, a national appeals board was set up in Norway.

27 UNECE, *Convention on Access to Information*, Article 10.

28 Ibid., Article 15.
29 The 'I' refers to the MoP at which the decision was taken, e.g. the first. The following number refers to the numbering of cases and decisions at each individual MoP.
30 UNECE, 'Background' (Unece.org, 2014). Available at http://www.unece.org/env/pp/ccbackground.html (accessed 15 September 2014).
31 UNECE, 'Report by the compliance committee'.
32 To my knowledge, the requested reports following the 2008 decision were not submitted every year, or if they were, they have not been made publicly available on UNECE's website where most of the other information is posted. In 2008, however, it was anticipated that Armenia would submit these reports as requested.
33 UNECE, 'Report by the compliance committee'.
34 Riles, *The Network Inside Out*.
35 Julia Brunnée and Stephen J. Toope, 'Interactional international law and the practices of legality', in E. Adler and V. Pouliot (eds), *International Practices* (Cambridge: Cambridge University Press, 2011), p. 131.
36 UNECE, *Convention on Access to Information*.
37 Ibid.
38 Riles, *The Network Inside Out*, p. 84.
39 UNECE, *Convention on Access to Information*, Article 15.
40 Riles, *The Network Inside Out*, p. 172.
41 UNECE, 'Fourth session of the Meeting of the Parties: Overview' (UNECE.org, 2011). Available at http://www.unece.org/env/pp/mop4.html#/ (accessed 15 November 2015).
42 UNECE, *Convention on Access to Information*.
43 Interview, Yerevan, April 2007.
44 Michael Herzfeld, 'Political optics and the occlusion of intimate knowledge', *American Anthropologist* 107/3 (2005), p. 373.
45 Ulf Hannerz, *Cultural Complexity: Studies in the Social Organization of Meaning* (New York: Columbia University Press, 1992), p. 121.
46 Michael Herzfeld, *The Social Production of Indifference: Exploring the Symbolic Roots of Western Bureaucracy* (New York: Berg, 1992).
47 Herzfeld, 'Political optics', p. 372.
48 Ibid., p. 375.
49 Ibid.

50 James C. Scott, *Seeing Like a State: How Certain Schemes to Improve the Human Condition Have Failed* (New Haven, CT: Yale University Press, 1998), p. 8.
51 Herzfeld, 'Political optics', p. 372.
52 Martin King Whyte, 'Bureaucracy and antibureaucracy in China', in G. M. Britan and R. Cohen (eds), *Hierarchy & Society* (Philadelphia, PA: Institute for the Study of Human Issues [ISHI], 1980), p. 137.
53 Alena V. Ledeneva, *Russia's Economy of Favours: Blat, Networking and Informal Exchange* (Cambridge: Cambridge University Press, 1998), p. 1.
54 Hannerz, *Cultural Complexity*.
55 Alena Ledeneva, 'Telephone justice in Russia', *Post-Soviet Affairs* 24/4 (2008).
56 Armine Ishkanian, 'Is the personal political? The development of Armenia's NGO sector during the post-Soviet period', in *Berkeley Program in Soviet and Post-Soviet Studies Working Paper Series* (Berkeley: University of California, 2003).
57 Armine Ishkanian, *Democracy Building and Civil Society in Post-Soviet Armenia* (London: Routledge, 2008), p. 31.
58 Marta Bruno, 'Playing the co-operation game: Strategies around international aid in post-socialist Russia', in S. Bridger and F. Pine (eds), *Surviving Postsocialism: Local Strategies and Regional Responses in Eastern Europe and the Former Soviet Union* (London: Routledge, 1998).
59 Sarah L. Henderson, 'Selling civil society: Western aid and the nongovernmental organization sector in Russia', *Comparative Political Studies* 35/2 (2002); Sarah L. Henderson, *Building Democracy in Contemporary Russia: Western Support for Grassroots Organizations* (Ithaca, NY; London: Cornell University Press, 2003).
60 Riles, *The Network Inside Out*.
61 Karen Barad, 'Posthumanist performativity: Toward an understanding of how matter comes to matter', *Signs: Journal of Women in Culture and Society* 28/3 (2003).
62 ENVSEC addresses the links between the natural environment and human security. ENVSEC is a joint initiative by UNDP, UNEP, OSCE, NATO, UNECE and Regional Environmental Centre (REC).
63 OSCE, 'Decision No. 314' (1999). Available at http://www.osce.org/pc/28591?download=true (accessed 23 March 2015).
64 UNEP, 'ENVSEC projects by implementing organization' (Envsec.org, 2015). Available at http://www.envsec.org/index.php?option=com_content&view=article&id=79&lang=en (accessed 13 March 2015).

65   Anush has been working within the OSCE particularly on Aarhus-related activities.
66   *Mikri* – derivative of the Russian *mikroraion*: self-contained suburbs, largely built in the 1960s and 1970s to counter the housing crisis in Soviet cities.
67   PPT, e-mail correspondence, 20 April 2010.
68   The former minister of nature protection, Vartan Ayvazyan, has been accused of granting licenses to family and friends. He, too, has immunity from prosecution due to his position in parliament. The issue caused alarm bells to ring among NGOs and journalists alike, and in November 2008, the journalist Edik Bhagdasaryan was hospitalized after being beaten up in the streets the day after he published an article about the former minister's alleged acts of nepotism.
69   Anna Tsing, 'The global situation', *Cultural Anthropology* 15/3 (2000), p. 347.
70   Tsing, *Friction*, p. 57.
71   Tsing, 'The global situation', p. 347.
72   Ibid.
73   David Mosse, 'Introduction: The anthropology of expertise and professionals in international development', in D. Mosse (ed.), *Adventures in Aidland: The Anthropology of Professionals in International Development* (London: Berghahn, 2011), p. 4.
74   Ibid., p. 3.
75   UNECE, 'Environment for Europe – Home' (2014). Available at http://www.unece.org/env/efe/welcome.html (accessed 8 November 2018).
76   Riles, *The Network Inside Out*, p. 3.
77   Anna Lowenhaupt Tsing, 'Becoming a tribal elder, and other green development fantasies', in T. M. Li (ed.), *Transforming the Indonesian Uplands* (Singapore: Harwood Academic, 1999), p. 196.

3 Save Teghut!

1   James Ferguson, 'Power topographies', in D. Nugent and J. Vincent (eds), *A Companion to the Anthropology of Politics* (Malden, MA: Blackwell, 2007), p. 397.
2   Kay Milton, *Environmentalism and Cultural Theory: Exploring the Role of Anthropology in Environmental Discourse* (London: Routledge, 1996), p. 24.

3. Ibid., p. 33.
4. Armine Ishkanian et al., 'Civil Society, Development and Environmental Activism in Armenia' (London: London School of Economics, 2013), p. 43.
5. Ibid., pp. 71–2.
6. Armine Ishkanian, 'Challenging the gospel of neoliberalism? Civil society opposition to mining in Armenia', *Research in Social Movements, Conflicts and Change* 39/107–36 (2016), p. 110.
7. Ibid.
8. Ibid., p. 109.
9. Anna Lowenhaupt Tsing, *Friction: An Ethnography of Global Connection* (Princeton, NJ: Princeton University Press, 2005), p. 85.
10. Note on name: Ecodar later changed its name to Ecoera, but it remains the same organization with the same director with offices at the same address. I have chosen to use the two names as they appear in court cases and ensuing communication with the Aarhus Convention's Compliance Committee.
11. Administrative Court of the Republic of Armenia, *Decision on Denying Admission of the Claim* (Yerevan: Administrative Court of the Republic of Armenia, 2009), p. 4.
12. In law, standing refers to a party's ability to demonstrate sufficient connection and/or harm from a challenged action or law.
13. Administrative Court of the Republic of Armenia, *Judgment in the Name of the Republic of Armenia* (Yerevan: Administrative Court of the Republic of Armenia, 2010), p. 15.
14. G. Harutyunyan, *Decision of the Constitutional Court of the Republic of Armenia* (Constitutional Court of the Republic of Armenia, 2010). In this parallel case concerning legal standing, another organization had petitioned the Constitutional Court to determine the 'conformity with the Constitution of the Republic of Armenia of the word "its" after the word "violate" in ... the Administrative procedure code of ... Armenia'. According to the ruling, the wording was in conformity with the Armenian Constitution; see ibid., p. 1.
15. Compliance Committee, 'Draft Findings and Recommendations with Regard to Communication ACCC/C/2011/62 Concerning Compliance by Armenia' (2013). Available at http://www.unece.org/env/pp/compliance/compliancecommittee/62tablearm.html (accessed 15 September 2014).

16 Focal Point, 'Considerations on Communication ACCC/C/2009/43 sent by Armenia to Compliance Committee of Aarhus Convention' (Unece. org, 2009). Available at http://www.unece.org/fileadmin/DAM/env/pp/compliance/C2009-43/Correspondence/FrARMC43_Reply_16Dec2009.pdf (accessed 20 September 2014).
17 Tsing, *Friction*, p. 219.
18 Ibid., p. 221.
19 Lisa L. Gezon, 'Finding the global in the local: Environmental struggles in Northern Madagascar', in S. Paulson and L. L. Gezon (eds), *Political Ecology across Spaces, Scales and Social Groups* (New Brunswick, NJ: Rutgers University Press, 2005), p. 136.
20 Matthew S. Hull, 'Documents and bureaucracy', *Annual Review of Anthropology* 41 (2012).
21 Annelise Riles, *The Network Inside Out* (Ann Arbor: University of Michigan Press, 2001).
22 Hull, 'Documents and bureaucracy', p. 254.
23 Ann Laura Stoler, 'Colonial archives and the arts of governance', *Archival Science* 2/1–2 (2002), p. 87.
24 Hull, 'Documents and bureaucracy', p. 253.
25 Ibid.
26 Riles, *The Network Inside Out*, p. 3.
27 Julia Brunnée and Stephen J. Toope, 'Interactional international law and the practices of legality', in E. Adler and V. Pouliot (eds), *International Practices* (Cambridge: Cambridge University Press, 2011), p. 131.
28 Ibid., p. 109.
29 Ibid., p. 129.
30 Ibid.
31 Sally Engle Merry, 'Anthropology and international law', *Annual Review of Anthropology* 35 (2006), p. 100.
32 Ibid.
33 Ibid., pp. 100–1.
34 Ibid., p. 105.
35 Ibid., p. 106.
36 Ibid., p. 108.
37 Ibid.
38 Ibid.

39. Stephen J. Collier, 'Global assemblages', *Theory, Culture and Society* 23/2–3 (2006).
40. Maia Green, 'Globalizing development in Tanzania: Policy franchising through participatory project management', *Critique of Anthropology* 23/2 (2003), p. 140.
41. Riles, *The Network Inside Out*, p. 172.
42. David Mosse, *Cultivating Development: An Ethnography of Aid Policy and Practice* (London: Pluto Press, 2005), p. 16.
43. MoP III in 2008, Riga, Latvia, MoP IV in 2011, Chisinau, Moldova, and MoP V in 2014, Maastricht, the Netherlands.
44. These minutes are published at www.unece.org/env/pp/ccmeetings.html (downloaded 15 September 2015).
45. Brunnée and Toope, 'Interactional international law', p. 116.
46. Sona Ayvazyan, 'Dear Mr. Wates' (2009). Available at http://www.unece.org/env/pp/compliance/Compliancecommittee/43TableArmenia.html (accessed 20 September 2014).
47. Focal Point, 'Considerations on Communication ACCC/C/2009/43', p. 2.
48. UNECE, *Convention on Access to Information, Public Participation in Decision-Making and Access to Justice in Environmental Matters* (Geneva: United Nations Economic Commission for Europe, 1998), Article 9 (2A).
49. Focal Point, 'Considerations on Communication ACCC/C/2009/43', p. 2.
50. Sona Ayvazyan, 'Further Points After CC-27 [Re: Communication ACCC/C/2009/43 (Armenia)]' (2010). Available at http://www.unece.org/env/pp/compliance/Compliancecommittee/43TableArmenia.html (accessed 20 September 2014).
51. Focal Point, 'Additional information [Re: Communication ACCC/C/2009/43 (Armenia)]' (2010). Available at http://www.unece.org/env/pp/compliance/compliancecommittee/43tablearmenia.html (accessed 22 September 2014).
52. OECD, 'Armenia: Monitoring Report' (France: OECD, 2011), p. 16.
53. Compliance Committee, 'Draft Findings' (2010). Available at http://www.unece.org/fileadmin/DAM/env/pp/compliance/C2009-43/Findings/C43DraftFindings8.10.2010.pdf (accessed 20 September 2014).
54. Ibid.

55 Sona Ayvazyan, 'Comments from the Communicant on the Draft Findings [Re: Communication ACCC/C/2009/43 (Armenia)]' (2010). Available at http://www.unece.org/env/pp/compliance/Compliancecommittee/43TableArmenia.html (accessed 20 September 2014).
56 Focal Point, 'Comments from the Party Concerned [on the Draft findings]' (2010). Available at http://www.unece.org/env/pp/compliance/compliancecommittee/43tablearmenia.html (accessed 20 September 2014).
57 Compliance Committee, 'Draft Findings and Recommendations of the Compliance Committee with regard to Communication ACCC/C/2009/43 Concerning Compliance by Armenia' (2011). Available at http://www.unece.org/fileadmin/DAM/env/pp/compliance/C2009-43/Findings/C43DraftFindings8.10.2010.pdf (accessed 20 September 2014); Compliance Committee, 'Report of the Compliance Committee' (2011). Available at http://www.unece.org/fileadmin/DAM/env/pp/compliance/C2009-43/Findings/ece.mp.pp.2011.11.add.1.eng_040713.pdf (accessed 21 September 2014).
58 Environment Division UNECE Secretariat (UNECE.org, 2011). Available at http://www.unece.org/env/pp/compliance/compliancecommittee/62tablearm.html (accessed 10 September 2014).
59 Ecoera, 'Comments' (2012). Available at http://www.unece.org/env/pp/compliance/compliancecommittee/62tablearm.html (accessed 10 September 2014).
60 Focal Point, 'To the Secretariat of the Aarhus Convention' (2012). Available at http://www.unece.org/fileadmin/DAM/env/pp/compliance/C2011-62/Correspondence_with_the_Party/frARM_C62_comments20072012.pdf (accessed 10 September 2014).
61 Ibid., p. 2.
62 The hearings were held in Alaverdi, Lori Marz on 23 March 2006, and Teghut, Lori Marz on 12 October 2006.
63 Some of the people at one or both of these hearings later participated in the FNI seminars described in Chapter 5, including municipal mayors, NGO representatives and others.
64 Anon., 'Report of Public Hearings regarding opinions of affected communities, public units, citizens and competent state authorities'

(Unece.org, 2006). Available at http://www.unece.org/env/pp/compliance/compliancecommittee/62tablearm.html (accessed 10 September 2014).
65 Hrayr Savzyan, 'Answers: As to the request to provide a copy of the statement we made during the discussion with the Committee in 25 September 2012' (2012). Available at http://www.unece.org/env/pp/compliance/compliancecommittee/62tablearm.html (accessed 23 March 2015).
66 Ibid., p. 3.
67 Ibid., p. 4.
68 Ecoera, 'Answers [from the Communicant]', in ACCC/C/2011/62 (2012), p. 6.
69 Gevorg Danileyan, 'Board Decision [Decision of the Center of the Constitutional Law of the Republic of Armenia Board (Excerpt)]' (2012). Available at http://www.unece.org/env/pp/compliance/compliancecommittee/62tablearm.html (accessed 16 September 2014).
70 Ibid.
71 See Compliance Committee, 'Draft Findings and Recommendations'. This may sound familiar insofar as it invokes the term 'selective law enforcement'; see Håvard Bækken, 'Selective Law Enforcement in Russian Politics 2007–2011. Legal Action for Extra-Legal Purposes' (University of Oslo, 2012), and the Soviet term *telefonnij zakon*, see Alena Ledeneva, 'Telephone justice in Russia', *Post-Soviet Affairs* 24/4 (2008).
72 Tsing, *Friction*, p. 219.
73 Anthony Giddens, 'Living in a post-traditional society', in U. Beck, A. Giddens and S. Lash (eds), *Reflexive Modernization: Politics, Tradition and Aesthetics in the Modern Social Order* (Cambridge: Blackwell, 1994).
74 Ibid.; Stephen J. Collier and Aihwa Ong, 'Global assemblages, anthropological problems', in A. Ong and S. J. Collier (eds), *Global Assemblages: Technology, Politics and Ethics as Anthropological Problems* (Malden, MA: Blackwell, 2005), p. 9.
75 Merry, 'Anthropology and international law', p. 109.
76 Ibid.
77 Ibid., p. 102.
78 Brunnée and Toope, 'Interactional international law', p. 117.
79 Ibid., p. 121.

80 Philip Quarles van Ufford and Ananta Kumar Giri, 'Preface', in P. Quarles van Ufford and A. K. Giri (eds), *A Moral Critique of Development: In Search of Global Responsibilities* (Abingdon: Routledge, 2003).
81 Some of my hesitation stemmed from perceiving myself as acting like an activist while doing fieldwork (which is fine, I believe); but I was at the same time implementing the Armenia project in collaboration with Armenian ministries.
82 Transparency International Anticorruption Center: 'Statement of non-governmental organizations following the International Conference on the Environmental Safety of Teghut Copper-Molybdenum Mining Project held on December 14, 2010 in Yerevan, Armenia'. Available at https://transparency.am/en/statements/view/135 (accessed 12 February 2018).
83 In the same statement, Georgian authorities were urged to ratify the Espoo Convention on transboundary environmental impact assessments.
84 Riles, *The Network Inside Out*, p. 84.
85 Ibid., p. 172.
86 Ibid., p. 3.
87 Richard Sakwa, 'The dual state in Russia', *Post-Soviet Affairs* 26/3 (2010).
88 Ibid., p. 185.
89 Marina Kurkchiyan, 'The illegitimacy of law in post-Soviet societies', in D. J. Galligan and M. Kurkchiyan (eds), *Law and Informal Practices: The Post-Communist Experience* (Oxford: Oxford University Press, 2003).
90 Denis J. Galligan, 'Legal failure: Law and social norms in post-communist Europe', in D. J. Galligan and M. Kurkchiyan (eds), *Law and Informal Practices: The Post-Communist Experience* (Oxford: Oxford University Press, 2003).
91 Anna Lowenhaupt Tsing, 'Becoming a tribal elder, and other green development fantasies', in T. M. Li (ed.), *Transforming the Indonesian Uplands* (Singapore: Harwood Academic, 1999), p. 196.
92 Ibid.
93 Arun Agrawal, 'Environmentality: Community, intimate government, and the making of environmental subjects in Kumaon, India', *Current Anthropology* 46/2 (2005).
94 Maria Carmen Lemos and Arun Agrawal, 'Environmental governance', *Annual Review of Environment and Resources* (2006).
95 Agrawal, 'Environmentality'.

96 Arun Agrawal, *Environmentality: Technologies of Government and the Making of Subjects* (London: Duke University Press, 2005), p. 166.
97 Tania Murray Li, 'Beyond "the State" and Failed Schemes', *American Anthropologist* 107/3 (2005), p. 391.
98 Marlies Glasius and Armine Ishkanian, 'Surreptitious symbiosis: Engagement between activists and NGOs', *Voluntas: International Journal of Voluntary and Nonprofit Organizations* 26/6 (2014), pp. 2620–44.
99 Ferguson, 'Power topographies'.
100 Catherine Alexander, *Personal States: Making Connections between People and Bureaucracy in Turkey* (Oxford: Oxford University Press, 2002); Elif M. Babül, 'Training bureaucrats, practicing for Europe: Negotiating bureaucratic authority and governmental legitimacy in Turkey', *Political and Legal Anthropology Review* 35/1 (2012).
101 Armine Ishkanian, *Democracy Building and Civil Society in Post-Soviet Armenia* (London: Routledge, 2008).
102 Glasius and Ishkanian, 'Surreptitious symbiosis'.
103 Ibid.
104 Ishkanian, 'Challenging the gospel of neoliberalism?', p. 115.
105 Glasius and Ishkanian, 'Surreptitious symbiosis', p. 14.
106 Sharad Chari and Katherine Verdery, 'Thinking between the Posts: Postcolonialism, Postsocialism, and Ethnography after the Cold War', *Comparative Studies in Society and History* 51/1 (2009).
107 Tsing, *Friction*, p. 214.
108 Riles, *The Network Inside Out*, p. 84.
109 Ferguson, 'Power topographies', p. 397.

4 LOG framing: Donor legitimation and unattainable project goals

1 David Mosse, 'Is good policy unimplementable? Reflections on the ethnography of aid policy and practice', *Development and Change* 35/4 (2004), p. 646.
2 Philip Quarles van Ufford and Ananta Kumar Giri, 'Preface', in P. Quarles van Ufford and A. K. Giri (eds), *A Moral Critique of Development: In Search of Global Responsibilities* (Abingdon: Routledge, 2003).

3   Mosse, 'Is good policy unimplementable?', p. 665.
4   From revised application to MFA, June 2008. My translation.
5   UNECE, 'Report by the Compliance Committee. Addendum: DECISION III/6b Compliance by Armenia with its obligations under the convention' (2008). Available at https://www.unece.org/env/pp/compliance/compliancecommittee/ccimpldocsarmeniamop3.html (accessed 12 February 2018).
6   Ibid., p. 3.
7   FNI, 'Tillegg til søknaden "Miljøvernforvaltningen og det sivile samfunn i Armenia" 2008–2010 [Supplement to the Project Proposal: Environmental Management and Civil Society in Armenia 2008–2010]' (2008).
8   James C. Scott, *Seeing Like a State: How Certain Schemes to Improve the Human Condition Have Failed* (New Haven, CT: Yale University Press, 1998).
9   Janine R. Wedel, *Collision and Collusion: The Strange Case of Western Aid to Eastern Europe* (New York: Palgrave, 2001).
10 David Mosse, *Cultivating Development: An Ethnography of Aid Policy and Practice* (London: Pluto Press, 2005), p. 17.
11 Mosse, 'Is good policy unimplementable?', p. 665.
12 Maia Green, 'Globalizing development in Tanzania: Policy franchising through participatory project management', *Critique of Anthropology* 23/2 (2003), p. 129.
13 Ibid., p. 140.
14 From 2009 project proposal (translated from Norwegian).
15 James C. Scott, *Weapons of the Weak: Everyday Forms of Peasant Resistance* (New Haven, CT: Yale University Press, 1985), p. 2.
16 Mosse, *Cultivating Development*, p. 17.
17 James Ferguson, *The Anti-Politics Machine: 'Development', Depoliticization, and Bureaucratic Power in Lesotho* (Minneapolis: University of Minnesota Press, 1994).
18 Tania Murray Li, 'Beyond "the state" and failed schemes', *American Anthropologist* 107/3 (2005), p. 279.
19 Rosalind Eyben, 'Hiding relations: The irony of "effective aid"', *European Journal of Development Research* 22/3 (2010), p. 383.
20 Ibid., p. 385.
21 Ibid., pp. 386–7.

22 Ibid.
23 OECD, 'Paris Declaration and Accra Agenda for Action' (Organisation for Economic Co-operation and Development, 2015). Available at http://www.oecd.org/dac/effectiveness/parisdeclarationandaccraagendaforaction.htm (accessed 5 December 2015).
24 Des Gasper, 'Evaluating the "logical framework approach": Towards learning-oriented development evaluation', *Public Administration and Development* 20 (2000), p. 19.
25 Another example may help to illustrate the push to LOG-frame everything: Norwegian trade unions are involved in joint projects with trade unions in north-western Russia. The Norwegian trade unions had invited a representative of the Norwegian Agency for Development Cooperation (NORAD) to give them a crash course in 'management by objectives', to help them write more successful project proposals. I was there in the capacity of previously having evaluated this particular instance of trade union cooperation. It soon became apparent that success, according to the NORAD representative, hinged on the ability to formulate the project idea according to the management-by-objectives framework. Several trade union representatives raised objections, especially when the NORAD representative argued that one of the milestone achievements would be the formal negotiations between the trade unions and employer. At this, I also objected: 'What if this happens in an environment where formal negotiations do not take place and people rather meet informally and discuss over a meal with vodka?' The answer: 'You have to insist on formal meetings.' Apparently, we need to change local practices to fit the hierarchy of goals, which in the end makes it easier and more convenient for NORAD and/or the MFA to report results upwards in their respective organizations.
26 David M. Abramson, 'A critical look at NGOs and civil society as means to an end in Uzbekistan', *Human Organization* 58/3 (1999), p. 243.
27 Janine R. Wedel, 'US aid to Central and Eastern Europe, 1990–1994: An analysis of aid models and responses', in *East-Central European Economies in Transition: Study Papers submitted to Joint Economic Committee* (Washington, DC: Congress of the United States, 1994), p. 323.
28 Scott, *Weapons of the Weak*, p. 2.

29 My translation from the Norwegian. See Ministry of Foreign Affairs, 'St meld nr 47 (1994–1995) Om Handlingprogrammet for Øst-Europa [White paper 47 (1994–1995) on the Target Program for Eastern Europe]' (Oslo: Ministry of Foreign Affairs, 1994), p. 6.
30 Ministry of Foreign Affairs, 'Project Cooperation in the South Caucasus, Central Asia, Ukraine, Belarus and Moldova' (2008). Available at https://www.regjeringen.no/en/dokumenter/susprojects/id507666/ (accessed 15 October 2015).
31 Chapter 164, 'Peace, reconciliation and democracy', sub-chapter 73 'Other ODA-approved OSCE-countries'.
32 Statement at information meeting about the grant mechanism, MFA, Oslo, 2011.
33 Another incident occurred in 2008 when a state secretary from the Norwegian Ministry of the Environment visited Armenia and several Norwegian-funded projects with the Norwegian and Armenian partners, most notably WWF, to see a project ostensibly meant to improve the management of national parks in Armenia. Although this had nothing to do with the Armenia project, it served as a reminder of the possible diplomatic use of the project.
34 Emmanuel Adler and Vincent Pouliot (eds), *International Practices* (Cambridge: Cambridge University Press, 2011).
35 Green, 'Globalizing development in Tanzania', p. 124.
36 Arturo Escobar, *Encountering Development: The Making and Unmaking of the Third World* (Princeton, NJ: Princeton University Press, 1995).
37 Ferguson, *The Anti-Politics Machine*.
38 Sarah L. Henderson, 'Selling civil society: Western aid and the nongovernmental organization sector in Russia', *Comparative Political Studies* 35/2 (2002); Sarah L. Henderson, *Building Democracy in Contemporary Russia: Western Support for Grassroots Organizations* (London: Cornell University Press, 2003).
39 Mosse, 'Is good policy unimplementable?'; Mosse, *Cultivating Development*.
40 Green, 'Globalizing development in Tanzania', p. 140.
41 FNI, 'Environmental Management and Civil Society in Armenia' (2006). Available at www.fni.no/projects/armenia_environmental_management.html (accessed 23 March 2015).

42 FNI, 'Transparency in Armenian Environmental Governance' (2009). Available at www.fni.no/projects/armenia_environmental_governance_transparency.html (accessed 23 March 2015).
43 This particular centre no longer exists. Other environment-related centres have been established at the AUA, including the AUA Centre for Responsible Mining, partly in cooperation with the OSCE.
44 Mosse, *Cultivating Development*.
45 Anna Lowenhaupt Tsing, *Friction: An Ethnography of Global Connection* (Princeton, NJ: Princeton University Press, 2005), p. 58.
46 Mosse, 'Is good policy unimplementable?', p. 653.
47 Mosse, *Cultivating Development*, p. 16.
48 Ibid., p. 18.
49 Green, 'Globalizing development in Tanzania'.
50 Jeremy Gould, 'Timing, scale and style: Capacity as governmentality in Tanzania', in D. Mosse and D. Lewis (eds), *The Aid Effect: Giving and Governing in International Development* (London: Pluto Press, 2005).
51 Annelise Riles, *The Network Inside Out* (Ann Arbor: University of Michigan Press, 2001), p. 172.
52 Ibid., p. 3.
53 Scott, *Weapons of the Weak*, p. 2.
54 Mosse, *Cultivating Development*, p. 17.
55 Ferguson, *The Anti-Politics Machine*, p. xiv.
56 Ibid., p. xv.
57 Mosse, *Cultivating Development*, p. 17.
58 Ferguson, *The Anti-Politics Machine*, p. 258.
59 Raoul Beunen, Kristof Van Assche and Martijn Duinevel, 'Performing failure in conservation policy: The implementation of European Union directives in the Netherlands', *Land Use Policy* 31 (2013), p. 281.
60 Gould, 'Timing, scale and style'.
61 Mosse, *Cultivating Development*, p. 17.
62 Mark Schuller, 'Seeing like a "failed" NGO: Globalization's impacts on state and civil society in Haiti', *Political and Legal Anthropology Review* 30/1 (2007), p. 8.
63 Armine Ishkanian, *Democracy Building and Civil Society in Post-Soviet Armenia* (London: Routledge, 2008), p. 156.

64 Jim Igoe, 'Scaling up civil society: Donor money, NGOs and the pastoralist land rights movement in Tanzania', *Development and Change* 34/5 (2003), p. 867.
65 Tsing, *Friction*.
66 Mosse, *Cultivating Development*, p. 16.
67 Michael Burawoy and Katherine Verdery, 'Introduction', in M. Burawoy and K. Verdery (eds), *Uncertain Transition: Ethnographies of Change in the Postsocialist World* (Lanham, MD: Rowman & Littlefield, 1999).
68 Mosse, *Cultivating Development*, p. 19.

5 'Never mind, it's not a good idea'

1 Maia Green, 'Globalizing development in Tanzania: Policy franchising through participatory project management', *Critique of Anthropology* 23/2 (2003).
2 Annelise Riles, *The Network Inside Out* (Ann Arbor: University of Michigan Press, 2001).
3 Marta Bruno, 'Playing the co-operation game: Strategies around international aid in post-socialist Russia', in S. Bridger and F. Pine (eds), *Surviving Postsocialism: Local Strategies and Regional Responses in Eastern Europe and the Former Soviet Union* (London: Routledge, 1998).
4 Jeremy Gould, 'Timing, scale and style: Capacity as governmentality in Tanzania', in D. Mosse and D. Lewis (eds), *The Aid Effect: Giving and Governing in International Development* (London: Pluto Press, 2005), p. 71.
5 David M. Abramson, 'A critical look at NGOs and civil society as means to an end in Uzbekistan', *Human Organization* 58/3 (1999), p. 242.
6 Ibid., p. 243.
7 David Mosse, *Cultivating Development: An Ethnography of Aid Policy and Practice* (London: Pluto Press, 2005), p. 17.
8 Hovik Y. Sayadyan and Rafael Moreno-Sanchez, 'Forest policies, management and conservation in Soviet (1920–1991) and post-Soviet (1991–2005) Armenia', *Environmental Conservation* 33/1 (2006), p. 65.
9 Ibid.
10 Alena Ledeneva, 'Telephone justice in Russia', *Post-Soviet Affairs* 24/4 (2008).

11 Arun Agrawal, *Environmentality: Technologies of Government and the Making of Subjects* (London: Duke University Press, 2005).
12 Sharad Chari and Katherine Verdery, 'Thinking between the Posts: Postcolonialism, Postsocialism, and Ethnography after the Cold War', *Comparative Studies in Society and History* 51/1 (2009).
13 Philip Quarles van Ufford and Ananta Kumar Giri, 'Preface', in P. Quarles van Ufford and A. K. Giri (eds), *A Moral Critique of Development: In Search of Global Responsibilities* (Abingdon: Routledge, 2003).
14 The only exception being the project proposals for similar projects in Azerbaijan and Georgia.
15 Gould, 'Timing, scale and style'.
16 Armine and her family were some of the many Iranian Armenians who had fled Iran after the sacking of the Shah and the proclamation of the Islamic Republic. Many Armenians still live in Iran, however, and Teheran has its own Armenian quarter, known for its clandestine liquor stores. On the same note, Yerevan receives a significant number of Iranian tourists, who come to enjoy Yerevan's cafés, shops and more. The Teheran–Yerevan drive takes approximately twenty-four hours.
17 This Lada Niva had a large WWF sticker on it. The car was used by the *zapovedniki* guards, who, although under government control, were sponsored by the WWF.
18 Green, 'Globalizing development in Tanzania'.
19 Riles, *The Network Inside Out*.
20 Marc Augé, *Non-Places: Introduction to an Anthropology of Supermodernity* (London: Verso, 1995).
21 Green, 'Globalizing development in Tanzania', pp. 138–9.
22 Ibid., p. 139.
23 Ibid., pp. 138–9.
24 Riles, *The Network Inside Out*, pp. 26–7.
25 Karen Barad, 'Posthumanist performativity: Toward an understanding of how matter comes to matter', *Signs: Journal of Women in Culture and Society* 28/3 (2003).
26 Green, 'Globalizing development in Tanzania', p. 139.
27 Quarles van Ufford and Giri, 'Preface'.
28 Simon Abram and Marianne Elisabeth Lien, 'Performing nature at world's ends', *ETHNOS* 76/1 (2011), p. 3.

29 Barad, 'Posthumanist performativity'.
30 Ararat is a brand of Armenian brandy, what Armenians and Russians refer to as *armjanskij konjak*.
31 James C. Scott, *Weapons of the Weak: Everyday Forms of Peasant Resistance* (New Haven, CT: Yale University Press, 1985), p. 2.
32 Riles, *The Network Inside Out*.
33 Mosse, *Cultivating Development*, pp. 18–19.
34 Gould, 'Timing, scale and style', p. 69.
35 From a report compiled following the 2006 seminar, attachment to the 2007 project proposal.
36 Mosse, *Cultivating Development*, p. 18.
37 David Mosse, 'Is good policy unimplementable? Reflections on the ethnography of aid policy and practice', *Development and Change* 35/4 (2004).
38 Project proposal from 2009, my translation.
39 Tania Murray Li, 'Beyond "the state" and failed schemes', *American Anthropologist* 107/3 (2005), p. 268.
40 Ibid.
41 Mosse, *Cultivating Development*, p. 17.
42 Cf. David Mosse, 'Introduction: The anthropology of expertize and professionals in international development', in D. Mosse (ed.), *Adventures in Aidland, the Anthropology of Professionals in International Development* (London: Berghahn Books, 2011).
43 Raymond Apthorpe, 'Coda: With Alice in Aidland: A seriously satirical allegory', in D. Mosse (ed.), *Adventures in Aidland: the Anthropology of Professionals in International Development* (London: Berghahn Books, 2011); Raymond Apthorpe, 'Epilogue: Who is international aid? Some personal reflections', in A.-M. Fechter and H. Hindman (eds), *Inside the Everyday Lives of Development Workers: The Challenges and Futures of Aidland* (Sterling, VA: Kumarian Press, 2011).
44 Elizabeth Harrison, 'Beyond the looking glass? "Aidland" reconsidered', *Critique of Anthropology* 33/3 (2013).
45 Ibid., p. 274.
46 Mosse, 'Introduction', p. 2.
47 Harrison, 'Beyond the looking glass?', p. 274.
48 Janine R. Wedel, '"Studying through" a globalizing world: Building method through Aidnographies', in J. Gould and H. S. Marcussen (eds),

Ethnographies of Aid: Exploring Development Texts and Encounters (Occasional Paper 24: Roskilde University Centre, 2004).
49 Ibid., pp. 168–9.
50 Li, 'Beyond "the state"', p. 268.
51 Riles, *The Network Inside Out*.
52 Li, 'Beyond "the state"', p. 385.
53 Mosse, *Cultivating Development*, p. 242.
54 Barad, 'Posthumanist performativity'.
55 Jim Igoe, 'Scaling up civil society: Donor money, NGOs and the pastoralist land rights movement in Tanzania', *Development and Change* 34/5 (2003), p. 867.
56 Mark Schuller, 'Seeing like a "failed" NGO: Globalization's impacts on state and civil society in Haiti', *PoLAR: Political and Legal Anthropology Review* 30/1 (2007), p. 8.
57 Armine Ishkanian, *Democracy Building and Civil Society in Post-Soviet Armenia* (London: Routledge, 2008), p. 156.
58 Mosse, *Cultivating Development*, p. 14.
59 Ibid., pp. 16–17.
60 Gerald W. Creed and Janine R. Wedel, 'Second thoughts from the Second World: Interpreting aid in post-communist Eastern Europe', *Human Organization* 3/56 (1997).
61 Anna Lowenhaupt Tsing, *Friction: An Ethnography of Global Connection* (Princeton, NJ: Princeton University Press, 2005).
62 Quarles van Ufford and Giri, 'Preface'.

Conclusion

1 Paul Rabinow, 'Midst anthropology's problems', in A. Ong and S. J. Collier (eds), *Global Assemblages: Technology, Politics, and Ethics as Anthroplogical Problems* (Malden, MA: Blackwell, 2005), p. 45.
2 Maia Green, 'Globalizing development in Tanzania: Policy franchising through participatory project management', *Critique of Anthropology* 23/1 (2003).
3 Annelise Riles, *The Network Inside Out* (Ann Arbor: University of Michigan Press, 2001), p. 3.

4 Ibid., p. 84.
5 Michael Burawoy and Katherine Verdery, 'Introduction', in M. Burawoy and K. Verdery (eds), *Uncertain Transition: Ethnographies of Change in the Postsocialist World* (Lanham, MD: Rowman & Littlefield, 1999).
6 Armine Ishkanian, *Democracy Building and Civil Society in Post-Soviet Armenia* (London: Routledge, 2008), p. 156.
7 David Mosse, *Cultivating Development: An Ethnography of Aid Policy and Practice* (London: Pluto Press, 2005), p. 16.
8 Stephen J. Collier, *Post-Soviet Social* (Princeton, NJ: Princeton University Press, 2011), p. 29.
9 Nikolas Rose, *Powers of Freedom: Reframing Political Thought* (Cambridge: Cambridge University Press, 1999), pp. 27–30; Tania Murray Li, 'Beyond "the state" and failed schemes', *American Anthropologist* 107/3 (2005), p. 386.
10 Sharad Chari and Katherine Verdery, 'Thinking between the posts: Postcolonialism, postsocialism, and ethnography after the Cold War', *Comparative Studies in Society and History* 51/1 (2009), p. 18.
11 Ibid., pp. 18–19.
12 Susan Buck-Morss, *Dreamworld and Catastrophe: The Passing of Mass Utopia in East and West* (Cambridge: MIT Press, 2002).
13 Susanne Brandtstädter, 'Transitional spaces: Postsocialism as a cultural process: Introduction', *Critique of Anthropology* 27/2 (2007), pp. 132–3.
14 Chari and Verdery, 'Thinking between the posts'.
15 Ibid., p. 19.
16 Philip Quarles van Ufford, Ananta Kumar Giri and David Mosse, 'Interventions in development: Towards a new moral understanding of our experiences and an agenda for the future', in P. Quarles van Ufford and A. K. Giri (eds), *A Moral Critique of Development: In Search of Global Responsibilities* (Abingdon: Routledge, 2003), p. 24.
17 Ibid.
18 Maia Green, 'Doing development and writing culture', *Anthropological Theory* 9/4 (2009); Quarles van Ufford, Giri and Mosse, 'Interventions in development', p. 24.
19 Quarles van Ufford, Giri and Mosse, 'Interventions in development', p. 18.
20 Green, 'Doing development and writing culture', p. 396.
21 Ibid., p. 397.

22 Raymond Apthorpe, 'Writing development policy and policy analysis plain or clear: On language, genre and power', in C. Shore and S. Wright (eds), *Anthropology of Policy: Critical Perspectives on Governance and Power* (Abingdon: Routledge, 1997), p. 56.
23 Green, 'Doing development and writing culture', p. 399.
24 Trevor Parfitt, 'A post-structuralist agenda for development?' E-International Relations (2012). Available at http://www.e-ir.info/2012/04/10/a-post-structuralist-agenda-for-development/ (accessed 23 September 2015).
25 Green, 'Doing development and writing culture', p. 405.
26 Marlies Glasius and Armine Ishkanian, 'Surreptitious symbiosis: Engagement between activists and NGOs', *Voluntas: International Journal of Voluntary and Nonprofit Organizations* 26/6 (2014), pp. 2620–44.
27 Rosalind Eyben, 'Hiding relations: The irony of "Effective Aid"', *European Journal of Development Research* 22/3 (2010), p. 383.
28 Ibid., pp. 385–6.
29 Glasius and Ishkanian, 'Surreptitious symbiosis'.

Bibliography

Anon., 'Report of Public Hearings regarding opinions of affected communities, public units, citizens and competent state authorities'. Unece.org, 2006. Available at http://www.unece.org/env/pp/compliance/compliancecommittee/62tablearm.html (accessed 10 September 2014).

Abram, Simon, and Marianne Elisabeth Lien, 'Performing nature at world's ends', *ETHNOS* 76/1 (2011), pp. 3–18.

Abramson, David M., 'A critical look at NGOs and civil society as means to an end in Uzbekistan', *Human Organization* 58/3 (1999), pp. 240–50.

Adler, Emmanuel, and Vincent Pouliot (eds), *International Practices*. Cambridge: Cambridge University Press, 2011.

Administrative Court of the Republic of Armenia, 'Decision on Denying Admission of the Claim'. In *VD/3275/05/09*, edited by Administrative Court of the Republic of Armenia. Yerevan, Armenia, 2009.

Administrative Court of the Republic of Armenia, 'Judgment in the Name of the Republic of Armenia'. In *VD/3275/05/09*, edited by Administrative Court of the Republic of Armenia. Yerevan, Armenia, 2010.

Agrawal, Arun, 'Environmentality: Community, intimate government, and the making of environmental subjects in Kumaon, India', *Current Anthropology* 46/2 (2005), pp. 161–90.

Agrawal, Arun, *Environmentality: Technologies of Government and the Making of Subjects*. London: Duke University Press, 2005.

Ahmedbeyli, Samira, and Armeni Karapetyan, 'Concerns Grow Over Nagorny Karabakh' (2016). Available at https://iwpr.net/global-voices/concerns-grow-over-nagorny-karabakh (accessed 26 April 2016).

Alexander, Catherine, *Personal States: Making Connections between People and Bureaucracy in Turkey*. Oxford: Oxford University Press, 2002.

Alexander, Catherine, 'Privatization: Jokes, scandal, and absurdity in a time of rapid change', in K. Sykes (ed.), *Ethnographies of Moral Reasoning: Living Paradoxes of a Global Age*. New York: Palgrave Macmillan, 2009.

Alexander, Catherine, Victor Buchli and Caroline Humphrey (eds), *Urban Life in Post-Soviet Asia*. New York: Routledge, 2007.

Anderson, David G., 'Bringing civil society to an uncivilised place: Citizenship regimes in Russia's Arctic frontier', in C. Hann and E.

Dunn (eds), *Civil Society: Challenging Western Models*. London: Routledge, 1996, pp. 99–120.

Apthorpe, Raymond, 'Coda: With Alice in Aidland: A seriously satirical allegory', in D. Mosse (ed.), *Adventures in Aidland, the Anthropology of Professionals in International Development*. London: Berghahn Books, 2011, pp. 199–220.

Apthorpe, Raymond, 'Epilogue: Who is international aid? Some personal reflections', in A.-M. Fechter and H. Hindman (eds), *Inside the Everyday Lives of Development Workers: The Challenges and Futures of Aidland*. Sterling, VA: Kumarian Press, 2011, pp. 193–210.

Apthorpe, Raymond, 'Writing development policy and policy analysis plain or clear: On language, genre and power', in C. Shore and S. Wright (eds), *Anthropology of Policy: Critical Perspectives on Governance and Power*. Abingdon, Oxon: Routledge, 1997, pp. 43–58.

Armenian Aarhus Centers, 'Memorandum of Understanding' (2007). Available at http://aarhus.am/?page_id=662&lang=en (accessed 15 December 2015).

Augé, Marc, *Non-Places: Introduction to an Anthropology of Supermodernity*. London: Verso, 1995.Ayvazyan, Sona, 'Comments from the communicant on the Draft Findings [Re: Communication ACCC/C/2009/43 (Armenia)]' (2010). Available at http://www.unece.org/env/pp/compliance/Compliance committee/43TableArmenia.html (accessed 20 September 2014).

Ayvazyan, Sona, 'Dear Mr. Wates' (2009). Available at http://www.unece.org/env/pp/compliance/Compliancecommittee/43TableArmenia.html (accessed 20 September 2014).

Ayvazyan, Sona, 'Further Points after CC-27 [Re: Communication ACCC/C/2009/43 (Armenia)]' (2010). Available at http://www.unece.org/env/pp/compliance/Compliancecommittee/43TableArmenia.html (accessed 20 September 2014).

Babül, Elif M., 'Training bureaucrats, practicing for Europe: Negotiating bureaucratic authority and governmental legitimacy in Turkey', *PoLAR Political and Legal Anthropology Review* 35/1 (2012), pp. 30–52.

Barad, Karen, 'Posthumanist performativity: Toward an understanding of how matter comes to matter', *Signs: Journal of Women in Culture and Society* 28/3 (2003), pp. 801–31.

Baran, Paul, 'Some remarks on digital distributed communications networks'. Santa Monica, CA: RAND Corporation, 1967.

Beunen, Raoul, Kristof Van Assche and Martijn Duinevel, 'Performing failure in conservation policy: The implementation of European Union directives in the Netherlands', *Land Use Policy* 31 (2013), pp. 280–8.

Boyer, Dominic, *The Life Informatic: Newsmaking in the Digital Era*. Ithaca, NY: Cornell University Press, 2013.

Brandtstädter, Susanne, 'Transitional spaces: Postsocialism as a cultural process: Introduction', *Critique of Anthropology* 27/2 (2007), pp. 131–45.

Breit, Eric, Lars Rowe and Pål Wilter Skedsmo, 'Evaluering av støtteordningen BarentsKult ("Evaluation of the Funding Mechanism BarentsKult")'. In *FNI Report 11/2014*. Lysaker: Fridtjof Nansen Institute, 2014.

Brunnée, Julia, and Stephen J. Toope, 'Interactional international law and the practices of legality', in E. Adler and V. Pouliot (eds), *International Practices*. Cambridge: Cambridge University Press, 2011, pp. 108–35.

Bruno, Marta, 'Playing the co-operation game: Strategies around international aid in post-socialist Russia', in S. Bridger and F. Pine (eds), *Surviving Postsocialism: Local Strategies and Regional Responses in Eastern Europe and the Former Soviet Union*. London: Routledge, 1998, pp. 79–98.

Buchowski, Michal, 'The shifting meanings of civil and civic society in Poland', in C. Hann and E. Dunn (eds), *Civil Society: Challenging Western Models*. London: Routledge, 1996, pp. 79–98.

Buck-Morss, Susan, *Dreamworld and Catastrophe: The Passing of Mass Utopia in East and West*. Cambridge: MIT Press, 2002.

Burawoy, Michael and Katherine Verdery, 'Introduction', in M. Burawoy and K. Verdery (eds), *Uncertain Transition: Ethnographies of Change in the Postsocialist World*. Lanham, MD: Rowman & Littlefield, 1999, pp. 1–18.

Burawoy, Michael and Katherine Verdery (eds), *Uncertain Transition: Ethnographies of Change in the Postsocialist World*. Lanham, MD: Rowman & Littlefield, 1999.

Bækken, Håvard, 'Selective Law Enforcement in Russian Politics 2007–2011. Legal Action for Extra-Legal Purposes'. University of Oslo, 2012.

Central Intelligence Agency, 'Eastern Turkey and Vicinity'. Washington, DC: Library of Congress, 2002.

Chari, Sharad and Katherine Verdery, 'Thinking between the Posts: Postcolonialism, Postsocialism, and Ethnography after the Cold War', *Comparative Studies in Society and History* 51/1 (2009), pp. 6–34.

Collier, Stephen J., 'Global assemblages', *Theory, Culture and Society* 23/2–3 (2006), pp. 399–401.

Collier, Stephen J., *Post-Soviet Social*. Princeton, NJ: Princeton University Press, 2011.

Collier, Stephen J. and Aihwa Ong, 'Global assemblages, anthropological problems', in A. Ong and S. J. Collier (eds), *Global Assemblages: Technology, Politics and Ethics as Anthropological Problems*. Malden, MA: Blackwell, 2005, pp. 3–21.

Compliance Committee, 'Draft Findings' (2010). Available at http://www.unece.org/fileadmin/DAM/env/pp/compliance/C2009-43/Findings/C43DraftFindings8.10.2010.pdf (accessed 20 September 2014).

Compliance Committee, 'Draft Findings and Recommendations of the Compliance Committee with Regard to Communication ACCC/C/2009/43 Concerning Compliance by Armenia' (2011). Available at http://www.unece.org/fileadmin/DAM/env/pp/compliance/C2009-43/Findings/C43DraftFindings8.10.2010.pdf (accessed 20 September 2014).

Compliance Committee, 'Draft Findings and Recommendations with Regard to Communication ACCC/C/2011/62 Concerning Compliance by Armenia' (2013). Available at http://www.unece.org/env/pp/compliance/compliancecommittee/62tablearm.html (accessed 15 September 2014).

Compliance Committee, 'Report of the Compliance Committee' (2011). Available at http://www.unece.org/fileadmin/DAM/env/pp/compliance/C2009-43/Findings/ece.mp.pp.2011.11.add.1.eng_040713.pdf (accessed 21 September 2014).

Creed, Gerald W. and Janine R. Wedel, 'Second thoughts from the Second World: Interpreting aid in post-communist Eastern Europe', *Human Organization* 3/56 (1997), pp. 253–64.

Danileyan, Gevorg, 'Board Decision [Decision of the Center of the Constitutional Law of the Republic of Armenia Board (Excerpt)]' (2012). Available at http://www.unece.org/env/pp/compliance/compliancecommittee/62tablearm.html (accessed 16 September 2014).

de Waal, Thomas, *Black Garden: Armenia and Azerbaijan Through Peace and War*. New York: New York University Press, 2004.

Deleuze, Gilles and Félix Guattari, *A Thousand Plateaus: Capitalism and Schizophrenia*. Minneapolis: University of Minnesota Press, 1987.

Dilley, Roy, 'Introduction: The problem of context', in R. Dilley (ed.), *The Problem of Context*. New York: Berghahn Books, 1999, pp. 1–46.

Dresen, F. Joseph, 'The Aarhus Convention Test: Environmentalists and Freedom of Information in Post-Soviet States'. Woodrow

Wilson International Center for Scholars, 2011. Available at https://www.wilsoncenter.org/publication/the-aarhus-convention-test-environmentalists-and-freedom-information-post-soviet-states (accessed 15 October 2014).

Dunn, Elisabeth Cullen and Katherine Verdery, 'Dead ends in the critique of (post)socialist anthropology: Reply to Thelen', *Critique of Anthropology* 31/3 (2011), pp. 251–5.

Ebbesson, Jonas, 'Public participation', in D. Bodansky, J. Brunnée and E. Hey (eds), *The Oxford Handbook of International Environmental Law*. Oxford: Oxford University Press, 2008, pp. 681–703.

Ecoera, 'Answers [from the Communicant]', in *ACCC/C/2011/62* (2012).

Ecoera, 'Comments' (2012). Available at http://www.unece.org/env/pp/compliance/compliancecommittee/62tablearm.html (accessed 10 September 2014).

Escobar, Arturo, *Encountering Development: The Making and Unmaking of the Third World*. Princeton, NJ: Princeton University Press, 1995.

European External Action Service, 'EU Relations with Armenia'. European External Action Service, 2016. Available at http://eeas.europa.eu/armenia/index_en.htm (accessed 29 February 2016).

Evans, Alfred B., Jr., Laura A. Henry and Lisa McIntosh Sundstrom (eds), *Russian Civil Society: A Critical Assessment*. Armonk, NY: M. E. Sharpe, 2006.

Eyben, Rosalind, 'Hiding relations: The irony of "effective aid"', *European Journal of Development Research* 22/3 (2010), pp. 382–97.

Fechter, Anne-Meike and Heather Hindman (eds), *Inside the Everyday Lives of Development Workers: The Challenges and Futures of Aidland*. Sterling, VA: Kumarian Press, 2011.

Ferguson, James, *The Anti-Politics Machine: 'Development', Depoliticization, and Bureaucratic Power in Lesotho*. Minneapolis: University of Minnesota Press, 1994.

Ferguson, James, 'Global disconnect: Abjection and the aftermath of modernism', in Jonathan Xavier Inda and Renato Rosaldo (eds), *The Anthropology of Globalization: A Reader*. Oxford: Blackwell, 2002, pp. 136–53.

Ferguson, James, 'Power topographies', in D. Nugent and J. Vincent (eds), *A Companion to the Anthropology of Politics*. Malden, MA: Blackwell, 2007.

Fisher, William F., 'DOING GOOD? The politics and antipolitics of NGO practices', *Annual Review of Anthropology* 26 (1997), pp. 439–64.

FNI, 'Environmental Management and Civil Society in Armenia' (2006). Available at www.fni.no/projects/armenia_environmental_management.html (accessed 23 March 2015).

FNI, 'Tillegg til søknaden "Miljøvernforvaltningen og det sivile samfunn i Armenia" 2008–2010 [Supplement to the Project Proposal: Environmental Management and Civil Society in Armenia 2008–2010]' (2008).

FNI, 'Transparency in Armenian Environmental Governance' (2009). Available at www.fni.no/projects/armenia_environmental_governance_transparency.html (accessed 23 March 2015).

Focal Point, 'Additional information [Re: Communication ACCC/C/2009/43(Armenia)]' (2010). Available at http://www.unece.org/env/pp/compliance/compliancecommittee/43tablearmenia.html (accessed 22 September 2014).

Focal Point, 'Comments from the Party Concerned [on the Draft findings]' (2010). Available at http://www.unece.org/env/pp/compliance/compliancecommittee/43tablearmenia.html (accessed 20 September 2014).

Focal Point, 'Considerations on Communication ACCC/C/2009/43 sent by Armenia to Compliance Committee of Aarhus Convention'. Unece.org, 2009. Available at http://www.unece.org/fileadmin/DAM/env/pp/compliance/C2009-43/Correspondence/FrARMC43_Reply_16Dec2009.pdf (accessed 20 September 2014).

Focal Point, 'To the Secretariat of the Aarhus Convention' (2012). Available at http://www.unece.org/fileadmin/DAM/env/pp/compliance/C2011-62/Correspondence_with_the_Party/frARM_C62_comments20072012.pdf (accessed 10 September 2014).

Galligan, Denis J., 'Legal failure: Law and social norms in post-communist Europe', in D. J. Galligan and M. Kurkchiyan (eds), *Law and Informal Practices: The Post-Communist Experience*. Oxford: Oxford University Press, 2003.

Gans-Morse, Jordan, 'Searching for transitologists: Contemporary theories of post-communist transitions and the myth of a dominant paradigm', *Post-Soviet Affairs* 20/4 (2004), pp. 320–49.

Gasper, Des., 'Evaluating the "logical framework approach": Towards learning-oriented development evaluation', *Public Administration and Development* 20 (2000), pp. 17–28.

Gezon, Lisa L., 'Finding the global in the local: Environmental struggles in Northern Madagascar', in S. Paulson and L. L. Gezon (eds), *Political*

Ecology across Spaces, Scales and Social Groups. New Brunswick, NJ: Rutgers University Press, 2005, pp. 135–53.

Giddens, Anthony, 'Living in a post-traditional society', in U. Beck, A. Giddens and S. Lash (eds), *Reflexive Modernization: Politics, Tradition and Aesthetics in the Modern Social Order.* Cambridge: Blackwell, 1994, pp. 56–109.

Giordano, Christian and Dobrinka Kostova, 'The social production of mistrust', in C. Hann (ed.), *Postsocialism: Ideal, Ideologies and Practices in Eurasia.* London: Routledge, 2002, pp. 74–91.

Glasius, Marlies and Armine Ishkanian, 'Surreptitious symbiosis: Engagement between activists and NGOs', *Voluntas: International Journal of Voluntary and Nonprofit Organizations* 26/6 (2014), pp. 2620–44.

Goffman, Erving, *The Presentation of Self in Everyday Life.* Harmondsworth: Penguin Books, 1971.

Gould, Jeremy, 'Timing, scale and style: Capacity as governmentality in Tanzania', in D. Mosse and D. Lewis (eds), *The Aid Effect: Giving and Governing in International Development.* London: Pluto Press, 2005, pp. 61–84.

Green, Maia, 'Doing development and writing culture', *Anthropological Theory* 9/4 (2009), pp. 395–417.

Green, Maia, 'Globalizing development in Tanzania: Policy franchising through participatory project management', *Critique of Anthropology* 23/2 (2003), pp. 123–43.

Gupta, Akhil and James Ferguson, 'Beyond "culture": Space, identity, and the politics of difference', *Cultural Anthropology* 7/1 (1992), pp. 6–23.

Hann, Chris, 'Introduction: Political society and civil anthropology', in C. Hann and E. Dunn (eds), *Civil Society: Challenging Western Models.* London: Routledge, 1996, pp. 1–26.

Hann, Chris, Caroline Humphrey and Katherine Verdery, 'Introduction: Postsocialism as a topic of anthropological investigation', in C. Hann (ed.), *Postsocialism: Ideals, Ideologies and Practices in Eurasia.* London: Routledge, 2002, pp. 1–11.

Hann, Chris and Elisabeth Dunn (eds), *Civil Society: Challenging Western Models.* London: Routledge, 1996.

Hann, Chris M. (ed.), *Postsocialism: Ideals, Ideologies and Practices in Eurasia.* London: Routledge, 2002.

Hannerz, Ulf, *Cultural Complexity: Studies in the Social Organization of Meaning.* New York: Columbia University Press, 1992.

Harper, Janice, *Endangered Species: Health, Illness and Death among Madagascar's People of the Forest*. Durham, NC: Carolina Academic Press, 2002.

Harrison, Elizabeth, 'Beyond the looking glass? "Aidland" reconsidered', *Critique of Anthropology* 33/3 (2013), pp. 263–79.

Harutyunyan, G., 'Decision of the Constitutional Court of the Republic of Armenia'. *SDO-906*. Constitutional Court of the Republic of Armenia, 2010.

Hemment, Julie, 'The riddle of the third sector: Civil society, international aid, and NGOs in Russia', *Anthropological Quarterly* 77/2 (2004), pp. 215–41.

Henderson, Sarah L., *Building Democracy in Contemporary Russia: Western Support for Grassroots Organizations*. London: Cornell University Press, 2003.

Henderson, Sarah L., 'Selling civil society: Western aid and the nongovernmental organization sector in Russia', *Comparative Political Studies* 35/2 (2002), pp. 139–67.

Herzfeld, Michael, 'Political optics and the occlusion of intimate knowledge', *American Anthropologist* 107/3 (2005), pp. 369–76.

Herzfeld, Michael, *The Social Production of Indifference: Exploring the Symbolic Roots of Western Bureaucracy*. New York: Berg, 1992.

Holy, Ladislav, 'Contextualisation and paradigm shifts', in R. Dilley (ed.), *The Problem of Context*. New York: Berghahn Books, 1999, pp. 47–60.

Huen, Chi W., 'What is context? An ethnophilosophical account', *Anthropological Theory* 9/2 (2009), pp. 149–69.

Hull, Matthew S., 'Documents and bureaucracy', *Annual Review of Anthropology* 41 (2012), pp. 251–67.

Humphrey, Caroline, 'New subjects and situated interdependence: After privatisation in Ulan-Ude', in C. Alexander, V. Buchli and C. Humphrey (eds), *Urban Life in Post-Soviet Asia*. New York: Routledge, 2007, pp. 175–207.

Humphrey, Caroline, *The Unmaking of Soviet Life: Everyday Economies after Socialism*. New York: Cornell University Press, 2002.

Igoe, Jim, 'Scaling up civil society: Donor money, NGOs and the pastoralist land rights movement in Tanzania', *Development and Change* 34/5 (2003), pp. 863–85.

Ishkanian, Armine, 'Challenging the gospel of neoliberalism? Civil society opposition to mining in Armenia', *Research in Social Movements, Conflicts and Change* 39 (2016), pp. 107–36.

Ishkanian, Armine, *Democracy Building and Civil Society in Post-Soviet Armenia*. London: Routledge, 2008.

Ishkanian, Armine, 'From inclusion to exclusion: Armenian NGOs participation in the PRSP', *Journal of International Development* 18 (2006), pp. 729–40.

Ishkanian, Armine, 'Is the personal political? The development of Armenia's NGO sector during the post-Soviet period', in *Berkeley Program in Soviet and Post-Soviet Studies Working Paper Series*. Berkeley: University of California, 2003.

Ishkanian, Armine, Evelina Gyulkhandanyan, Sona Manusyan and Arpy Manusyan, 'Civil Society, Development and Environmental Activism in Armenia'. London: London School of Economics, 2013.

King, Charles, 'The benefits of ethnic war: Understanding Eurasia's unrecognized states', *World Politics* 53/4 (2001), pp. 524–52.

King, Charles, *The Ghost of Freedom: A History of the Caucasus*. Oxford: Oxford University Press, 2008.

Kolstø, Pål, 'The sustainability and future of unrecognized quasi-states', *Journal of Peace Research* 43/6 (2006), pp. 723–40.

Kolstø, Pål and Helge Blakkisrud, 'Living with non-recognition: State- and nation-building in South Caucasian quasi-states', *Europe-Asia Studies* 60/3 (2008), pp. 483–509.

Kornai, János, *Economics of Shortage: Contributions to Economic Analysis*. Amsterdam: North-Holland, 1980.

Kurkchiyan, Marina, 'The illegitimacy of law in post-Soviet societies', in D. J. Galligan and M. Kurkchiyan (eds), *Law and Informal Practices: The Post-Communist Experience*. Oxford: Oxford University Press, 2003.

Ledeneva, Alena, 'Telephone justice in Russia', *Post-Soviet Affairs* 24/4 (2008), pp. 324–50.

Ledeneva, Alena V., *Russia's Economy of Favours: Blat, Networking and Informal Exchange*. Cambridge: Cambridge University Press, 1998.

Lemos, Maria Carmen and Arun Agrawal, 'Environmental governance', *Annual Review of Environment and Resources* (2006), pp. 297–325.

Li, Tania Murray, 'Beyond "the state" and failed schemes', *American Anthropologist* 107/3 (2005), pp. 383–94.

Martirosyan, Armine, 'End in Sight for Last Armenia Quake Refugees?' Institute for War and Peace Reporting, 2015. Available at https://iwpr.net/global-voices/end-sight-last-armenia-quake-refugees (accessed 3 December 2015).

Mason, Michael, 'So far but no further? Transparency and disclosure in the Aarhus Convention', in A. Gupta and M. Mason (eds), *Transparency in Global Environmental Governance: Critical Perspectives*. Cambridge: MIT Press, 2014, pp. 83–106.

Mason, Michael and Aarti Gupta, 'Transparency revisited', in A. Gupta and M. Mason (eds), *Transparency in Global Environmental Governance: Critical Perspectives*. Cambridge: MIT Press, 2014, pp. 321–39.

Merry, Sally Engle, 'Anthropology and international law', *Annual Review of Anthropology* 35 (2006), pp. 99–116.

Milton, Kay, *Environmentalism and Cultural Theory: Exploring the Role of Anthropology in Environmental Discourse*. London: Routledge, 1996.

Ministry of Foreign Affairs, 'Project cooperation in the South Caucasus, Central Asia, Ukraine, Belarus and Moldova' (2008). Available at https://www.regjeringen.no/en/dokumenter/susprojects/id507666/ (accessed 15 October 2015).

Ministry of Foreign Affairs, 'St meld nr 47 (1994–1995) Om Handlingprogrammet for Øst-Europa [White paper 47 (1994–1995) On the Target Program for Eastern Europe]'. Oslo: Ministry of Foreign Affairs, 1994.

Mirzoyan, Alla, *Armenia, the Regional Powers, and the West: Between History and Geopolitics*. New York: Palgrave Macmillan, 2010.

Mosse, David, *Cultivating Development: An Ethnography of Aid Policy and Practice*. London: Pluto Press, 2005.

Mosse, David, 'Global governance and the ethnography of international aid', in D. Mosse and D. Lewis (eds), *The Aid Effect: Giving and Governing in International Development*. London: Pluto Press, 2005, pp. 1–36.

Mosse, David, 'Introduction: The anthropology of expertize and professionals in international development', in D. Mosse (ed.), *Adventures in Aidland, the Anthropology of Professionals in International Development*. London: Berghahn Books, 2011, pp. 1–32.

Mosse, David, 'Is good policy unimplementable? Reflections on the ethnography of aid policy and practice', *Development and Change* 35/4 (2004), pp. 639–71.

Mosse, David, 'The making and marketing of participatory development', in P. Quarles van Ufford and A. K. Giri (eds), *A Moral Critique of Development: In Search of Global Responsibilities*. Abingdon: Routledge, 2003, pp. 43–75.

Nustad, Knut G., *Creating Africas: Struggles over Nature, Conservation and Land*. London: Hurst, 2015.

Nustad, Knut G., *Gavens makt: norsk utviklingshjelp som formynderskap*, Makt- og globaliseringsutredningen. Oslo: Pax, 2003.

OECD, 'Armenia: Monitoring Report'. France: OECD, 2011.

OECD, 'Compare Your Country: Aid Statistics by Donor, Recipient and Sector'. OECD, 2015. Available at http://www.compareyourcountry.org/aid-statistics?cr=302&cr1=oecd&lg=en&page=1 (accessed 16 November 2015).

OECD, 'Paris Declaration and Accra Agenda for Action'. Organisation for Economic Co-operation and Development, 2015. Available at http://www.oecd.org/dac/effectiveness/parisdeclarationandaccraagendaforaction.htm (accessed 5 December 2015).

OSCE, 'Decision No. 314' (1999). Available at http://www.osce.org/pc/28591?download=true (accessed 23 March 2015).

Parfitt, Trevor, 'A Post-Structuralist Agenda for Development?' E-International Relations (2012). Available at http://www.e-ir.info/2012/04/10/a-post-structuralist-agenda-for-development/ (accessed 23 September 2015).

Quarles van Ufford, Philip and Ananta Kumar Giri (eds), *A Moral Critique of Development: In Search of Global Responsibilities*. Abingdon: Routledge, 2003.

Quarles van Ufford, Philip and Ananta Kumar Giri (eds), 'Preface', in P. Quarles van Ufford and A. K. Giri (eds), *A Moral Critique of Development: In Search of Global Responsibilities*. Abingdon: Routledge, 2003, pp. xi–xiii.

Quarles van Ufford, Philip, Ananta Kumar Giri and David Mosse, 'Interventions in development: Towards a new moral understanding of our experiences and an agenda for the future', in P. Quarles van Ufford and A. K. Giri (eds), *A Moral Critique of Development: In Search of Global Responsibilities*. Abingdon: Routledge, 2003, pp. 3–40.

Rabinow, Paul, 'Midst anthropology's problems', in A. Ong and S. J. Collier (eds), *Global Assemblages: Technology, Politics, and Ethics as Anthropological Problems*. Malden, MA: Blackwell, 2005, pp. 40–53.

Ries, Nancy, *Russian talk: Culture and Conversation during Perestroika*. Ithaca, NY: Cornell University Press, 1997.

Riles, Annelise, 'Models and documents: Artifacts of international legal knowledge', *International and Comparative Law Quarterly* 48 (1999), pp. 805–25.

Riles, Annelise, *The Network Inside Out*. Ann Arbor: University of Michigan Press, 2001.

Rose, Nikolas, *Powers of Freedom: Reframing Political Thought*. Cambridge: Cambridge University Press, 1999.

Sakwa, Richard, 'The dual state in Russia', *Post-Soviet Affairs* 26/3 (2010), pp. 185–206.

Sampson, Steven, 'Beyond transition: Rethinking elite configurations in the Balkans', in C. Hann (ed.), *Postsocialism: Ideals, Ideologies and Practices*. London: Routledge, 2002, pp. 297–316.

Sampson, Steven, 'The social life of projects', in C. Hann and E. Dunn (eds), *Civil Society: Challenging Western Models*. New York: Routledge, 1996, pp. 121–42.

Sampson, Steven, 'Weak States, Uncivil Societies and Thousands of NGOs' (2002). Available at http://www.anthrobase.com/Txt/S/Sampson_S_01.htm (accessed 19 January 2005).

Savzyan, Hrayr, 'Answers: As to the request to provide a copy of the statement we made during the discussion with the Committee in 25 September 2012' (2012). Available at http://www.unece.org/env/pp/compliance/compliancecommittee/62tablearm.html (accessed 23 March 2015).

Sayadyan, Hovik Y. and Rafael Moreno-Sanchez, 'Forest policies, management and conservation in Soviet (1920–1991) and post-Soviet (1991–2005) Armenia', *Environmental Conservation* 33/1 (2006), pp. 60–72.

Schuller, Mark, 'Seeing like a "failed" NGO: Globalization's impacts on state and civil society in Haiti', *PoLAR: Political and Legal Anthropology Review* 30/1 (2007), pp. 67–89.

Scott, James C., *Seeing Like a State: How Certain Schemes to Improve the Human Condition Have Failed*. New Haven, CT: Yale University Press, 1998.

Scott, James C., *Weapons of the Weak: Everyday Forms of Peasant Resistance*. New Haven: Yale University Press, 1985.

Skedsmo, Pål, 'Demokratisering og miljøkamp på Kolahalvøya ("Democratisation and environmentalism on the Kola Peninsula")', *Norsk Antropologisk Tidsskrift* 18/3–4 (2007), pp. 241–52.

Skedsmo, Pål, 'Doing good' in Murmansk?: Civil society, ideology and everyday practices in a Russian environmental NGO, FNI Report 14/2005. Lysaker: Fridtjof Nansens Institutt, 2005.

Skedsmo, Pål Wilter, 'Europeanizing Armenia: Assemblages of Environmental Rights and Development in Post-Soviet Armenia'. University of Oslo, 2017.

Skedsmo, Pål Wilter, 'Evaluering av Demokratimidlene ("Evaluation of the democracy funds")'. In FNI Report 8/2008. Lysaker: Fridtjof Nansen Institute, 2008.

Skedsmo, Pål Wilter, 'Evaluering av samarbeidet mellom LO og FNPR 2001–2010 ("Evaluation of Co-operation Between LO and FNPR 2001–2010")'. In *FNI Report 05/2011* Lysaker: Fridtjof Nansen Institute, 2011.

Skedsmo, Pål Wilter, *Russisk sivilsamfunn og norske hjelpere (Russian Civil Society and its Norwegian Benefactors)*. Trondheim: Tapir Akademisk Forlag, 2010.

Stan, Sabina, 'Looking for a place to stand: Theory, field and holism in contemporary anthropology', in J. G. Carrier (ed.), *After the Crisis: Anthropological Thought, Neoliberalism and the Aftermath*. London: Routledge, 2016, pp. 114–23.

Stoler, Ann Laura, 'Colonial archives and the arts of governance', *Archival Science* 2/1–2 (2002), pp. 89–109.

The World Bank, 'Armenia'. The World Bank Group, 2018. Available at http://data.worldbank.org/country/armenia (accessed 12 February 2018).

Thelen, Tatjana, 'Economic concepts, common grounds and "new" diversity in the anthropology of post-socialism: Reply to Dunn and Verdery', *Critique of Anthropology* 32/1 (2012), pp. 87–90.

Thelen, Tatjana, 'Shortage, fuzzy property and other dead ends in the anthropological analysis of (post)socialism', *Critique of Anthropology* 31/1 (2011), pp. 43–61.

Transparency International Anticorruption Center, 'Statement of nongovernmental organizations following the International Conference on the Environmental Safety of Teghut Copper-Molybdenum Mining Project held on December 14, 2010 in Yerevan, Armenia'. Available at https://transparency.am/en/statements/view/135 (accessed 12 February 2018).

Tsing, Anna, 'The global situation', *Cultural Anthropology* 15/3 (2000), pp. 327–60.

Tsing, Anna Lowenhaupt, 'Becoming a tribal elder, and other green development fantasies', in T. M. Li (ed.), *Transforming the Indonesian Uplands*. Singapore: Harwood Academic, 1999, pp. 159–202.

Tsing, Anna Lowenhaupt, *Friction: An Ethnography of Global Connection*. Princeton, NJ: Princeton University Press, 2005.

UNECE, Addendum: Riga Declaration. Adopted at the third meeting of the Parties held from 11 to 13 June 2008 in Riga UNECE (2008). Available at http://www.unece.org/env/pp/mop3/web/Riga%20declaration_v_2008_07_21.pdf (accessed 15 February 2018).

UNECE, 'Background'. Unece.org, 2014. Available at http://www.unece.org/env/pp/ccbackground.html (accessed 15 September 2014).

UNECE, *Convention on Access to Information, Public Participation in Decision-Making and Access to Justice in Environmental Matters*. United Nations Economic Commission for Europe, 1998.

UNECE, 'Environment' (2012). Available at http://www.unece.org/leginstr/env.html (accessed 7 November 2014).

UNECE, 'Environment for Europe – Home' (2014). Available at http://www.unece.org/env/efe/welcome.html (accessed 8 November 2014).

UNECE, 'Fourth session of the Meeting of the Parties: Overview'. UNECE.org, 2011. Available at http://www.unece.org/env/pp/mop4.html#/ (accessed 15 November 2015).

UNECE, 'Report by the compliance committee. Addendum: DECISION III/6b Compliance by Armenia with its obligations under the convention' (2008). Available at https://www.unece.org/env/pp/compliance/compliancecommittee/ccimpldocsarmeniamop3.html (accessed 12 February 2018).

UNECE, 'Third Ministerial Conference "Environment for Europe"'. UNECE.org, 2011. Available at http://www.unece.org/env/efe/historyofefe/history.en2011_3.html#/ (accessed 8 November 2014).

UNECE Secretariat, 'Environment Division'. UNECE.org, 2011. Available at http://www.unece.org/env/pp/compliance/compliancecommittee/62tablearm.html (accessed 10 September 2014).

UNEP, 'ENVSEC Projects by Implementing Organization'. Envsec.org, 2015. Available at http://www.envsec.org/index.php?option=com_content&view=article&id=79&lang=en (accessed 13 March 2015).

United States Central Intelligence Agency, *Armenia*. Washington, DC: Central Intelligence Agency, 2002. Map. Retrieved from the Library of Congress.

Available at https://www.loc.gov/item/2002625531/ (accessed 15 February 2018).

Verdery, Katherine, *What Was Socialism and What Comes Next?* Princeton, NJ: Princeton University Press, 1996.

Verdery, Katherine, 'The "new" Eastern Europe in an anthropology of Europe', *American Anthropologist* 99/4 (1997), pp. 713–30.

Verdery, Katherine and Caroline Humphrey (eds), *Property in Question: Value Transformation in the Global Economy*. Oxford: Berg, 2004.

Wedel, Janine R., *Collision and Collusion: The Strange Case of Western Aid to Eastern Europe*. New York: Palgrave, 2001.

Wedel, Janine R., '"Studying through" a globalizing world: Building method through Aidnographies', in J. Gould and H. S. Marcussen (eds), *Ethnographies of Aid: Exploring Development Texts and Encounters*. Occasional Paper 24: Roskilde University Centre, 2004, pp. 149–73.

Wedel, Janine R., 'US aid to Central and Eastern Europe, 1990–1994: An analysis of aid models and responses', in *East-Central European Economies in Transition: Study Papers submitted to Joint Economic Committee*. Washington, DC: Congress of the United States, 1994.

Whyte, Martin King, 'Bureaucracy and antibureaucracy in China', in G. M. Britain and R. Cohen (eds), *Hierarchy & Society*. Philadelphia, PA: Institute for the Study of Human Issues (ISHI), 1980.

Zaharchenko, Tatiana R. and Gretta Goldenmann, 'Accountability in governance: The challenge of implementing the Aarhus Convention in Eastern Europe and Central Asia', *International Environmental Agreements: Politics, Law and Economics* 4 (2004), pp. 229–51.

Index

Aarhus centres 49, 53, 59, 70–3, 105, 110, 128
   ELRC and 66
   in Hrazdan 74–6
Aarhus community 63
Aarhus Convention 1, 2, 4, 5, 27, 38, 103, 137, 158, 205 n.1 *see also* Armenia
   Aarhus centres 49, 53, 59, 66, 70–6, 105, 110, 128
   access to information 53–4
   access to justice 55–7
   access to participation 54–5
   as assemblage 76–7
   authentic versions 59–60
   Chisinau 61–3
   Compliance Committee 13, 53, 81, 83, 89, 94, 187
   compliance mechanism 57–9
   creation and legitimization 42
   European context 8
   European standards 30–2
   excerpt 201–2
   focal point 59, 63–70
   government-appointed focal point 49
   institutional proliferation 42
   legitimization of 42, 184
   Moldova, international meeting of Convention parties 49, 50–2
   project of scale-making 10, 185–7
   proliferation of 49
   repercussions 115
   sections 6, 61
   translations 59
   unpacking 59–61
abstractability 42
ACCC/C/2009/43 93, 94, 95
ACCC/C/2011/62 93, 99
access to environmental information 32, 53, 108, 222 n.26
access to information 31, 34, 49, 53–4, 61
   in Georgia 67
access to justice 55–7, 59, 61, 63, 101, 110, 205 n.1
access to participation 54–5, 59, 108
ACP *see* Armenia Copper Programme (ACP)
acquiring funding 132
actio popularis 88, 96, 108
adherence 3, 16, 17, 82, 86, 130, 192
Administrative Procedural Code of the Republic of Armenia 87, 101
administrative regime 107
afforestation 154
Aidnographies 178
Alaverdi 100–1
Albania 93
alignment 77, 130
American Anthropological Association 208 n.46
American University of Armenia (AUA) 74, 139
anchoring 134, 148, 166–71
anthropological problems 4–9, 184
anthropology 7, 13, 36, 197
   post-Cold War 195–6
anti-bureaucratic practices 67
anti-corruption 149, 155, 191
anti-politics 129
anti-politics machine 145
Arax river 22
Armenia 93, 140 *see also* Aarhus Convention
   agricultural sector 154
   in Aidland 176–8

bureaucratic *habitus* 67
claims, universals and assemblages 42–4
contextualizing 3
development 39–41
earthquake (1988) 25
ethnography 4, 119
Europeanizing 3, 26–8
European standards 30–2
focal point 63–70
foreign aid per capita 35
independence and crisis 24–6
journalists 170
map 23
natural environment and mining 2
and Norway 134
open-pit mining 82
post-socialism 35–9
post-Soviet transition 30–5
project practices 42
seminars and preparatory work 156–61
topography 22–4
transparency and Europe 77–9
UNECE framework 28–30
Armenia Copper Programme (ACP) 66, 83, 87, 89, 101, 103, 104
Armenian authorities 166–71
Armenian civil society activists 9
Armenian Constitutional Court 87
Armenian environmental legislation 122
Armenian legislation 122
Armenian Ministries of Nature Protection and Territorial Administration 53
Armenian Socialist Soviet Republic (ASSR) 32
Armenia project 10, 11, 171
formalities and informalities 178–81
Armenia project seminars 153–6
ARPANET 4
Arthsakh movement 25
article 15 57
article 20–1 55–6
Ashot 76–6, 183, 186
assemblages 2, 10, 16, 38, 42–4
environmental rights 84, 86, 194
of human rights 82
asymmetrical power relations 166
Augé's conception of airports 164
Ayvazyan, Vartan 75, 170–1, 225 n.68
Azerbaijan 70, 121, 133, 137, 140, 141
Azerbaijani Ministry of Ecology and Natural Resources 141

Baku State University in Azerbaijan 138
Baltic republics 133
Barad, Karen 69
Baran, Paul 4
Belarus 133
Bhagdasaryan, Edik 170
bilateral development projects 2
blat 68, 69
Boyer, Dominic 4
Brunnée, Julia 90
Building a Network 73
bureaucrats 66–7
businesses 133

capacity building 10, 34, 81, 149, 173, 191
centralized network 5
Chari, Sharad 45
Chisinau, Moldova 50–2, 61–3
Civil Procedure Code of Armenia 101
civil servant 153
civil society 3, 9, 26, 34, 36, 39, 81–2, 106, 131, 132, 137, 149, 158, 187, 191, 193
and democratization 146
and NGOs 26
post-Soviet societies 124
Cold War 30, 33, 35, 36, 91, 113
see also post-Cold War
collective patterning of intention 114

Index

Collective Security Treaty
  Organization (CSTO) 27
Collier, Stephen J. 7, 8, 43
competence transfer 131
Compliance Committee 13, 57, 58,
  66, 78, 101
compliance mechanism 57
Conference of Parties (CoP) 212 n.37
Convention on Biological Diversity
  137, 158
Convention on Wetlands 158
Convention principles 52
Convention to Combat
  Desertification in Armenia 158
copper 83
Court of Cassation 87
cultural change 82

data collection and fieldwork 12–17
decentralized environmental
  governance 109
decentralized network 5
decision making 63, 68, 96
decisions on compliance 52
decontextualization 42
deforestation 83
democracy 9, 39
  export 173
democratization 34, 49, 69, 138, 149,
  171, 191
  and civil society 146
  initiatives 26
  scalability 140
Department of Bioresources 153
deterritorialization 164
development 39–41
  encounter 166
  policies 166
disarticulation 175
discursive formation 193
disillusionment 37
distributed network 5
document-related networks 163
donor 33, 180

cycle 131
implementer relationship 119, 120
legitimation 119–50
dual state 107

Eastern Partnership (EaP) 27
Ecodar 86
Ecoera 94
economic rationalism 42
economic reforms 36
environmental activism in Armenia
  1, 16, 76, 112–14
  ethnography of 82
  political imagination 88
environmental activists 59
environmental commitments 136–7
environmental democracy 29, 31, 141
environmental governance 34
environmental impact assessment
  (EIA) 74–6, 106
environmental information 77
Environmental Information Act 56,
  222 n.26
environmentalism 34, 82
environmentalists 81, 82
environmentality 109, 158
Environmental Law Resource Centre
  (ELRC) 66, 139
environmental management 113,
  154, 158, 176
Environmental Management and
  Civil Society in Armenia 207
  n.37, 233 n.7, 235 n.41
environmental NGOs 133
environmental politics 60
  legitimization 16
environmental protection 87, 97
environmental rights 1, 2, 6, 9–12,
  85, 106, 184, 188, 193
  assemblages 84, 86
  pan-European legal framework 18
  violations 82
Environment and Security Initiative
  (ENVSEC) 53, 70–1

Environment for Europe process 28
epistemological experiments 90
erosion 154
ethnography
  post-Cold War 159
Europeanization 3, 6, 76, 133, 166, 171, 183
  consequences of 133
  post-Soviet impediments 140
European semi-integration 27
Eyben, Rosalind 129

fashionable transitology 37
Ferguson, James 2, 135, 145
fetishization of participation 152
FNI–MFA relationship 180
foreign aid 9–12
  projects 183
formal rights 85
friction 50
Fridtjof Nansen Institute (FNI) 10, 11, 44, 121, 124, 128, 135, 139, 144, 151, 169, 193
fuzzy property 215 n.73

genuine NGOs 26
Georgia 35, 121, 137, 140
Georgian Aarhus Centre 142
Georgian Ministry of Environmental Protection 141
Gezon, Lisa L. 89
Giddens, Anthony 102
global community 81
global connections 2
good governance 149, 191
government-appointed officials 69
grant-eaters *(grantagerner)* NGOs 26
Green, Maia 136, 138, 143, 164, 165
Green Union of Armenia 26
Gyumri 25

harmonization 77, 130
Hasmik 65
Hayastan *see* Armenia

Helsinki Citizens' Assembly Vanadzor 86, 87
Hrazdan, Aarhus centres 74–6
Hrazdan River 154
human rights 5, 9, 29, 31, 39, 43, 49, 91
  organizations 133
hydropower plants 154

internally displaced persons (IDPs)
  in Azerbaijan 24
international development aid 3
international donors 165
international environmental politics 183
international law 52, 59, 91
International Monetary Fund (IMF) 43
international obligations 149, 191
irrigation projects 154
Ishkanian, Armine 38
Istanbul, Turkey 73
Ivane Javakhishvili Tbilisi State University in Georgia 138

journalists, attack on 170–1

Karabakh Armenians 25
Karabakh movement 25
Kazakhstan 93, 133, 140
Khosrov State Reserve 162
Kocharyan, Robert 25
Komitas Conservatory 85
Koyoto Protocol 137
Kyrgyzstan 35, 133

Lake Sevan 154, 155
land for agricultural purposes 154
larger-scale political processes 28
lavash 162
League of Nations High Commissioner for Refugees 135
legal framework 128
legitimacy 36
Leninakan *see* Gyumri

lex superior 56, 103
Li, Tania Murray 10, 110
liberalism 114
liberal market democracies 138
Lithuania 93
localized operational system 152
local legitimacy 143
logical framework (LOG frame) approach 11, 90, 119–21
  adjustments 146
  Armenia project 2009 128
  hierarchy 125, 126, 130, 189
  Norwegian development policies 132–3
  perception 145–7
  plenary information meetings at Norwegian MFA 133–8
  project management, diversions in 147–50
  seminar 121–32
  South Caucasus, project in 140–5
  submission 123
Lukashenko regime 62

makeshift links 12
management by objectives 18, 122, 127, 133
marketization of economy 132
market liberalism 29
Marz., Ararat 161
Meeting of Parties (MoP) 31, 57, 60, 185, 212 n.37
  Chisinau 98
  Lucca, Italy 31, 57
  Riga, Latvia 58, 123
Merry, Sally Engle 91
Metsamor 25
mikri 72
Ministries of Nature Protection and Territorial Administration 135
Ministry of Ecology and Natural Resources 70
Ministry of Foreign Affairs (MFA) 10, 44, 121
  Armenian 153, 189
  Norwegian 134
Ministry of Nature Protection (MNP) 68, 72, 153, 155
Moldova 35, 133
molybdenum 83
Mosse, David 12, 16, 40, 77, 122, 125, 126, 129, 145, 150, 175
Mount Aragats 22
multilateral environmental agreements (MEAs) 2, 55–6, 127, 158
multilateral policy 164, 166
municipal officials 100
municipal tax collection 158
mutual accountability 130

Nagorny Karabakh 25
nation state 81
neo-liberal governance 35
neo-liberalism 77
neo-liberal reforms 6
networking 82, 151, 170
Network Inside Out, The 163
networks 2
  distributed 5, 19
  document-related networks 163
  informal 37
  invocation 4–5, 12
  NGOs 4, 37
  private 153
  professional 151, 153
  project 7
  project spaces and 181–2
  semi-professional 153
  social aspects 153
  social networks 163
  support 41
NGOs *see* non-governmental organizations (NGOs)
non-governmental organizations (NGOs) 3, 81, 87, 123, 184
  activism 106
  and civil society 26

networks 4
organized civil society 112
statutory goals 103
types 26
non-places argument 164
NORAD *see* Norwegian Agency for Development Cooperation (NORAD)
normative state 107
Norway 1, 2, 3, 12, 31, 32, 42, 56, 62, 63, 78, 132, 134, 135, 137, 138, 141, 145, 147, 161, 172, 179, 183, 192, 199
Norwegian Agency for Development Cooperation (NORAD) 132, 207 n.35, 234 n.25
Norwegian–Armenian relations 135
Norwegian development interventions 189
Norwegian development policies 132-3
Norwegian foreign aid project 3, 8, 10
Norwegian-funded Armenia project 183
Norwegian-funded development cooperation 1
Norwegian-funded projects 235 n.33
Norwegian MFA 124
notion of networking 151

official development assistance (ODA) 132
Ong, Aihwa 43
open-pit mining 82
operational system 119, 121, 125, 147
Organization for Security and Cooperation in Europe (OSCE) 9-12, 53, 70, 105, 161, 173-4, 186
ownership 130

pan-European network 62
Paris Declaration on Aid Effectiveness (2005) 130

participation 49
patterned intention 59
patterning of intention 106
plenary information meetings at Norwegian MFA 133-8
pocket *(grbanayin)* NGOs 26
Polhøgda 135
policies 1, 3, 5, 6, 10, 41
    development 16, 18, 41
    donor 33
    environmental 16, 18
    frameworks 44
    ideas 40, 44
    judgements 146
    Norwegian 29, 39
    and practice 40
political leadership 122
post-Civil War 191
post-Cold War 3, 17, 30, 45
    anthropology 195-6
    ethnography 159
post-colonial literatures 3, 17, 35, 38-9, 45
post-socialism 35-9
    anthropology 37, 38, 50
    contribution 177
    transformation 92
    transition 34-5, 166
post-Soviet Caucasus 1, 4
post-Soviet governance 125
post-Soviet societies 132
post-Soviet states 138, 190
post-Soviet transition 30-5
poverty 129
private networks 153
privatization 36
problematization 6, 7
professional networks 151, 153
project(s) 166
    acquisitions 131
    documentation 127
    management 129-30
    participants 164
    practices 42, 131

spaces 18, 151, 165
project-speak 37
project-within-a-project 170
public concerned 55
Public Environmental Information Centres (PEICs) 73
public participation 54–5

ramifications 166
Ramsar Convention 158
reactive mode 122
recontextualization 42
reforestation 100, 101, 154
relationalism 130
Republic of Armenia *see* Armenia
Republic of Nagorny Karabakh 24
research professionals 133
results 129, 130
rights 129
rights-based environmentalism 113–14
Riles, Annelise 59, 62, 69, 163, 165
Rio Declaration on Environment and Development (1992) 60
ritual lip-service 37, 152
Road Map 73
Russia 133
Russian Federation 27

Sakwa, Richard 107
Sargsyan, Serzh 25
Save Teghut campaigners 106
Save Teghut Civic Initiative (STCI) 81, 84
    activism 115
    in Armenian courts 86–9
    beyond Armenia 94–104
    in conference halls 104–7
    environmental activism 112–14
    environmental rights, documenting 92–4
    international law 89–92
    practising Aarhus 107–12
    in the streets 84–6

scale-making efforts 158
    project 30
scales 16, 42, 44
Scott, James C. 10, 124
semi-authoritarian state 88
seminars and workshops 122
semi-professional networks 153
servants of the people 66
Skedsmo, Pål Wilter 205 n.1, 217 n.91, 218 n.92
small-scale development projects 28
social change 82
social life 93
social networks 151, 163
South Caucasus, project in 140–5
Soviet republics 133
Soviet socialism 152
Soviet *telefonnii zakon* 68
state-like entities 25
Stockholm Declaration on Human Environment (1972) 60
strategies of extraversion 148
structural adjustment programmes (SAPs) 43
substantialism 129
surreptitious symbiosis 198
sustainable development 158

Tajikistan 133
Tanzania 41
Target Programme for Eastern Europe 132
techno-bureaucratic terms 129
technoscience 42
Teghut *see also* Save Teghut Civic Initiative (STCI)
    conference 105, 203–4
    mines 83, 84
    mining license 82, 86–7, 93, 96
telefonnij zakon (telephone law) 156
Ter-Petrosyan, Levon 25
Toope, Stephen J. 90
trade organizations 133

Trans-Caucasian organization 141–2
Transcaucasian Socialist Federative Soviet Republic (TSFSR) 24
transition 30–5, 36, 49–50
transnationalized locals 81
transparency 9, 16, 45, 49, 193
 and anti-corruption 96
 and Europe 77–9
Transparency in Armenian Environmental Governance 207 n.37
Transparency International Anticorruption Center 86, 87, 94, 96, 177, 231 n.82
triumphalism 37
Tsing, Anna 8, 10, 50, 88, 108
Tsitsernakaberd 159
Turkmenistan 93, 133

Ukraine 93, 133
UNECE Convention on Access to Information, Public Participation in Decision-making and Access to Justice in Environmental Matters *see* Aarhus Convention

United Nations Development Programme (UNDP) 53, 105
United Nations Economic Commission for Europe (UNECE) 27, 28, 29, 30, 123, 124, 137, 191, 212 n.38
United Nations Environmental Programme (UNEP) 53
University of Oslo 137
US Peace Corps 74
Uzbekistan 133

Vavrousek, Josef 28
Verdery, Katherine 45
vertical topography of power 6
vibrant civil society 158
vulnerability problem 5

western democracy export 3
World Wide Fund for Nature (WWF) 141, 180

Yerevan 173
Yerevan State University (YSU) 138

Lightning Source UK Ltd.
Milton Keynes UK
UKHW020047210521
384105UK00009B/223